Dynamic Optics in Economics:
Quantitative, Experimental and Econometric Analyses

Hale Kırer Silva Lecuna (ed.)

Dynamic Optics in Economics: Quantitative, Experimental and Econometric Analyses

PETER LANG

Bibliographic Information published by the Deutsche Nationalbibliothek
The Deutsche Nationalbibliothek lists this publication in the Deutsche Nationalbibliografie; detailed bibliographic data is available online at http://dnb.d-nb.de.

Library of Congress Cataloging-in-Publication Data
A CIP catalog record for this book has been applied for at the Library of Congress.

Cover Illustration: © Jackie niam/istockphoto.com

ISBN 978-3-631-83191-5 (Print)
E-ISBN 978-3-631-84254-6 (E-PDF)
E-ISBN 978-3-631-84255-3 (EPUB)
E-ISBN 978-3-631-84256-0 (MOBI)
DOI 10.3726/b17871

Peter Lang – Berlin · Bern · Bruxelles · New York · Oxford · Warszawa · Wien

This publication has been double-blind peer reviewed.

www.peterlang.com

Preface and Acknowledgments

Economy as a complex system consists of different agents and several factors that interact in every level. Since the existence of the economics as a science, the focus on the studies has always been to understand the dynamics in it. At this point the key role of the mathematical formalizations is undeniable in the development of the economic thoughts[1]. In economics, mathematical approaches first appeared with marginalism in 1870s. In the 20th century, this trend gained an increasing speed. Besides the mathematicalization in economics, in all times, the interaction between physics and economics has been inevitable. It was first believed that human mind could understand the nature and predict its behavior, which can be seen through the Determinism approach proposed by Newton and Laplace[2]. Classical economists mostly tried to build their models by adopting Newtonian physics, where homoeconomicus can be linked to Newton. Parallel to 19th century discoveries on quantum physics and chaos, their influence on economics in terms of unpredictability of human-being behavior came into question.

In the recent years, the number of interdisciplinary studies that employ the tools from mathematics, physics and biology has increased. The reason behind this is, beyond any doubt, insufficiency of mainstream economics to explain complex structures by simplification. In this context, this book, entitled "Dynamic Optics in Economics: Quantitative, Experimental and Econometric Analyses" intends to gather empirical studies, which try to explain the real world more realistically and accordingly, it consists of thirteen chapters that examine the economic issues, such as exchange rate fluctuations, international trade, stock exchange market-interbank relationship, monetary and fiscal policies, economic growth, unemployment, income inequality, economic development, environmental and health economics, from a dynamic perspective by using econometric and complexity approaches.

Within this framework, the first chapter analyzes the exchange rate fluctuations by employing the Principal component-Guided Sparse Regression model, which is particularly appropriate for wide data. Asymmetric behavior in

1 Hodgson, G.M. (2013). On the Complexity of Economic reality. Filosofia de la Economia, 1(1): 25–45.

2 Eren, E. & Şahin, S. (2017). Sunuş, in "Komplesite and İktisat" edited by E. Eren, S. Şahin, Efil yayınevi, Ankara Turkey. pp. v–vii.

exchange rate through inflation is examined by using smooth transition regression models that allow capturing the non-linearity, in Chapter 2. The time-varying parameter causality test is introduced in Chapter 3, and the causality relationship between exchange rate and uncertainties in Turkey is examined through this perspective. The Chapter 4 models international trade as a complex adaptive system. In the chapter, agent based modeling is conducted and evolutionary strategies are used in the simulations. The dynamic volatility spillover between stock exchange and interbank market is investigated in Chapter 5 by employing EGARCH model to estimate the asymmetric volatility. Markov Regime Switching, which assumes that the observed time series follow a non-linear process, is used in Chapter 6 to test the validity of the real interest differential model for Turkey. The Chapter 7 analyzes the interactions between the monetary and fiscal policies from a game theoretical view. The Dynamic Stochastic Equilibrium Model is employed to examine the interactions between policymakers. The Chapter 8 performs a Panel causality test to investigate the relationship between unemployment and economic growth in the OECD countries. Entropy based GRA and WASPAS methods were employed in Chapter 9 to analyze the Better Living Index in the OECD countries. The Chapter 10 examines income distribution inequality from a complexity perspective. Fractal dimension of income distribution is calculated on the basis of scaling indicator for Turkey and its regions and its relationship with some of the development indicators are analyzed. Environmental degradation and economic development is investigated in Chapter 11 using a panel ARDL model. The Chapter 12 examines the extent of generic competition in different European countries under different price regulations in the EU pharmaceutical industry by performing the Fully Interacted Model. Finally, Chapter 13 illustrates how to switch from individual level data to aggregate level data analysis within a difference in differences setting for OLS estimation by using aggregate data in the evaluation of hospital interventions in the UK.

I would like to express my special thanks to all the authors who contributed with their time and expertise. My grateful thanks also to my spouse Elias Esteban Silva Lecuna for all his readings, constructive recommendations, endless patience and support during the preparation of the manuscript.

Editor; Hale Kırer Silva Lecuna, PhD

Table of Contents

List of Authors

Akın Usupbeyli, *Asst. Prof., PhD, Ankara University*
ORCID: 0000-0003-2792-8805

Ali İlhan, *PhD, Tekirdağ Namık Kemal University*
ORCID: 0000-0001-6201-5353

Ayça Özkekin, *Asst. Prof., PhD, Bandırma Onyedi Eylül University*
ORCID: 0000-0002-0566-7168

Aykut Karakaya, *PhD, Recep Tayyip Erdoğan University*
ORCID: 0000-0001-6491-132X

Berna Tuncay, *PhD, Koç University*
ORCID: 0000-0001-6398-1123

Bilgin Bari, *Asst. Prof., PhD, Anadolu University*
ORCID: 0000-0001-7665-2740

Coşkun Akdeniz, *PhD, Tekirdağ Namık Kemal University*
ORCID: 0000-0002-3973-754X

Erdal Alancıoğlu, *PhD, Harran University*
ORCID: 0000-0002-5008-4957

Frank Windmeijer, *Professorial Research Fellow, University of Oxford*
ORCID: 0000-0002-4232-2783

Hakan Ulucan, *Asst. Prof., PhD, Pamukkale University*
ORCID: 0000-0002-1769-9407

Hale Kırer Silva Lecuna, *Asst. Prof., PhD, Bandırma Onyedi Eylül University*
ORCID: 0000-0002-1879-3315

Melih Kutlu, *PhD, Samsun University*
ORCID: 0000-0002-8634-6330

Merve Ertok Onurlu, *Asst. Prof., PhD Çanakkale 18 Mart University*
ORCID: 0000-0001-5187-1568

Metin Tetik, *Asst. Prof. PhD, Uşak University*
ORCID: 0000-0003-2741-7175

Özlem Ayvaz Kızılgöl, *Asst. Prof., PhD, Bandırma Onyedi Eylül University*
ORCID: 0000-0001-9996-7892

Özlem Kuvat, *Asst. Prof., PhD, Balıkesir University*
ORCID: 0000-0001-7017-4557

Pınar Deniz, *Asst. Prof., PhD, Marmara University*
ORCID: 0000-0001-5693-1144

Reşat Ceylan, *Prof. Dr., Pamukkale University*
ORCID: 0000-0003-3727-6644

Rüya Eser, *PhD, Mimar Sinan University*
ORCID: 0000-0003-0763-5423

Suna Korkmaz, *Prof. Dr.,*
Bandırma Onyedi Eylül University
ORCID: 0000-0001-6221-2322

Uğur Akkoç, *PhD,*
Pamukkale University
ORCID: 0000-0002-9949-2097

Pınar Deniz

Chapter 1 A Nonlinear Approach for the Determinants of Exchange Rate Volatility: Evidence from Turkey

Abstract: Emerging markets are reflecting highly volatile exchange rates. Turkish economy, apart from being exposed to exchange rate fluctuations, is fragile due to its dependence on imports. The aim of this paper is to analyze the exchange rate fluctuations in Turkish economy under the following steps: (i) to run principal component-guided sparse regression (PC-LASSO) which is a method for large data to shrink predictions toward the most important variable for volatility out of many potential domestic and international macroeconomic indicators, (ii) to estimate a threshold level for the main determinant of the volatility and examine the impact of these macroeconomic indicators using structural threshold regression model. The empirical findings suggest the international reserves of the central bank as the most important variable for volatility and that the threshold regression reflects the nonlinearity of the model.

Keywords: Financial Markets, Exchange Rate, International Reserves, PC-LASSO, Threshold Regression Models

1. Introduction

After the breakdown of Bretton Woods, countries adopted various exchange rate policies depending on their conditions. Exchange rate is a critical indicator for open economy transactions as import and export levels are dependent on their relevant prices in the international markets. Leaving all other links to a side, stable exchange rate is crucial to enhance trade volume which is – from the perspective of neoclassical theories – argued to be beneficial for consumers and producers together with a rise in the variety of goods and services and a trigger for innovation due to the rise in the level of competition. Prices of domestic products in the international market are theoretically one of the determinants of exports of a domestic country and prices of foreign products in a domestic market are one the determinants of imports the country. Hence, determination of the exchange rate is important to specify the trade balance, which is one of the determinants of the GDP growth as it is a component of GDP. When it comes to developing countries, adjustments in the exchange rate are way more critical due to their fragilities. Regarding the export levels, relatively lower value added and lack of competitiveness, and regarding the import levels, dependence on foreign products highlights the importance of developing an effective exchange regime. Emerging economies carry the vulnerabilities of developing countries however their growth potential is very high compared to all others. Relatively higher returns attract global capital searching for best options regarding risk-return rates. Thereby, these countries have become the short-term harbors of the global liquidity. During relatively higher risks or lower returns, capital outflows from one harbor and inflows to another one with lower risks and/or higher returns. Capital inflows bring in international currency triggering an appreciation whereas capital outflow lowers international currency triggering a depreciation of the local currency. Being open to short term capital in and outflows, emerging countries are the countries most exposed to exchange rate volatilities.

Even though the main objective of most central banks worldwide is to maintain price stability, there may be dual mandates including achieving a target for unemployment rate, growth rate, exchange rate or these objectives can be implicitly targeted with a flexibility. Many central banks, explicitly or implicitly, intervene to lower currency and/or exchange rate volatilities due to lack of information regarding the determinants of exchange rates. Trade flows, interest rates, speculations, and several other macroeconomic indicators are unknown and comes as a shock that ends up with a deviation from a steady state or a target level. The hyperglobalization starting by 1990s, as defined by Rodrik (2011), has increased capital flows and increased the accumulation of portfolio investments, which can be used for currency wars. Due to the severe impacts of exchange rate volatility on economies under currency crisis, analyzing the determinants of fluctuations and the searching for policies to best intervene the fluctuations (achievement of a long term impact) has gained importance together with globalization. Fratzscher et al. (2019) argues that after global financial crisis (2008–2009), the importance of limiting exchange rate volatilities has increased more.

Early papers disregard the strength of policy intervention for a long-lasting adjustment in the exchange rate (Dominguez and Frankel, 1993; Lewis, 1994; Kaminsky and Lewis, 1996; Dominguez, 1998; Ramchander and Sant, 2002). On the other hand, recent papers concentrate on optimality regarding foreign exchange intervention. For instance, Cavallino (2019) identifies three endogenous target, namely as the consumption wedge, the domestic net foreign assets and foreign reserves, to follow an optimal exchange rate intervention policy. Some studies signify the role of public announcement in the success of interventions (Dominguez, 1998; Fratzscher et al., 2019).

The necessity to intervene exchange rate is relatively rare for advanced countries whereas it is frequent for emerging/developing countries (Fratzscher et al., 2019). Chamon et al. (2019) states that emerging countries have relatively smaller foreign reserves compared to advanced countries and that this is one of the main indicators of vulnerabilities. Turkey is one of the emerging countries with the highest exchange rate volatility. In light of the earlier literature, this study concentrates on Turkish exchange rate volatility to investigate the main determinant so as to identify the optimal exchange rate intervention policy as most emerging countries require to do so.

This study aims to identify the most important variable for the exchange rate volatility using a novel technique, principal component-guided sparse regression (PC-LASSO) model, by Tay et al. (2018) and use this as a threshold variable for an asymmetric analysis. Asymmetric modeling is employed as a tool for nonlinear models when the coefficients change depending on the period or on the economic conditions. Most asymmetric models assign the threshold exogenously which is purely decided by the researcher rather than a rule. Structural threshold model of Kourtellos et al. (2016) allows for an endogenous threshold variable that is estimated using 2SLS or GMM methodology. The findings highlight international reserves as the most relevant variable for exchange rate volatility and that during the low reserve periods, trade balance and policy rate (besides reserves) affect exchange rate volatility negatively; whereas during high reserves period, global economic policy uncertainty is positively effective on volatility.

The empirical findings are in the literature on other countries highlights several macroeconomic indicators. Hooper and Morton (1982) highlight changes in current account in the determination of the fluctuations in the exchange rate. Kriljenko and Habermeier (2004), using cross section analysis for 85 developing and transition economies for the year 2001, states that inflation, fiscal deficits positively affect exchange rate volatility whereas GDP growth and openness have negatively effect. Several papers highlight the impact of uncertainty on capital flights leading to depreciation in the local currency (Krol, 2014; Balcilar et al., 2016; Abid, 2019; Nilavongse et al., 2020). Nowak et al. (2004) using a panel of 28 countries observe that holding adequate reserves reduces exchange rate volatility. Devereux and Lane (2003) using several industrial and developing countries, find that trade openness and international finance (proxied by liquid liabilities) reduces exchange rate volatility but economic size increases.

The following section explains the model, data and the methodology. Section 3 presents empirical findings and last section concludes the study.

2. Model, Data and Methodology

The determinants of exchange rate volatility are examined for Turkey using key indicators highlighted in the empirical and theoretical literature. The dataset covers the flexible exchange rate regime (de jure) period using monthly data between February 2006 and February 2020. All domestic variables are obtained from Central Bank of Republic of Turkey (CBRT) database. Dependent variable, exchange rate volatility is the standard deviation of daily nominal exchange rate which is measured as Turkish Lira per US Dollar. Domestic determinants are as follows: inflation rate (*INF*) is CPI annual inflation; domestic interest rate (*INT*) is the policy rate of the central bank; budget balance (*BB*) is in domestic currency; trade balance (*TB*) is in US dollar; financial openness (*FO*) is measured as the summation of net portfolio investment and net foreign direct investment (assets minus liabilities); industrial production index (*IPI*) is used for a monthly proxy for total production; foreign reserves (*RES*) is the foreign assets in US dollar terms. External determinants are as follows: oil price (*OIL*) is the daily average of closing spot Brent oil prices from US Energy Information Administration (EIA); federal funds rate (*FFR*) (effective) is from Federal Reserve Bank of Saint Louis (FRED); global economic policy uncertainty index[1] (*EPU*) is retrieved from and the "Economic Policy Uncertainty" webpage[2] which is based on PPP-adjusted GDP measured by Davis (2016). The regression for the determination of exchange rate volatility is represented with the following model specification:

$$\begin{aligned}\sigma_t^{XR} = &\, I\left(q_t \leq \gamma\right)\left(\beta_{0i}^{L} + \beta_{1i}^{L}M_t + \beta_{2i}^{L}R_t + \beta_{3i}^{L}E_t\right) \\ &+ I\left(q_t > \gamma\right)\left(\beta_{0i}^{H} + \beta_{1i}^{H}M_t + \beta_{2i}^{H}R_t + \beta_{3i}^{H}E_t\right) + \varepsilon_t\end{aligned}$$

where σ_t^{XR} the is the standard deviation of the exchange rate as a proxy for volatility, M_t is a vector of domestic monetary macroeconomic indicators (*INF, INT, FO, RES*), R_t is a vector of real macroeconomic indicators (*BB, TB, IPI*) and E_t is a vector of external shocks (*FFR, OIL, EPU*).

1 Country wise measurement of EPU (economic policy uncertainty index) is available but not for Turkey. However, global EPU Index is the GDP-weighted average of national EPU indices for 16 countries that account for a great majority of global output and includes Turkey. Global developments may affect emerging countries through fluctuations in international capital.

2 http://www.policyuncertainty.com.

The regression model allows for an asymmetric approach to examine the effect of potential macroeconomic indicator taking a threshold variable (q_t) into account. After the determination of the threshold variable, Kourtellos et al. (2016) structural regression model is employed to estimate the threshold parameter (γ) and the parameters of the coefficients (β) under different regimes. Higher regime (H) is reflecting the period when the threshold variable is higher than estimate of the threshold parameter, and low regime (L) is reflecting the period when the threshold variable is lower than estimate of the threshold parameter. $I(.)$ is the indicator function for the presentation of the subsamples obtained from structural break via Kourtellos et al. (2016). The methodology also allows for the endogeneity of the slope variables using instrumental variables[3]. For the determination of the threshold variable, principal component-guided sparse regression (pcLasso[4]) model of Tay et al. (2018) is employed which is the combination of lasso and principle components (pc) that shrinks the coefficient vector to the leading principal components and hence provides the most important variable within a group of variables.

3. Empirical Findings

Historically, Turkey has adopted fixed exchange rate regime until 1980. After that period, several different regimes were adopted such as crawling peg, crawling band, managed floating, real exchange rate targeting until one of the deepest economic downturns of Turkish history in February 2001. Following the crisis, inflation targeting regime with floating exchange rate regime was adopted motivated by the success stories of several other inflation targeters. However, as an emerging economy, Turkey is subjected to capital flows and exchange rate volatilities are very high accordingly. Fig. 1.1 depicts the rise in the volatility of exchange rate around the neighborhood of global financial crisis and after coup attempt. The figures of all variables vis-à-vis exchange rate volatility are available in the Appendix.

Tab. 1.1 presents the descriptive statistics for all variables and Tab. 1.2 shows ADF unit root test results for different periods. Unit root variables are transformed into stationary form considering the period. Variables in rate or index form are differenced (monthly) whereas variables in level form are

3 Two-stages least squares method is employed to allow for endogeneity.
4 R package codes are available under the command "pcLasso" taking the ratio of shrinkage equal to 0.8.

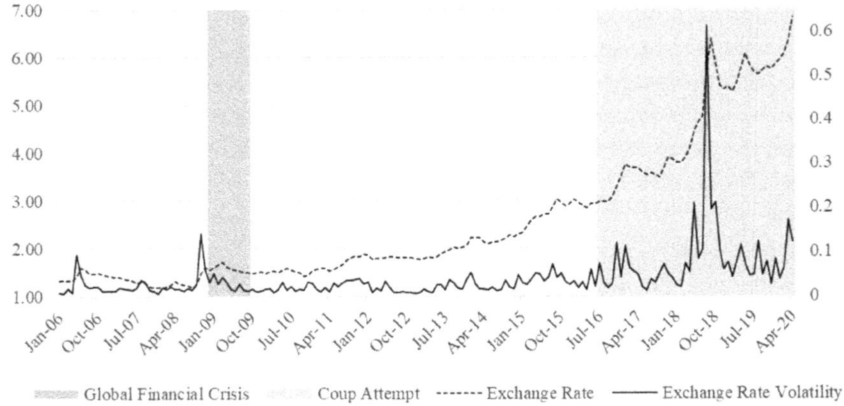

Fig. 1.1: Exchange Rate and Volatility (US Dollar/Turkish Lira), Source: Author's own construction. **Note:** Global financial crisis hit Turkish economy within the period December 2008 – September 2009. The date of the coup attempt is July 15, 2016. Exchange rate volatility is depicted in the right axis.

Tab. 1.1: Descriptive Statistics, Source: Author's own calculations

	VOL	INF	IPI	TB	RES	INT	FO	BB	OIL	FFR	EPU
Mean	0.05	0.04	0.09	-0.20	0.36	-0.30	-0.05	0.03	0.01	0.01	-0.02
Max	10.95	4.67	2.15	2.37	1.62	0.94	2.37	2.77	2.20	2.34	3.26
Min	-0.59	-1.61	-1.71	-2.48	-0.96	-1.04	-3.39	-3.77	-1.86	-0.72	-1.43
Std	1.06	1.06	0.97	0.98	0.67	0.66	1.06	0.94	0.99	1.00	0.97

Note: TB, Reserve, FO variables are in billion US $, BB variable is in billion TL. Std is short for standard deviation.

logarithmic differenced (monthly). All variables are standardized for a comparison of the coefficients[5].

Tab. 1.3 presents pcLasso coefficients for full period and subsamples regarding dramatic changes within the period such as global financial crisis that affected Turkish economy in the period December 2008 – September 2009[6] and coup attempt on June 15th, 2016. Hence, besides the full period, the following subsamples are investigated: pre global financial crisis period (February

5 Standardization is calculated simply using Excel "standardize" function.

6 According to the dropdown of the industrial production.

Tab. 1.2: ADF Unit Root Test (Constant and Trend Case), Source: Author's own calculations

	Full Period		**Pre-crisis**		**Post-crisis**		**Pre-coup attempt**		**Post-coup attempt**	
	Coef.	**I(0)/I(1)**	**Coef.**	**I(0)/I(1)**	**Coef.**	**I(0)/I(1)**	**Coef.**	**I(0)/I(1)**	**Coef.**	**I(0)/I(1)**
VOL	-5.86	I(0)	-4.20	I(0)	-5.34	I(0)	-7.54	I(0)	-4.75	I(0)
INF	-1.33	I(1)	-4.43	I(0)	-3.36	I(1)	-3.63	I(0)	-2.26	I(1)
IPI	-3.18	I(1)	-3.23	I(1)	-1.87	I(1)	-1.65	I(1)	-6.38	I(0)
TB	-3.21	I(1)	-2.76	I(1)	-3.69	I(0)	-2.95	I(1)	-2.66	I(1)
RES	-1.26	I(1)	-0.72	I(1)	-1.36	I(1)	-1.68	I(1)	-2.07	I(1)
INT	-2.31	I(1)	-2.25	I(1)	-2.99	I(1)	-1.37	I(1)	-0.35	I(1)
FO	-10.12	I(0)	-4.92	I(0)	-8.55	I(0)	-8.72	I(0)	-5.52	I(0)
BB	-1.72	I(1)	-6.88	I(0)	-1.98	I(1)	-2.10	I(1)	-4.95	I(0)
OIL	-2.78	I(1)	-2.64	I(1)	-2.64	I(1)	-2.29	I(1)	-1.55	I(1)
FFR	-1.54	I(1)	-1.17	I(1)	-1.79	I(1)	-1.22	I(1)	-2.73	I(1)
EPU	-4.90	I(0)	-3.02	I(1)	-4.46	I(0)	-3.98	I(0)	-3.41	I(1)

Note: Values above are ADF test coefficients with constant and trend case. Critical value for 5 % significance level is -3.436634. In ambiguity, the decision regarding the order of integration is left to the ADF test with constant case.

Tab. 1.3: PC-LASSO Coefficients, Source: Author's own calculations

	Full period	**Pre-crisis**	**Post-crisis**	**Pre-coup attempt**	**Post-coup attempt**
INF	0.0334	0.0231	0.0288	0.0000	0.0621
IPI	0.0000	0.0000	0.0000	0.0000	0.0000
TB	0.0000	0.0000	0.0667	0.0000	-0.0059
RES	**-0.0949**	**-0.1421**	**-0.0730**	**-0.1507**	**-0.0987**
INT	0.0000	0.0000	0.0024	0.0000	0.0000
FO	0.0597	0.0166	0.0686	0.0654	0.0499
BB	0.0000	0.0000	0.0000	0.0000	0.0000
OIL	0.0000	-0.1059	0.0000	-0.0887	0.0000
FFR	0.0000	-0.0616	0.0000	-0.0429	0.0000
EPU	0.0851	0.0000	0.0724	0.0187	0.0000

2006 – December 2008); post global financial crisis period (October 2009 – February 2020); pre coup attempt period (February 2006 – June 2016); post-coup attempt period (July 2016 – February 2020). Out of 10 domestic and external macroeconomic variables, international reserves of the central bank (*RES*) is observed to be the most important variable for exchange rate volatility and has a negative association. This negative link is observed in the Turkish economic history during the depletion of international reserves – following crises – leading to devaluations (Kasman and Ayhan, 2008). In the similar manner, Parlaktuna (2005) explains that exchange market pressure in Turkey is reduced by adjustments in the foreign reserves. In the post-crisis subperiod, *EPU* is very close to *RES* and is positively associated to exchange rate volatility. This finding is in line with the recent empirical literature regarding the positive and significant impact of economic policy uncertainty index on exchange rate volatility for different country groups (Krol, 2014; Abid, 2019; Bartsch, 2019; Chen et al., 2020).

After the specification of the most relevant variable for the exchange rate volatility, structural threshold model is investigated with the international reserve as the threshold variable. In order to control for multicollinearity, correlation matrix is examined, given in Tab. 1.A1. The threshold model estimations are presented in Tab. 1.4 with low and high regime distinction for the overall period of February 2006 – February 2020. Low regime reflects the period when the threshold variable is below the threshold level, that is, the estimated threshold parameter; whereas high regime reflects the period when the threshold variable is above the threshold level. Hence, low (high) regime provides the effects of 10 internal and external macroeconomic variables on exchange rate volatility when the international reserves are below (above) a threshold level.

During low regime, that is, when international reserves are lower than an estimated threshold level, trade balance (*TB*), international reserves (*RES*) and policy rate (*INT*) reflect negative and significant impact on exchange rate volatility. These findings reflect that as trade deficit deepens, due to the rise in the necessity of foreign currency, exchange rate volatility rises; and, lower international reserves lead to higher volatility which can be attributed to capital flight due the rise in risk perceptions of the foreign investors; and as the policy rate declines, due to decline in the returns of domestic assets together with arbitrage, exchange volatility increases. During high regime, that is, when international reserves are higher than an estimated threshold level, policy uncertainty and budget balance are observed to have positive and significant impact on volatility, whereas the impact of trade balance is negative, as observed in the low regime period. The positive impact of *EPU* reflects that the rise in global political uncertainties increases exchange rate volatility due to capital flight in

Tab. 1.4: Structural Threshold Model, Source: Author's own calculations

Variable	Low Regime	High Regime	Delta
Constant	-0.6596	-0.2959	-0.3637
	(2.376)	(0.1912)	(2.5198)
OIL	0.4998	-0.0125	0.5123
	(0.3845)	(0.0317)	(0.3868)
FFR	-0.133	0.0633	-0.1964
	(0.2564)	(0.0413)	(0.2596)
EPU	-0.3042	0.3127**	-0.6169
	(0.414)	(0.0493)	(0.4163)
INF	0.3434	-0.0029	0.3463
	(0.3729)	(0.0525)	(0.3657)
IPI	-0.0471	0.0076	-0.0547
	(0.3525)	(0.0308)	(0.3536)
TB	-4.4087**	-0.1124*	-4.2963**
	(0.9034)	(0.061)	(0.9023)
RES	-2.1626**	-0.0496	-2.1129**
	(0.6582)	(0.0373)	(0.6586)
INT	-0.8396**	-0.0119	-0.8278**
	(0.1905)	(0.0929)	(0.1967)
FO	0.4326	-0.0134	0.446
	(0.492)	(0.0916)	(0.4356)
BB	-0.1156	0.2213*	-0.3369**
	(0.1634)	(0.1189)	(0.1567)

Note: Variables in paranthesis are standard errors. (*), (**) indicates significance at 10 %, 5 %, successively. Joint Sum of Squares (JSSE = 35.49), n1 = 16, n2 = 153. Threshold Estimate: -1.4695 with confidence interval [-1.4695 1.0894].

the times of rising risks. The positive impact of *BB* reflects that as budget balance improves, exchange rate volatility rises which can be linked to an indirect transmission mechanism: as budget balance improves, the return from holding domestic government bond declines which renders domestic treasury securities less attractive for the foreign investors and lead to capital outflow.

4. Conclusion

This study concentrates on the determination of exchange rate volatility for Turkey as an example for highly fragile emerging economies. The capital flows have increased tremendously after 1990s due to hyperglobalization (Rodrik, 2011). Emerging countries are one of the main stops of international capital, searching for the highest yield. However, due to instabilities in emerging countries, from time to time there are relatively higher risks compared to normal times. During risky periods, capital outflows from emerging countries which leads to depreciations in the domestic currencies. These risks can result from several reasons such as a decline in growth rate, a lower yield in domestic assets, deepening of trade deficit, decline in financial openness, fluctuations in budget, oil prices, increase in international policy rate, global uncertainties and decrease in international reserves of the central bank, all of which can lead to capital outflows. Turkey is a perfect example to examine the determinants of exchange rate volatility due to the high fluctuations.

The main empirical findings suggest international reserves as the main determinant of exchange rate volatility. The analysis is also controlled for different time periods, such as before/after global financial crisis as the globalization loses its strength and there are capital outflows from many emerging countries (van Bergeijk, 2019); and before/after coup attempt, which is argued to be a strong political break for Turkey. After the identification of the main determinant, a nonlinear model is investigated to examine the effects of several macroeconomic indicators on exchange rate volatility. The findings suggest the existence of a nonlinear model as determinants and coefficients change from one regime to another one. The model identifies that during the times when the international reserves are depleted, trade balance, international reserves and interest rates are effective; whereas during the times when international reserves of the central bank is above a specific level, global uncertainties, trade balance and budget balance become effective in the determination of exchange rate volatility.

It may be argued that during lower international reserves, the economy is doomed to the trade markets to bring more foreign currency via relatively higher net exports or to alternative resources to fill reserves of the central bank or to a rise in the interest rates to attract foreign investors in spite of the risks carried by low reserves. All other variables are not effective on exchange rate volatility during low regime. On the other hand, during the times when there is not an alarm for international reserves, global uncertainties, developments in the trade markets and fiscal stance of the economy matter for exchange rate volatility. Hence, central bank intervention to exchange rate considering the conditionalities in light of these findings may provide optimal policies.

References

Abid, A. (2019). Economic policy uncertainty and exchange rates in emerging markets: Short and long runs evidence. Finance Research Letters, 101378, Retrieved from https://doi.org/10.1016/j.frl.2019.101378 (15.11.2020).

Balcilar, M., Gupta, R., Kyei, C., & Wohar, M. E. (2016). Does economic policy uncertainty predict exchange rate returns and volatility? Evidence from a nonparametric causality-in-quantiles test. Open Economies Review, 27(2), 229–250.

Bartsch, Z. (2019). Economic policy uncertainty and dollar-pound exchange rate return volatility. Journal of International Money and Finance, 98, 102067.

Cavallino, P. (2019). Capital flows and foreign exchange intervention. American Economic Journal: Macroeconomics, 11(2), 127–70.

Chamon, M., Hofman, D. J., Magud, N. E., & Werner, A. (2019). Foreign exchange intervention in inflation targeters in Latin America. International Monetary Fund, Retrieved from https://www.elibrary.imf.org/doc/IMF073/25492-FXILAEAEX/25492-FXILAEAEX/Other_formats/Source_PDF/25492-FXILAETEX.pdf (15.11.2020).

Chen, L., Du, Z., & Hu, Z. (2020). Impact of economic policy uncertainty on exchange rate volatility of China. Finance Research Letters, 32, 101266.

Davis, S. J. (2016). An index of global economic policy uncertainty (No. w22740). National Bureau of Economic Research.

Devereux, M. B., & Lane, P. R. (2003). Understanding bilateral exchange rate volatility. Journal of International Economics, 60(1), 109–132.

Dominguez, K. M. (1998). Central bank intervention and exchange rate volatility. Journal of International Money and Finance, 17(1), 161–190.

Dominguez, K. M., & Frankel, J. A. (1993). Does foreign-exchange intervention matter? The portfolio effect. The American Economic Review, 83(5), 1356–1369.

Economic Policy Uncertainty, Retrieved from http://www.policyuncertainty.com/ (04.05.2020).

Fratzscher, M., Gloede, O., Menkhoff, L., Sarno, L., & Stöhr, T. (2019). When is foreign exchange intervention effective? Evidence from 33 countries. American Economic Journal: Macroeconomics, 11(1), 132–56.

Hooper, P., & Morton, J. (1982). Fluctuations in the dollar: A model of nominal and real exchange rate determination. Journal of International Money and Finance, 1, 39–56.

Kaminsky, G. L., & Lewis, K. K. (1996). Does foreign exchange intervention signal future monetary policy?. Journal of Monetary Economics, 37(2), 285–312.

Kasman, A., & Ayhan, D. (2008). Foreign exchange reserves and exchange rates in Turkey: Structural breaks, unit roots and cointegration. Economic Modelling, 25(1), 83–92.

Kourtellos, A., Stengos, T., & Tan, C. M. (2016). Structural threshold regression. Econometric Theory, 32(4), 827–860.

Kriljenko, J. I. C., & Habermeier, K. F. (2004). Structural factors affecting exchange rate volatility: A cross-section study (No. 4–147). International Monetary Fund.

Krol, R. (2014). Economic policy uncertainty and exchange rate volatility. International Finance, 17(2), 241–256.

Lewis, K. K. (1994). Puzzles in international financial markets (No. w4951). National Bureau of economic research.

Nilavongse, R., Michał, R., & Uddin, G. S. (2020). Economic policy uncertainty shocks, economic activity, and exchange rate adjustments. Economics Letters, 186, 108765.

Nowak, M. M., Hviding, M. K., & Ricci, M. L. A. (2004). Can higher reserves help reduce exchange rate volatility? (No. 4–189). International Monetary Fund.

Parlaktuna, I. (2005). Exchange market pressure in Turkey 1993–2004: An application of the girton–roper monetary model. International Economic Journal, 19(1), 51–62.

Ramchander, S., & Sant, R. R. (2002). The impact of Federal Reserve intervention on exchange rate volatility: Evidence from the futures markets. Applied Financial Economics, 12(4), 231–240.

Rodrik, D. (2011). The globalization paradox: Democracy and the future of the world economy. WW Norton & Company, New York.

Tay, J. K., Friedman, J., & Tibshirani, R. (2018). Principal component-guided sparse regression. arXiv preprint arXiv:1810.04651.

van Bergeijk, P. A. (2019). Deglobalization 2.0: Trade and openness during the great depression and the great recession. Edward Elgar Publishing, Cheltenham, UK.

Appendix A

Tab. 1.A1: Correlation Matrix, Source: Author's own calculations

	VOL	INF	IPI	TB	RES	INT	FO	BB	OIL	FFR	EPU
VOL	1.00										
INF	0.23	1.00									
IPI	-0.11	-0.01	1.00								
TB	-0.13	-0.09	-0.07	1.00							
RES	-0.37	-0.23	0.00	-0.04	1.00						
INT	0.11	0.44	-0.04	-0.02	-0.23	1.00					
FO	0.26	0.12	0.01	-0.02	-0.41	0.01	1.00				
BB	0.02	-0.03	-0.05	-0.07	0.18	-0.02	-0.04	1.00			
OIL	-0.10	0.12	0.18	0.03	0.10	0.03	-0.09	0.09	1.00		
FFR	0.01	0.03	0.03	-0.01	0.04	0.21	-0.17	-0.06	0.20	1.00	
EPU	0.38	-0.07	-0.09	0.08	-0.14	-0.12	0.14	0.00	-0.15	0.01	1.00

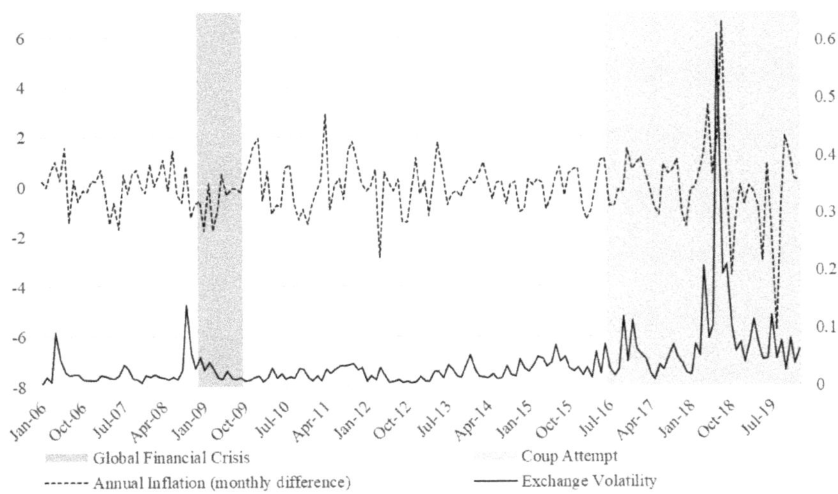

Fig. 1.A1: Exchange Rate Volatility and Inflation Rate, Source: Author's own construction. Note: Exchange rate volatility is depicted on the right axis.

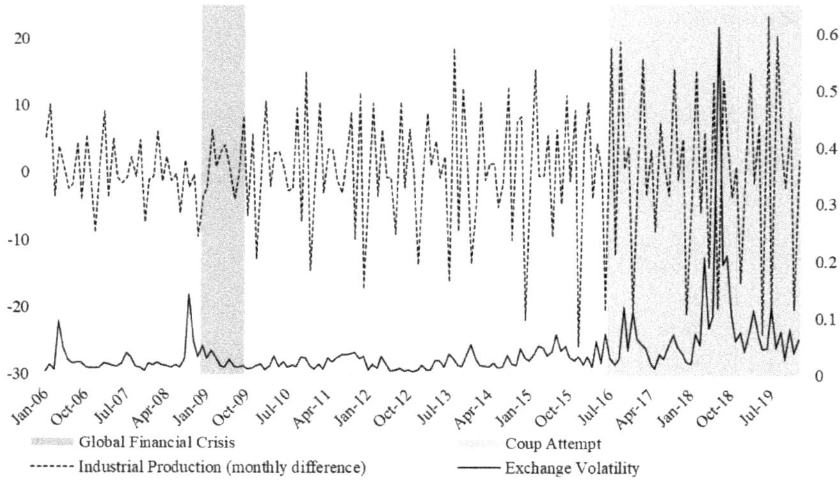

Fig. 1.A2: Exchange Rate Volatility and Industrial Production, Source: Author's own construction

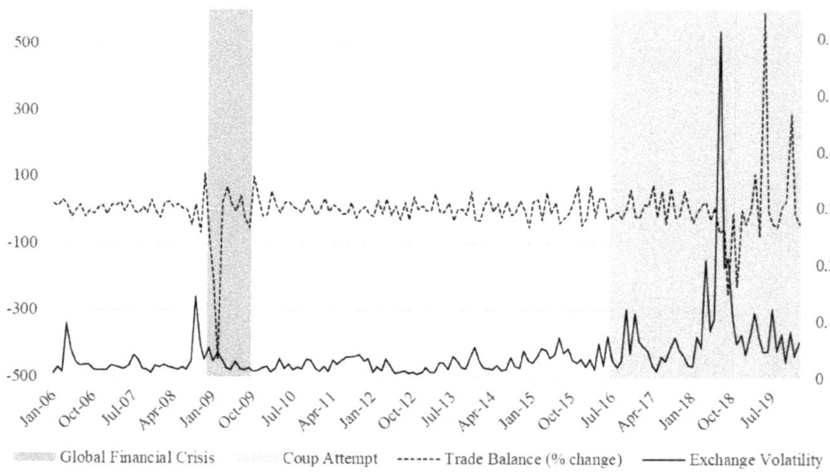

Fig. 1.A3: Exchange Rate Volatility and Trade Balance, Source: Author's own construction

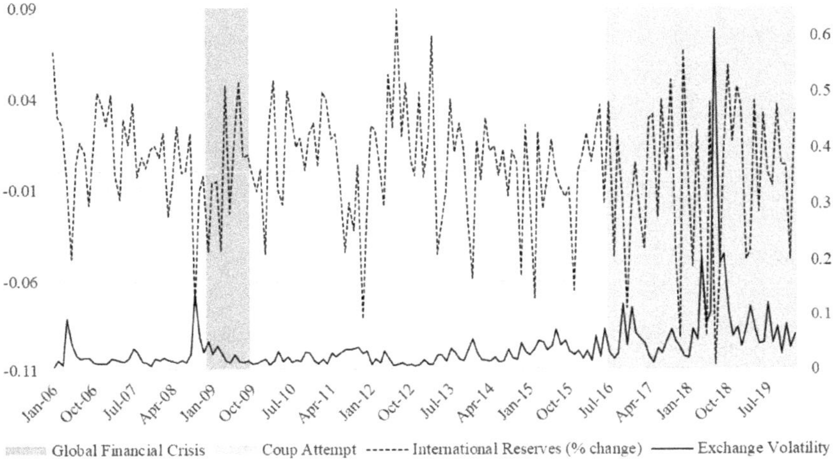

Fig. 1.A4: Exchange Rate Volatility and International Reserves, Source: Author's own construction

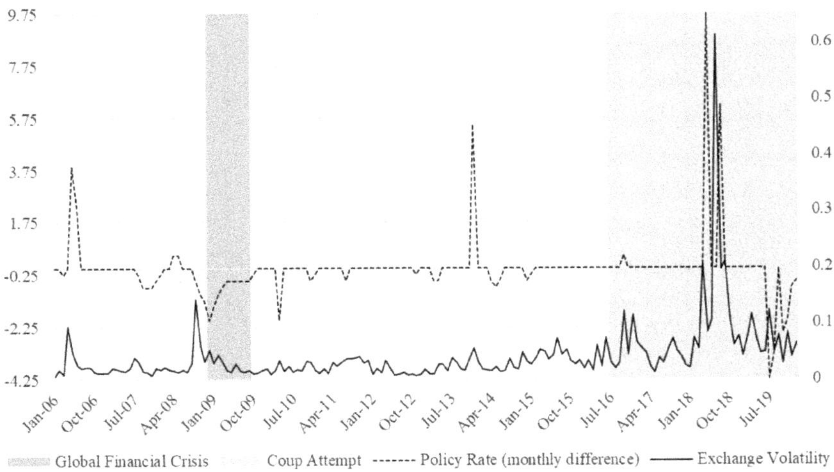

Fig. 1.A5: Exchange Rate Volatility and Policy Rate, Source: Author's own construction

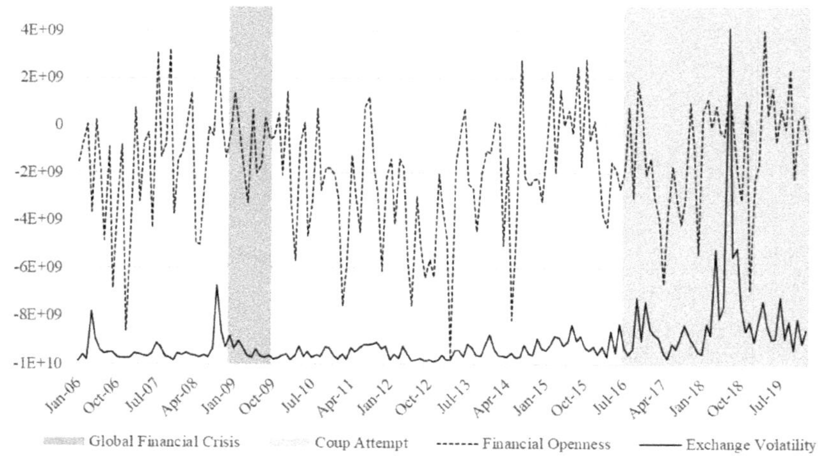

Fig. 1.A6: Exchange Rate Volatility and Financial Openness, Source: Author's own construction

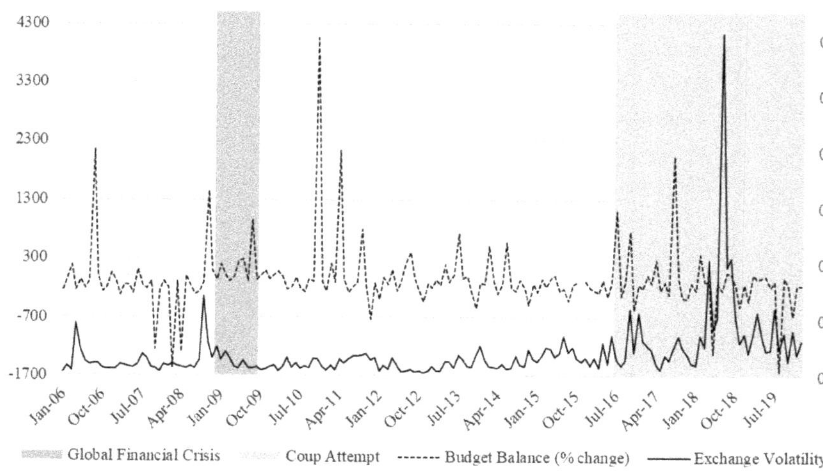

Fig. 1.A7: Exchange Rate Volatility and Budget Balance, Source: Author's own construction. Note: There is great dropdown in the budget balance (%change) in September 2015 which is omitted from the graph for a better visuality,

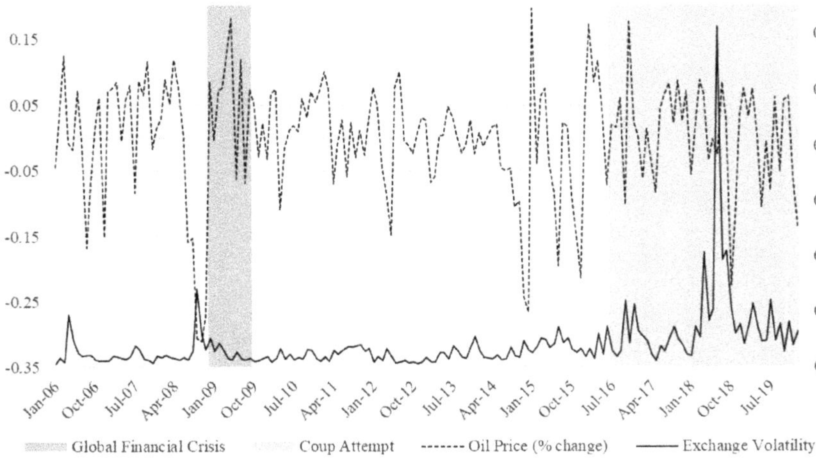

Fig. 1.A8: Exchange Rate Volatility and Oil Price, Source: Author's own construction

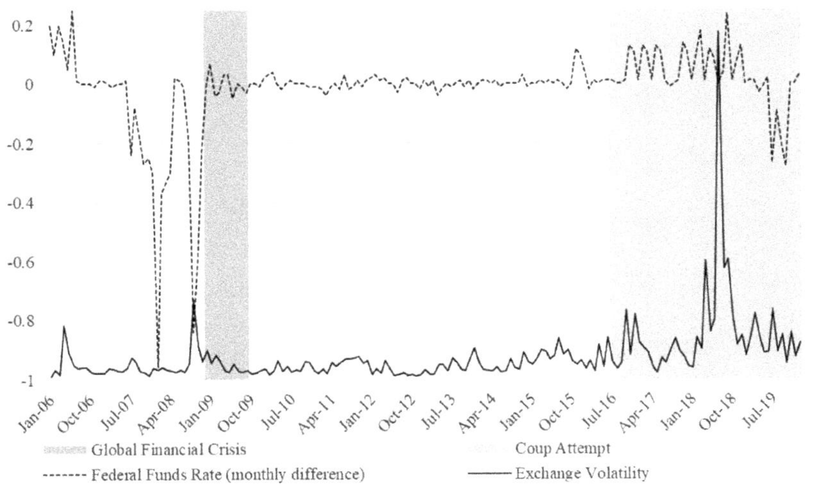

Fig. 1.A9: Exchange Rate Volatility and Federal Funds Rate, Source: Author's own construction

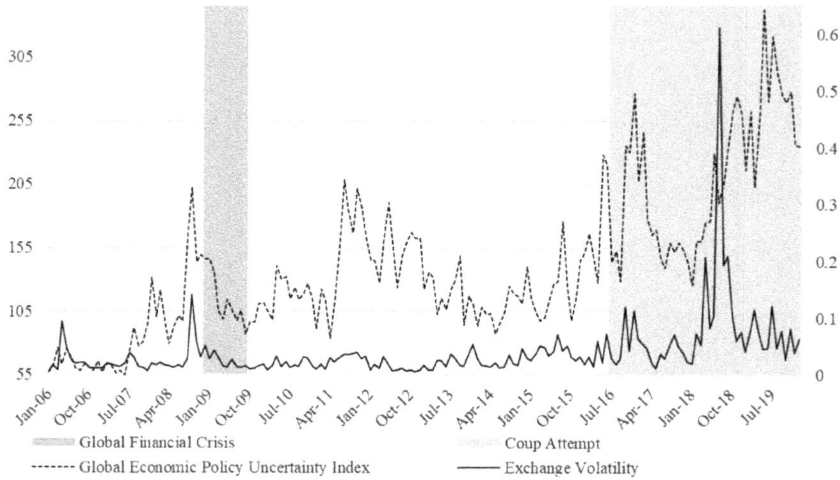

Fig. 1.A10: Exchange Rate Volatility and Global Economic Policy Uncertainty Index, Source: Author's own construction

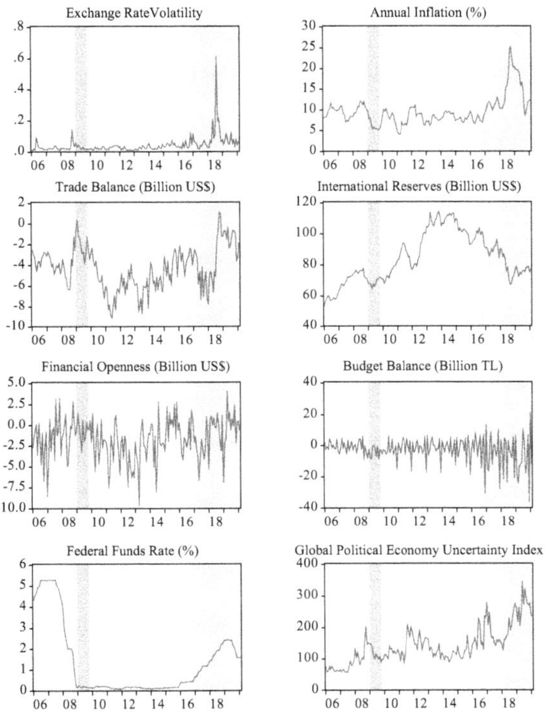

Fig. 1.A11: All Variables in Levels Form, Source: Author's own construction

Akın Usupbeyli

Chapter 2 Asymmetric Exchange Rate Pass-through in Turkey: Evidence from Smooth Transition Models

Abstract: This study examines the presence of asymmetric behavior in exchange rate pass- through (ERPT) to CPI inflation in Turkey for the period 2003:06– 2019:10 by using monthly data. Applying exponential nonlinear smooth transition models, the author tests to capture the asymmetry causing by the size of exchange rate changes. The findings show evidence that ERPT responds asymmetrically to the size of exchange rate changes as a result of presence of menu costs. The results indicate that when the exchange rate deviations are over 2 %, pass through to CPI inflation strengthens.

Keywords: Exchange Rate Pass Through, CPI Inflation, Asymmetric Adjustment, Smooth Transition Regression

1. Introduction

In a small open economy, especially where floating exchange rate regime is adopted, the reaction of the domestic prices to exchange rates constructs a major importance. Although exchange rate pass through is very easy to understand as a concept and can be considered as a natural process, its mechanism is complex and not easy to comprehend. This limited comprehension of the pass-through mechanism creates a frustration for the central banks of small open economies whose main task is to fight against inflation and to set monetary policies (Mishkin, 2008; Forbes et al., 2015).

Technically, exchange rate pass through refers to the percentage change in domestic prices caused by a 1 % change in the exchange rate (Goldberg & Knetter, 1996). Rincón-Castro and Rodríguez (2016) present the factors that determine the magnitude of pass through as the degree of trade openness of the country, the degree of competition in which exporter and importers are faced in this market, the duration, the direction and the magnitude of the change in exchange rate and the share of imported input used in domestic production.

Independent of the factors determines the magnitude of pass through, exchange rate monetary models, based on the validity of the law of one price, theoretically assume that the exchange rate pass-through on prices will be complete. In other words, domestic inflation will change in the same magnitude and direction with a fluctuation in exchange rate. Nevertheless, Dornbousch (1987), Floden and Wilander (2006) and Takhtamanova (2010) show that in noncompetitive markets, the pass through will be incomplete. Yang (2007) emphasized that varying demand elasticity is determinant for the firms in a noncompetitive market in explaining price adjustments following exchange rate changes. If exporter firms act in a competitive market, this means consumers will be more sensitive to price changes. Partial pass-through will occur if demand becomes more elastic as price increases. On the contrary, in lack of competition, the exporter prices will be less sensitive to price changes, which lead to a higher pass through (Goldberg and Campa, 2006). Meurers (2003) pays attention to the duration of exchange rate variation as other sources of incomplete pass through. If the appreciation in exchange rate is considered temporary by the firms, they may choose to lower their profit margin to protect their market share. Contrary, if they consider that this appreciation is persistent, the pass through is more likely to be complete.

These reasons of incomplete transmission give a nonlinear and asymmetric character to the pass-through mechanism. Rincón-Castro and Rodríguez (2016) associates this nonlinear and asymmetric behavior of pass through with the size, sign and nature of the exchange rate shocks (whether the shock is transitory or permanent). The past behavior of inflation (for example the size of the deviation from central bank's target) and the past performance of nominal exchange rates (for example its volatility and its misalignment from equilibrium rate) can also be considered as the source of asymmetric behavior of pass through.

Asymmetric behavior of pass through implies that prices react differently to an appreciation or a depreciation of exchange rate changes. To explain this asymmetric behavior further, let's consider an appreciation in exporter's currency. They can end up with the absorption of this appreciation by keeping their product's price unchanged on the importers currency in order to preserve their market share. This situation exhibits a low or incomplete pass through. But, when it comes to depreciation in exporter's currency, this promotes a decrease in price of the product in importer's market in order to attract consumers. In this situation, a complete pass through will occur. Thus, we observe an incomplete pass through in the case of an appreciation and a complete pass through in the case of a depreciation, which implies an asymmetric behavior (Goldberg & Knetter, 1996).

Bussiere (2013) states that an asymmetric pattern could be seen when the prices are rigid downwards and quantities are rigid upwards. An exporter gets price advantages in the case of depreciation. Even if the prices remain same in domestic currency, exporters can earn more by augmenting the quantity of the exported good. However, when the full capacity is attained or production costs are very high, it won't be possible to increase the quantity, which leads them to adjust the prices upwards. In the case of appreciation, a different scenario will occur. This time, keeping the prices unchanged leads the exporters to lose their competitiveness, which clarifies the reason why the exporters utilize "pricing-to-market"[1] in order to limit their loss of competitiveness causing by an appreciation (Boussier, 2013). We can conclude that in an economy where the prices are rigid to downward, export prices react more to depreciation than appreciation and on the contrary import prices tend to response more to appreciations.

Besides, exporters or importers may not change their prices if the exchange rate changes are insignificant, and change their prices only when the exchange rate change is above a given threshold (El bejaoui, 2013). In other words, in the presence of menu costs or switching costs, the exchange rate pass-through can be symmetric but nonlinear. Therefore, linearity and symmetry can't be considered as a given. Asymmetry and nonlinearity must be tested depending on the underlying economic structure of the country.

After a serious banking crisis in 2001, Turkey has abandoned the fixed exchange rate regime and has passed to the floating exchange rate regime. In addition, Turkey has adopted the inflation targeting policy to combat inflation after the standby agreement with IMF. Until the 2009 global crisis, there was a serious success in the fight against inflation with the stable exchange rate. However, after the global crisis, Turkey, like most countries, began to experience severe fluctuations in the exchange rate. The fight against inflation was interrupted and inflation increased to two-digits due to high depreciation of Turkish Lira. Central Bank of the Republic of Turkey has also emphasized the negative impact of the exchange rate fluctuations on prices in their inflation reports.

Taylor (2000) stated that if a country can sustain its inflation at a low level, pass through would be low too. But when a country experiences a high inflation era, the opposite will be true. Turkish economy kept the inflation credibly low

---

1 "The pricing to market" defines that in the international markets where there is with imperfect competitions, the mark-up of foreign firms differs from country to country depending on market conditions and sometimes cause incomplete pass through of exchange rates to prices. For further literature on the relation between exchange rate and pricing to market see Goldberg and Knetter (1996).

and stable between 2002 and 2009 but lost its control on it after and couldn't prevent it to rocket to 25 % in 2018. Hence, it won't be realistic to consider a linear and symmetric pass through mechanism for Turkish economy.

The purpose of this study is to study whether the pass-through of exchange rate fluctuations on consumer prices is symmetric or the adjustment of the prices differs depending on the magnitude of the exchange rate changes. Our analysis is conducted for Turkey and uses monthly data from 2003 to 2019. The recent fluctuations in the Turkish lira and the reincarnation of two-digit inflation rates are the reasons for focusing on Turkey. As widely discussed in literature, understanding the respond of the prices to transitory exchange rate movements is a determinant for the ability of Central Banks to attain their inflation targets. To this end, we use exponential smooth transition regression (ESTR) model in order to capture the possible nonlinearity caused by the size of exchange rate changes. To our knowledge, this study will be the first study testing for asymmetries and nonlinearities in ERPT using a smooth transition regression for Turkish economy.

2. Literature Review

There is a vast literature presenting the extent of exchange rate variations to import/export/domestic prices assuming empirically that this relation is both linear and symmetric. However, large exchange rate movements especially observed in emerging market emphasize the importance of asymmetric and nonlinear character of the pass-through mechanisms. Therefore, we concentrate on asymmetric and nonlinear pass through literature in this section.

Pollard and Coughlin (2004) analyze asymmetries and nonlinearities at the industry level for import prices in the United States following a profit maximization model. Their data set covers 9 industries at the two-digit and 20 industries at the three-digit level of classification between 1978:Q1 and 2000:Q4. Although their findings demonstrate an evidence of asymmetric behavior in 5 of two- and 10 of three-digit industries, they conclude that the aggregate results may not provide an evidence of asymmetry. They also add that import prices respond more to the large changes in the exchange rates.

Yang (2007) studies whether depreciation and appreciation of US Dollar in the early 1980s have symmetric effects on import prices across different sectors of United States. Examining import price data for 98 disaggregated SIC industries in the US manufacturing sector and the US import price for all commodities, the author detects mixed evidence regarding the stability of exchange rate pass-through. Covering a period from 1980:12 to 1991:12, Yang (2007) examines the effects of nominal exchange rate index for the US dollar and domestic price index on the import price index.

Bussière (2013) tests if the response of export and import prices of G7 countries to exchange rate changes are symmetric and linear. In his study, he used a standard linear model with polynomial functions of the exchange rate and interactive dummy variables by using Terasvirta's (1994) nonlinearity tests. His findings demonstrate a clear evidence of a non-linear effect and asymmetric behavior and emphasizes that large appreciations have a more than proportional effect on prices.

Nogueira and León-Ledesma (2007) investigate the asymmetry and nonlinearities of exchange rate pass– through into inflation (ERPT) for a set of emerging and developed economies. According to the results obtained by Smooth Transition Model, the nonlinearity is evident although its sources can vary across countries.

Delatte and López-Villavicencio (2012) combined asymmetric long-run relationships with a dynamically flexible ARDL model to analyze the asymmetry of exchange rate pass-through in four major economies (Japan, Germany, United Kingdom and United States) for the period 1980:Q1–2009:Q3. They state that the exchange has a clear effect on the determination of the consumer prices, especially in the long run. They also emphasized that this effect of exchange rate is not linear. The response of prices to an appreciation is smaller the to a depreciation. They consider these results as a sign of weak market competition and downward price rigidities.

Nidhaleddin (2012) investigates nonlinearities and the asymmetry of exchange rate pass through to consumer prices in 12 country of Euro zone. Applying logistic and exponential smooth transition models, the author examines the asymmetry with respect to the direction and the magnitude of exchange rate changes. Although no clear evidence about the direction of asymmetry is detected, the author shows asymmetric pass-through related to exchange rate appreciations and depreciations in 5 countries. The author states that size of exchange rate fluctuations causes asymmetric respond in prices especially in the presence of menu costs.

Rincón-Castro and Rodríguez-Niño (2016) examine a smooth transition autoregressive vector model estimated by Bayesian methods as a tool in order to examine the behavior of exchange rate pass through in Colombia. Their findings show that pass through is incomplete in Colombia and the nature of exchange rate pass through is nonlinear and asymmetric in both short and long run in this small open economy.

These studies have demonstrated the importance of testing and detecting the nonlinear and asymmetric characteristic of pass through mechanism in developed or developing countries. Similarly, in recent years, many studies have been conducted in order to investigate the nonlinearity and asymmetry in pass through mechanism in Turkish economy.

Arbatlı (2003) applies Threshold VAR model to assess a possible asymmetric reaction of wholesale and consumer prices to exchange rate changes in Turkey. Annual change in the industrial production index and inflation are used as a threshold variable, the main threshold variable is the deviation of the change in annual exchange rate from its sample that detects the asymmetric reaction to small and big changes in exchange rate. The author concludes that bigger changes in exchange rate are associated with lower pass through.

Mihaljek and Klau (2008) report that exchange rate passes through to domestic prices in Turkey, which experienced a structural break after 2003. They find that variation of exchange rates exceeding 5 % reflects into the inflation, which shows a threshold effect of pass through in Turkey. Besides, they reported that depreciations have higher coefficients while appreciations have lower confirming an asymmetry in exchange rate pass through in Turkey.

Çiçek and Boz (2013) examine inflation-targeting period of Turkey for the expansion and recession cycles by applying a co-integrating nonlinear autoregression distributed lag (NARDL) model in order to investigate the asymmetric effect of exchange rate movement to domestic inflation rate. Their findings show that because of downward price rigidity in Turkey, the depreciation is passed through the prices, but appreciation is not.

Akkoç and Yücel (2017) analyze the pass-through of the exchange rate movements to the consumer prices in Turkey by Markov regime switching model. Due to their findings, there exist two regimes, stable versus unstable regime, for 2002–2027 period in Turkey and the pass-through varies considerably depending on the regimes. Nevertheless, the change in foreign prices has powerful effects on the domestic consumer prices in both regimes.

Another NARDL model application is applied by Göktaş (2019) for Turkey to examine the relationship between nominal exchange rate and consumer prices for monthly data. The author reports that depreciation has a greater effect than appreciation on consumer prices in Turkey.

3. Empirical Approach

Linear modeling used systematically in Economics since Adam Smith as the linearity assumption is easy to adopt and it allows a simple mathematical treatment. Because of their numerous advantages, they have been frequently applied to reveal the relationship between economic and financial variables. Especially the methodological difficulty, the absence of efficient quantitative tools and the weakness of mathematical tools led researchers to adapt the theory of linear oscillations to economic phenomena in the beginning. Nevertheless, the dominant aspect of these linear processes should not make us forget the limitations and disadvantages that have been attributed to them. Linear models can only generate a symmetrical behavior of the series and therefore cannot account for asymmetry phenomena. Indeed, several studies have shown that the class of linear models is inadequate and that these models may conceal the important properties of cyclical fluctuations in series such as self-sustaining oscillations, excessive variability of certain series, regime changes, trend breaks and cycle asymmetry, which means that the expansion and recession phases do not have the same durations, nor the same amplitudes. Linear formulation is limited to generating similar phases of expansion and recession, thus inducing incomplete exploitation of the information contained in the series. Non-linear models can thus allow us to account for notions of asymmetry and non-linearity.

3.1. Smooth Transition Regression Models

Luukkonen, Saikkonen and Teräsvirta (1988), Teräsvirta (1994) construct STAR (Smooth Transition Autoregressive) models as an extension of TAR (Threshold Autoregressive) models to two regimes. STAR models define a relationship, which can be non-linear over a given period, but linear by sub-periods. In fact, the parameters of the linear relationships associated with the sub-periods differ and thus define the regimes, which enter action according to the previous realization of the transition variable with respect to a threshold. However, unlike the TAR models, where the transition from one regime to another takes place abruptly, the STAR models introduce progressiveness in the process of change (smooth or flexible transition). Granger and Teräsvirta (1997) generalize the STAR model to a STR (Smooth Transition Regression) model by replacing all or part of its regressors with exogenous variables (Uctum, 2007).

STR models are powerful candidates for capturing nonlinearities and regime switching in the analyses of different economic variables. As STR models can detect and model structural breaks naturally, these models are useful to analyze the emerging economies. Different from discrete switching models, smooth transition regression (STR) models transition as a continuous process dependent on the transition variable.

A STR model is defined as follows:

$$y_t = (\alpha_0+\alpha_1 z_{t-1}+...+\alpha_p z_{t-p}) + (\beta_0+\beta_1 z_{t-1}+...+\beta p z_{t-p}) F(s_{t-i}, \gamma, c) + \varepsilon(t) \quad (1)$$

where ε(t)⊱ iid (0, σ2) and z_t is a vector of explanatory variables consist of endogenous (y_t) and exogenous variables (x_t). s_{t-i} is the transition variable which can be a lagged endogenous variable or an exogenous variable or even a function of an exogenous variables. F represents the transition function bounded between 0 and 1. γ is the slope parameter, which measures the speed of transition from one regime to the other, and finally c is the threshold value.

There exist two main choices for the transition function:
Logistic function:

$$F(st; \gamma, c) = (1+\exp\{-\gamma(st - c)\})-1, \gamma > 0 \quad (2)$$

A STR model having this form of the transition function is called logistic STR or LSTR model. The logistics function defines an asymmetric dynamic behavior depend on the sign of the deviation of the transition variable from the threshold (Uctum, 2007). This model defines two extreme regimes associated with the values of s_t above and below the threshold c, between which the transition takes place gradually. The LSTAR model then allows us to describe the phenomena of asymmetry such as the transition of the economy from an expansion phase to a recession phase represented by its own dynamics. For example, if we take output growth as the transition variable and threshold, c, is close to zero, the model distinguishes between periods of positive and negative growth (Nidhaleddine, 2012). Besides, for the LSTAR model, when the transition speed tends to approach infinity (γ → ∞), the transition becomes abrupt and the LSTAR model merges with the TAR model. Conversely, when the transition speed tends towards zero, the model is transformed into a linear model since the transition function is equal to 0.5. Finally, as explained by Christopoulos and León–Ledesma (2007), the LSTR model indicates that the value of the nonlinear coefficient would change depending on whether the transition variable is below or above the threshold (Nogueira and León-Ledesma, 2007). In this sense, as (st-1–c) → −∞, the coefficient becomes α_1; if (st–c) → +∞ then the coefficient is $\alpha_1+\beta_1$; and if st = c it becomes $\alpha_1+\beta_1/2$.
Exponential function:

$$F(s_t; \gamma, c) = (1 - \exp(-\gamma(s_t - c)^2), \gamma > 0 \quad (3)$$

Unlike LSTR model, ESTR model generates symmetrical dynamics for the expansion and recession phases of the cycle, but the intermediate states can have different dynamics. In other words, this transition function is appropriate when the dynamic behavior is different for large and small value of transition variable. In this situation, the magnitude of the shock matters, not the sign. Therefore, the coefficients differ whether s_{t-I} is close or far away from threshold. Hence, when (st-i–c) $\rightarrow \pm\infty$ then the coefficient becomes $\alpha_1 + \beta_1$; and if st-i = c it becomes α_1. Besides, when the transition speed, γ, tends towards zero or infinity ($\gamma \rightarrow 0$ or $\gamma \rightarrow \infty$), the ESTR model becomes a linear model.

As we can clearly see, LSTR and ESTR models specify different nonlinear behaviors. If we choose exchange rate as a transition variable and LSTR as model, then we analyze the asymmetric behavior of exchange rate pass through for currency appreciations and depreciations. In other words, we consider the direction of exchange rate as the source of asymmetry. For ESTR model, the interpretation is different, and this time, it is the magnitude of exchange rate changes, that is whether exchange rate fluctuations are large or small, which cause the asymmetric pass through behavior.

According to ERPT literature, in the presence of menu costs, firms tend to absorb small changes in exchange rate. Thus, Nogueira Jr. and Leon-Ledesma (2007) argue that the costs of changing prices may result in asymmetric pass-through for large and small exchange rate shocks and ESTR specification would be more appropriate in describing this kind of behavior. Terasvirta (1994) also discusses that ESTR models are popularly employed to capture possible nonlinearities in ERPT due to menu costs as firms are more likely to increase prices after large deviations than after small ones.

3.2. Model Specification and Data

In the empirical analysis, we define an ESTR model that enables us to test the presence of an asymmetric ERPT mechanism in Turkey. Our endogenous variable is the inflation rate in Turkey calculated by the changes in consumer price index. The lags of inflation (π_{t-j}) and changes in exchange rate are considered as explanatory variables in the empirical specification.

$$\pi_t = (\alpha_0 + \sum_{i=1}^{p} \alpha_{1i}\pi_{t-i} + \sum_{j=0}^{p} \alpha_{2j}\Delta e_{t-j}) + (\sum_{i=1}^{p} \beta_{1i}\Delta e_{t-i})$$
$$(1 - \exp(-\gamma(\Delta e_{t-d} - c)^2)) + \varepsilon(t) \tag{4}$$

where π_t is the inflation rate, Δe is the change in the exchange rate change and ε is an error term. Exchange rate changes will be transition variable.

There will be two basic outcomes of the equation (4) for ERPT. In the first one, if the transition variable is near the threshold for the ESTR model, ERPT is represented by the linear parameters $\sum_{i=1}^{p} \alpha_{1i}, \sum_{j=0}^{p} \alpha_{2j}$. In the second one, if the transition variable is far away from the threshold for the ESTR model, the coefficients will be $\sum_{i=1}^{p} \alpha_{1i}, \sum_{j=0}^{p} \alpha_{2j} + \sum_{i=1}^{p} \beta_{1i}$.

The data is obtained from the database of Central Bank of Republic of Turkey. Inflation is the change of Consumer Price Index (CPI) and exchange rate change is the change of the national currency per unit of dollar. An increase in exchange rate implies depreciation of the national currency. The data is monthly, and the period of estimation corresponds to the interval that spans from 2003:06 to 2019:10.

4. Empirical Results

In this section we investigate the presence of asymmetric behavior of exchange rate pass through for Turkey by applying ESTR model, which capture the asymmetry, related to size of the exchange rate deviation. We choose the relevant lagged of exchange rate variation Δe_{t-d} with d = 1,2,3,4 by the linearity test[2]. Test results shows that fourth lag of exchange rate change is the appropriate transition variable. The results are as follows[3]:

$$\pi_t = 0{,}52 + 0{,}34\,\pi_{t-1} - 0{,}2\,\pi_{t-2} - 4{,}27\,\Delta e_t - 0{,}18\,\Delta e_{t-2} + 4{,}89\,\Delta e_{t-3} +$$
$$[(4{,}34\,\Delta e_t + 0{,}18\,\Delta e_{t-2} - 4{,}90\,\Delta e_{t-3})\,(1 - \exp(-148{,}03\,(\Delta e_{t-4} - 1{,}96)^2))] + \varepsilon(t)$$
$$R^2 = 0{,}37,\ \text{S.E. of regression} = 0{,}72,\ \text{Fstat} = 7{,}03,\ \text{DW} = 1{,}96$$

We see that the sum of the exchange rate coefficients for change of exchange rate at time t (Δe_t) is 0,07 (-4,27 +4,34). Threshold value is 1,96 which means that %2 of exchange rate is threshold for the pass-through mechanism. Since the estimated threshold is different from zero, it suggests the presence of some adjustment costs of prices, for example menu costs. So, the exchange rate changes smaller than this threshold is not promptly transmitted to prices. The speed of transition is 148 and this high speed of transition shows that when the

2 The results of unit root tests and linearity test are not shown here for reasons of space but are available on request.

3 Only the significant results are shown.

exchange rate fluctuation is over the threshold value (%2), pass through mechanism strengthen.

5. Conclusion

In this study, we have investigated the possible asymmetric and nonlinear behavior of exchange rate pass through mechanism to consumer prices for Turkey. This analysis is conducted using the ESTR model for Turkey for the first time as our knowledge, which permits us to capture the non-linearity stem from the size of the exchange rate fluctuations. Using monthly data for the period 2003–2019, we find a nonlinear response of ERPT to inflation rate with respect to the magnitude of exchange rate changes for Turkey. The finding of our study shows that CPI inflation respond is higher for the exchange rate deviation larger than 2 %. This can be interpreted as an evidence of menu costs which creates a barrier before smaller changes. Central Bank of Republic of Turkey should take in consider this asymmetric nature of pass through in their model used for policy making.

References

Akkoç, U., & Yücel, M. E. (2017). Türkiye'de Döviz Kuru Geçişkenliğinin Asimetrik Davranışı. Uluslararası Yönetim İktisat ve İşletme Dergisi, ICMEB (Special Issue), 903–911.

Arbatlı, E. C. (2003). Exchange rate pass-through in Turkey: Looking for asymmetries. Central Bank Review, 3(2), 85–124.

Bussiere, M. (2013). Exchange rate pass–through to trade prices: The role of nonlinearities and asymmetries. Oxford Bulletin of Economics and Statistics, 75(5), 731–758.

Christopoulos, D. K., & León-Ledesma, M. A. (2007). A long–run non–linear approach to the fisher effect. Journal of Money, Credit and Banking, 39(2–3), 543–559.

Çiçek, S., veBoz, Ç. (2013). A new test of exchange rate pass-through in a small open economy: Evidence from asymmetric ARDL bounds approach. İktisat İşletme ve Finans, 28(June), 43–64.

Delatte, A. L., ve López-Villavicencio, A. (2012). Asymmetric exchange rate pass-through: Evidence from major countries. Journal of Macroeconomics, 34(3), 833–844.

Dornbusch, R. (1987). Exchange rates and prices. The American Economic Review, 77(1), 93–106.

El bejaoui, H. J. (2013). Asymmetric effects of exchange rate variations: AN empirical analysis for four advanced countries. International Economics, 135–136, 29–46.

Flodén, M., & Wilander, F. (2006). State dependent pricing, invoicing currency, and exchange rate pass-through. Journal of International Economics, 70(1), 178–196.

Forbes, K., Hjortsoe, I., & Nenova, T. (2015). The shocks matter: New evidence on exchange rate pass-through. Bank of England, External MPC Unit Discussion Paper, (43), Retrieved from https://www.bankofengland.co.uk/-/media/boe/files/external-mpc-discussion-paper/2015/the-shocks-matter-improving-our-estimates-of-exchange.pdf?la=en&hash=A2CB9E202EECC1F7EBFD3A3644431BE861E926C2 (15.11.2020).

Göktaş, P. (2019). Asymmetric Transition Effects of the Exchange Rate on Consumer Prices in Turkey. Sosyoekonomi, 27(42), 29–50.

Goldberg, L. S., & Campa, J. M. (2006). Distribution margins, imported inputs, and the sensitivity of the CPI to exchange rates (No. w12121). National Bureau of Economic Research, Retrieved from https://www.nber.org/system/files/working_papers/w12121/w12121.pdf (15.11.2020).

Goldberg, P. K., & Knetter, M. M. (1996). Goods prices and exchange rates: What have we learned? (No. w5862). National Bureau of Economic Research.

Granger, C. W. J., & Teräsvirta, T. (1997),.Modelling nonlinear economic relationships, Oxford University Press, Oxford.

Luukkonen, R., Saikkonen, P., & Teräsvirta, T. (1988). Testing linearity against smooth transition autoregressive models. Biometrika, 75(3), 491–499.

Meurers, M. (2003). Incomplete pass through in import markets and permanent versus transitory exchange rate shocks. Ifo, Discussion Paper (83), Retrieved from https://www.cesifo.org/DocDL/ifodpaper83.pdf (15.11.2019).

Mihaljek, D., & Klau, M. (2008). Exchange rate pass-through in emerging market economies: What has changed and why?. BIS Papers, 35, 103–130.

Mishkin, F. S. (2008). Exchange rate pass-through and monetary policy (No. w13889). National Bureau of Economic Research.

Nidhaleddin, B. C. (2012). Asymmetric exchange rate pass-through in the Euro area: New evidence from smooth transition models. Economics: The Open-Access, Open-Assessment E-Journal, 6(39), Retrieved from https://www.econstor.eu/bitstream/10419/65715/1/728676540.pdf (12.10.2019).

Nogueira, R. P., ve León-Ledesma, M. a. (2007). Exchange rate pass-through into inflation: The role of asymmetries and nonlinearities.

Pollard, P. S., & Coughlin, C. C. (2004). Size matters: Asymmetric exchange rate pass-through at the industry level. University of Nottingham Research Paper, (2004/13).

Rincon-Castro, H., & Rodríguez-Niño, N. (2016). Nonlinear pass-through of exchange rate shocks on inflation: A bayesian smooth transition VAR approach. Borradores de Economía; No. 930.

Takhtamanova, Y. F. (2010). Understanding changes in exchange rate pass-through. Journal of Macroeconomics, 32(4), 1118–1130.

Taylor, J. B. (2000). Low inflation, pass-through, and the pricing power of firms. European Economic Review, 44(7), 1389–1408.

Teräsvirta, T. (1994). Specification, estimation, and evaluation of smooth transition autoregressive models. Journal of the american Statistical association, 89(425), 208–218.

Uctum, R. (2007). Économétrie des modèles à changement de régimes: un essai de synthèse. L'Actualité économique, 83(4), 447–482.

Yang, J. (2007). Is exchange rate pass-through symmetric? Evidence from US imports. Applied Economics, 39(2), 169–178.

Uğur Akkoç

Chapter 3 Time Varying Nature of Causality between Exchange Rate and Uncertainties

Abstract: It is a well-known fact that economic uncertainties can affect investor and consumer behavior and pose a significant risk to economic performance. However, literature on the macroeconomic uncertainties related to Turkish economy mostly focuses on the exchange rate uncertainty. This study investigates the causal relationship between the local and global uncertainties with the exchange rate in Turkey by applying the time-varying parameter causality test. The period between 2006 and 2020, since when Turkey has started to implement open economy inflation targeting regime, was selected as sample and monthly data were employed. There are two main conclusions that can be summarized from the findings of time-dependent causality tests. Firstly, the causality relationship between inflation and interest rate uncertainty, which are local uncertainties, with the exchange rate, has been stable and explicitly continuing since 2017, when the high and volatile inflation period began. Secondly, it is noteworthy that there is a causal relationship from global uncertainties to the exchange rate especially in the period during the 2008 global crisis and immediately afterwards, where it has not been seen a casuality relationship between the variables in the whole sample. The causality relationship between global uncertainties and the exchange rate is more permanent in terms of real effective exchange rate.

Keywords: Time-Varying Parameter Causality Test, Exchange Rate, Uncertainties

1. Introduction

It is a well-known fact that economic uncertainties can affect investor and consumer behavior and pose a significant risk to economic performance. However, the 2008 global financial crisis reminded us that we all live in a world of risks and uncertainties (Nelson & Katzenstein, 2014). While the unpredictable 2008 crisis recalled the importance of uncertainties, the role of economic uncertainty in economic performance has become more controversial. It is seen that the question of how much increasing uncertainties are responsible for the 2008 crisis and the weak recovery afterwards is frequently discussed. According to the popular argument in this regard, the increase in economic uncertainties reduces the employment and investment of firms and the consumption of households. Therefore, in an environment of increased uncertainty, interruption of production and increase in unemployment are theoretically the first expected events.

It is seen that the literature on the subject is expanding gradually with Bloom's (2009) pioneering study. He tried to measure how uncertainties had an impact on the recession and unemployment in the US economy just after the 2008 crisis. In the subsequent studies, Baker et al. (2013) claims that 2.3 % of the revenue decline in the US economy during the period between 2006 and 2011 was due to policy uncertainty. Leduc and Liu (2014) stated that uncertainties were responsible for the one-point increase in unemployment in the similar period. Studies aiming to measure the macroeconomic effects of uncertainties during and after the 2008 crisis report analogous results[1].

Not only the effects of macroeconomic uncertainties during the 2008 crisis, but also various economic effects are discussed in the literature. Beckmann and Caudaj (2017) argue that economic uncertainties shape exchange rate expectations. Benigno et al. (2012) and Colombo (2013) state that local uncertainties in various areas are effective in explaining the exchange rate movements in the G-6 countries[2] and the USA, respectively. In addition, many studies report that macroeconomic uncertainties in a country are effective in investor behavior (Zhang, 2019) and have a negative impact on the stock market in that country (Özoğuz, 2009; Kang & Ratti, 2013; Dzielinski, 2012; Antonakakis et al., 2013; Brogaard & Detzel, 2015). According to another view, uncertainties in developed countries spread to the stock markets of other countries and have a negative effect (Trung, 2019; Jurado et al., 2015; Baker et al., 2016, Krol, 2014). Bekiros et al. (2015) show that uncertainties affect pricing in commodity markets. Finally, empirical analyses of the relationship between inflation and inflation uncertainty have often been studied (Balcılar & Özdemir, 2013; Nasr et al., 2015; Özdemir & Fisunoğlu, 2008; Su et al., 2017).

Literature on the macroeconomic uncertainties related to Turkish economy mostly focuses on the exchange rate uncertainty. In the literature, majority of the studies analyze the relationship between the exchange rate uncertainty and exports (Esen, 2012; Saatçioğlu & Karaca 2011; Tarı & Yıldırım, 2009; Acaravcı & Öztürk, 2002; Özer, 2012). Sarıoğlu (2013) expanded the effect of foreign exchange uncertainty on exports sectorally. Sever (2012) examines the impact of exchange rate uncertainty on the foreign trade performance of Turkish economy. Regarding to the studies about the effects of exchange rate uncertainty

1 For a detailed research, see Bloom (2014).
2 Ethiopia, Madagascar, Malawi, Sudan, Zambia, Zimbabwe.

on Turkish economy, Şahin and Sekmen (2013), Çevik et al. (2016) and Tiryaki and Tiryaki (2019) point out the negative effects of exchange rate uncertainty on Istanbul stoch exchange; whereas Öksüzler and Ekinci (2013) and Koç and Değer (2010) investigate the effect of exchange rate uncertainty on investments. Sever (2012) reports the bi-directional casuality relationship between exchange rate uncertainty and dolarization. In addition, Ceylan et al. (2018) analyzed the relationship between inflation uncertainty and interest rate.

The relationship between inflation uncertainty and inflation is an area widely examined in Turkey. It is observed that the validity of the Friedman (1977) – Ball (1992) hypothesis, which points to an increase of inflation uncertainty in the time of high inflation and the validity of the Cukierman and Meltzer (1986) hypothesis that mentions the effect of inflation uncertainty on inflation are frequently tested. Studies indicate that there is a causal relationship from inflation to inflation uncertainty as suggested by the Friedman-Ball hypothesis (Karahan, 2012; Korap, 2009; Sever & Demir, 2008; Oltulular & Terzi, 2006). Erkam (2008) claims that inflation uncertainty is the cause of inflation.

Finally, it is possible to mention the studies made on measuring macroeconomic uncertainty in Turkey. In this context, Yıldırım and Alkan (2018) using the time series properties of macroeconomic and financial variables have tried to measure the macroeconomic uncertainties in the economy of Turkey. In addition, Şahinöz and Coşar (2018), and Jirasavetakul and Spilimbergo (2018) have derived uncertainty indices with data mining methods, as it is often used in the international literature. Şahinöz and Coşar (2018) developed a unceraínty criterion by reviewing the news published in Turkish newspapers in order to observe the uncertainty in the market. Jirasavetalul and Spilimbergo (2018) carried out a similar method by examining the newspapers published abroad regarding to Turkish economy.

When the literature related to uncertainties in Turkish economy is considered, there has not been encountered an extensive study analyzing the effect of uncertainties on foreign exchange. The purpose of this study is to analyze the relationship between the exchange rate and macroeconomic uncertainties in the Turkish economy. In accordance with this object, the dynamic structure of the relationship between uncertainties and the exchange rate is analyzed by running the time-varying vector autoregressive (TV-VAR) causality tests. At the same time, the scope has been extended by using many alternative uncertainty criteria. The present study aims to fill the gap in the literature by examining the effects of local and global uncertainties on Turkey's exchange rates in terms of time varying structure and in an extensive format.

2. Method

In the empirical part of this study, Granger casuality test based on VAR model is employed to investigate the casuality relationship between foreign exchange (Forex) and macroeconomic uncertainties in Turkey. In this context, two-variable VAR models are established by using the exchange rate and each uncertainty criterion. After the estimation of these models, the existence of a causality relationship between the two variables is tested with the Granger causality test. The Granger causality test basically examines whether a second variable provides useful information in predicting future movements of a variable or not. The VAR model created for this purpose can be expressed as follows:

$$\begin{bmatrix} \text{Forex}_t \\ \text{Uncertainty}_t \end{bmatrix} = \begin{bmatrix} \varnothing_{10} \\ \varnothing_{20} \end{bmatrix} + \begin{bmatrix} \varnothing_{11}(\text{L}) & \varnothing_{12}(\text{L}) \\ \varnothing_{21}(\text{L}) & \varnothing_{22}(\text{L}) \end{bmatrix} \begin{bmatrix} \text{Forex}_t \\ \text{Uncertainty}_t \end{bmatrix} + \begin{bmatrix} \varepsilon_{1t} \\ \varepsilon_{2t} \end{bmatrix} \quad (1)$$

"Forex_t" and "Uncertainty_t" indicate the exchange rate and each of the macroeconomic uncertainty criteria variables respectively. Moreover "L" refers to the lag operator whereas ε is the error term. The parameters in the notation above are expressed as the sum of the coefficients of the lagged values. To generalize, it can be formulized as $\varnothing_{ij}(L) = \sum_{k=1}^{p+1} \varnothing_{ij,k} L^k$. Equation (1) is the VAR model that demonstrates the exchange rate and uncertainties simultaneously with both self- lagged values and cross-lagged values. The Granger causality test simply tests whether the sum of "$\varnothing_{12}$ and "$\varnothing_{21}$" parameters in this equation is equal to zero or not. For instance, zero sum "$\varnothing_{12}$ coefficient means that the level or any lag of the uncertainty variable does not take place in the exchange rate equation. This situation leads to the acceptance of the null hypothesis that the uncertainty is not the Granger cause of exchange rate. Likewise, whether the exchange rate is the Granger cause of macroeconomic uncertainties or not depends on if the exchange rate variable takes place statistically significant in the macroeconomic uncertainty equation. Then, aforesaid casuality relationship is tested as if the sum of "$\varnothing_{21}$" variable is equal to zero or not. If the parameter sum is not statistically different from zero, it is understood that there is no Granger causality relationship from exchange rate to uncertainty.

Structural changes or short-term cyclical fluctuations may prevent causality findings from being stable throughout the period. Similarly, it is thought that there may not be a permanent causal relationship between the exchange rate and macroeconomic uncertainty during the period under examination. In other words, while the causality relationship is significant in some sub-periods, in some other sub-periods, uncertainties and exchange rate can be independent from each other. In order to loosen the assumption that the relationship between the two variables is the same during the examined period, the Granger causality analysis applied in this study was expanded by the sliding windows method. In this method, time varing causality analysis is carried out through the sub-samples that are created and sequent nested during the examined period. The sliding windows approach basically provides two advantages. First, it allows causality relationship to change over time. Second, it allows taking into account the structural changes occurring in the studied period.

The sliding windows method is based on dividing the analyzed sample into sub-samples containing the fixed "l" size observation from the beginning to the end. To put a finer point on it, from the first observation of the sample, "l" observation forms the first sub-sample. The second sub-sample contains "l+1" observation including the second observation. In this way, while sub-samples are created sequentially and nested until the last observation, causality test is repeated in each sub-sample. In the sliding windows method, "l" refers to the window size. Although there is no consistent criterion recommended for determining the size of the window (Balcılar et al., 2010), the results of the applied test are expected to be of a size that can be significant (Brooks & Hinich, 1998).

The test statistics obtained from the each sub-sample are normalized with the unique bootstrap critical value of each sub-sample. Thus, standardized statistics are derived in order to facilitate decision-making while the test statistics and critical values obtained in each sub-sample change over time (e.g. Yılancı & Bozoklu, 2014). Since the test statistics for each sub-sample are normalized, the null hypothesis that there is no causality relationship in sub-samples with statistics exceeding the threshold value is rejected.

3. Data

To analyze the causality relationship between the exchange rate and macroeconomic uncertainties, several variations of these variables were used for the period 2006:01 – 2020:02 on a monthly basis. Firstly, the TRY/USD rate and real effective exchange rate (REER) were employed as proxy of exchange rate. Although TRY/USD exchange rate is a main indicator, the real effective exchange rate is a weighted currency basket, which is composed by the currencies of Turkey's foreign trade partners regarding to their share in Turkish foreign trade. Therefore, it can be claimed to be more inclusive. TRY/USD and the real effective exchange rate data were taken from the Electronic Data Delivery System (EVDS) of the Central Bank of the Republic of Turkey (CBRT).

It is possible to talk about many forms of macroeconomic uncertainties. Traditional uncertainty criteria are measured by the estimated variance series of macroeconomic variables (Jirasavetakul & Spilimbergo, 2018). For example, the variance of the policy interest rate is used to measure the uncertainties in monetary policy. In this context, to measure the macroeconomic uncertainties, five uncertainty criteria, two of which are global and three are local were employed. Interest rates and inflation uncertainty have been calculated in terms of representing the uncertainties related to Turkey's economy. The first one is the variance series of the CBRT's overnight average funding interest rate, which is accepted as a proxy of the policy interest rate in the market. Similarly, inflation uncertainty is the estimated variance series of inflation, which is measured as the percentage difference of the consumer price index.

To derive the interest rate and inflation uncertainty, conditional variances of these two series are estimated. Both variables were estimated by the autoregressive integrated moving average (ARIMA) and the generalized autoregressive conditional heteroskedasticity (GARCH) models for the prediction of conditional variances. Lags of AR and MA terms in ARIMA model and p and q parameters in GARCH model were determined by grid search. Accordingly, the highest lag was determined as 5. And among all model alternatives up to this lag, the model with the lowest information criteria was selected according to the Akaike and Schwarz information criteria. It can be argued that the selected model best reflects the motion of these two variables. Conditional variance series, derived from the estimates made by the selected method, were used as uncertainty criteria. Interest and inflation data are also taken from EVDS.

The third local uncertainty regarding to Turkish economy, besides the interest rate and inflation uncertainties, is discussed as geopolitical risks. Caldara and Iacoviello (2017) generated a geopolitical risk index for 18 developing countries including the USA by using data mining method. As the value of the index increases, it means that the geopolitical risk increases and the index is normalized to take an average value of 100 in the 2000–2009 decade. Turkey's geopolitical risk data were obtained from Economic Policy Uncertainty web page.

It can be argued that in Turkey as a typical developing country, exchange rates are not only affected by local uncertainties but also international uncertainties. Liquidity conditions in the global markets or uncertainties in the developed markets present a significant impact on Turkish economy. It can be said that the exchange rate is affected by global uncertainties both through foreign trade relations and through foreign exchange liquidity. In this context, the global uncertainty index developed by Davis (2016) and the US uncertainty index measured by Baker et al. (2016) were used as proxy of global uncertainties in the study. The global uncertainty index is obtained from the Federal Reserve System (FED) database, while the uncertainty index for the US economy is taken from Economic Policy Uncertainty web page.

4. Findings

Before examining the relationship between exchange rate and macroeconomic uncertainties within the scope of the sample described in the previous section, it is necessary to determine whether the variables used are stationary or not. For this purpose, the results of the Augmented Dickey–Fuller (ADF) unit root test applied to the level values and first differences of the variables are given in Tab. 3.1. According to the results in the table, georisk expressing geopolitical risk, uncertainties in the US economy and inflation uncertainty are seemed to be stationary. For these variables, the null hypothesis in the form of the unit root existence is rejected. However, the TRY/USD exchange rate and the real effective exchange rate variables, as well as the global uncertainty index and the interest rate uncertainty variable, become stationary at the first difference. Therefore, the first difference of exchange rate variables and interest rate uncertainty and global uncertainty variables are included in the analysis, while the level values of other variables are employed.

Tab. 3.1. ADF Unit Root Test Results, Source: Author's own calculations

	Level			**First Difference**		
	Constant	**Trend and Constant**	**None**	**Constant**	**Trend and Constant**	**None**
Dolar	1.805	-0.683	3.219	-6.75***	-11.23***	-6.32***
Real Effective Exchange Rate	-0.857	-2.591	-1.232	-10.330***	-10.322***	-10.260***
Interest rate Uncertainty	-2.632*	-2.624	-1.395	-4.468***	-4.448***	-4.478***
Inflation Uncertainty	-9.890***	-9.880***	-1.564	-	-	-10.49***
Georisk	-3.676***	-3.948**	-0.436	-11.618***	-11.591***	-11.647***
Global Uncertainty	-2.376	-4.901***	-0.313	-17.064***	-17.012***	-17.084***
USA Uncertainty	-4.642***	-4.639***	-1.580	-	-	-10.113***

Note: *, ** and *** indicate that the null hypothesis was rejected at the %10, %5 and %1 significance level, respectively.

Tab. 3.2 shows the results of the causality relationship between the variables that have been made stationary. In the first step of causality analysis, causality test was done for the whole sample. The first column of the Tab. 3.2 indicates the number of lags used in the VAR estimate performed before the causality test. The optimal lags in the VAR models are determined according to the Akaike Information Criterion. The other columns of the Tab. 3.2 represent the test statistics of the Granger causality tests between the dollar and the real effective exchange rate as proxy of the exchange rate, and the local and global uncertainties; and the numbers in parentheses illustrate the p values.

According to the results in the Tab. 3.2, there is no causal relationship in any direction between exchange rate and global uncertainty, US uncertainty and geopolitical risk. All p values of the relevant test statistics are higher than 5 %, and the null hypothesis that indicates there is no causal relationship cannot be

Tab. 3.2. Granger Causality Test Results for the Whole Sample, Source: Author's own calculations

Optimal Lag	Hypothesis	Test Statistics	Hypothesis	Test Statistics
TRY/USD Exchange Rate				
3	Inflation Uncertainty -> Dollar	12.84 (0.005)	Dollar -> Inflation Uncertainty	51.208 (0.00)
2	Interest Rate Uncertainty -> Dollar	7.091 (0.028)	Dollar -> Interest Rate Uncertainty	0.602 (0.739)
2	Georisk -> Dollar	0.013 (0.99)	Dollar -> Georisk	0.118 (0.94)
2	Global Uncertainty -> Dollar	3.383 (0.18)	Dollar -> Global Uncertainty	2.199 (0.33)
2	USA Uncertainty -> Dollar	0.040 (0.98)	Dollar -> USA Uncertainty	1.390 (0.49)
Real Effective Exchange Rate				
2	Inflation Uncertainty -> REER	5.472 (0.06)	REER -> Inflation Uncertainty	10.267 (0.005)
1	Interest Rate Uncertainty -> REER	2.34 (0.125)	REER -> Interest Rate Uncertainty	0.20 (0.88)
4	Georisk -> REER	0.969 (0.91)	REER -> Georisk	1.278 (0.86)
2	Global Uncertainty -> REER	0.479 (0.78)	REER -> Global Uncertainty	0.207 (0.90)
2	USA Uncertainty -> REER	0.329 (0.827)	REER -> USA Uncertainty	6.676 (0.43)

rejected. On the other hand, it is observed that there is a causality relationship between the interest rate and inflation uncertainties, which are proxy of local uncertainties, and the exchange rate. The same results were obtained with the tests performed using both the TRY/USD and the real effective exchange rate variables. Accordingly, it is possible to talk about the existence of a bidirectional causality relationship between inflation uncertainty and exchange rate. In other words, the relationship between the uncertainty in inflation rates and the exchange rate is reported, while the level of the exchange rate affects the inflation uncertainty. When the transitivity from the exchange rate to inflation is considered, this is an expected result. The causality relationship between interest rate uncertainty and exchange rate is unidirectional. Only the uncertainty of interest arises as the cause of the exchange rate.

The results in Tab. 3.2 are based on the assumption that the causality relationship is constant all over the examined period. However, the focus of the study is that these relationships may change over time. Therefore, the study was expanded with time-dependent causality analysis by repeating the mentioned causality relationships throughout the sub-samples. The size of each sub-sample should be small enough to reveal the time-varying dynamic structure, but wide enough to allow the test to be reliably performed. In this context, each of the sub-samples was determined to include twenty observations. Thus, the whole sample was divided into 150 sub-samples consisting of twenty observations, and Granger causality test results were obtained based on the VAR estimation for each sub-sample.

Fig. 3.1 visualizes the results of Granger causality tests performed on sub-samples. All charts in the figure contain the results of causality relationships from macroeconomic uncertainties to the exchange rate. While the null hypothesis states that there is no causal relationship, the null hypothesis is rejected during the periods when the normalized test statistics is greater than one. Therefore, it can be said that the relevant macroeconomic uncertainty is the Granger cause of the exchange rate in the areas where the test statistics expressed in colored and dashed lines exceed a limit.

First of all, in the causality relation from inflation uncertainty to exchange rate, the normalized test statistics are higher than one in the majority of the period examined. Another remarkable point in this relationship is that the continuous causality relationship between inflation and exchange rate has been found out since the beginning of 2017. Inflation in Turkey has been increasing in an unstable trend since the beginning of 2017. In a period of high and volatile inflation, it is possible to say that the relationship between inflation uncertainty and exchange rate is maintained consistently. Interest rate uncertainty,

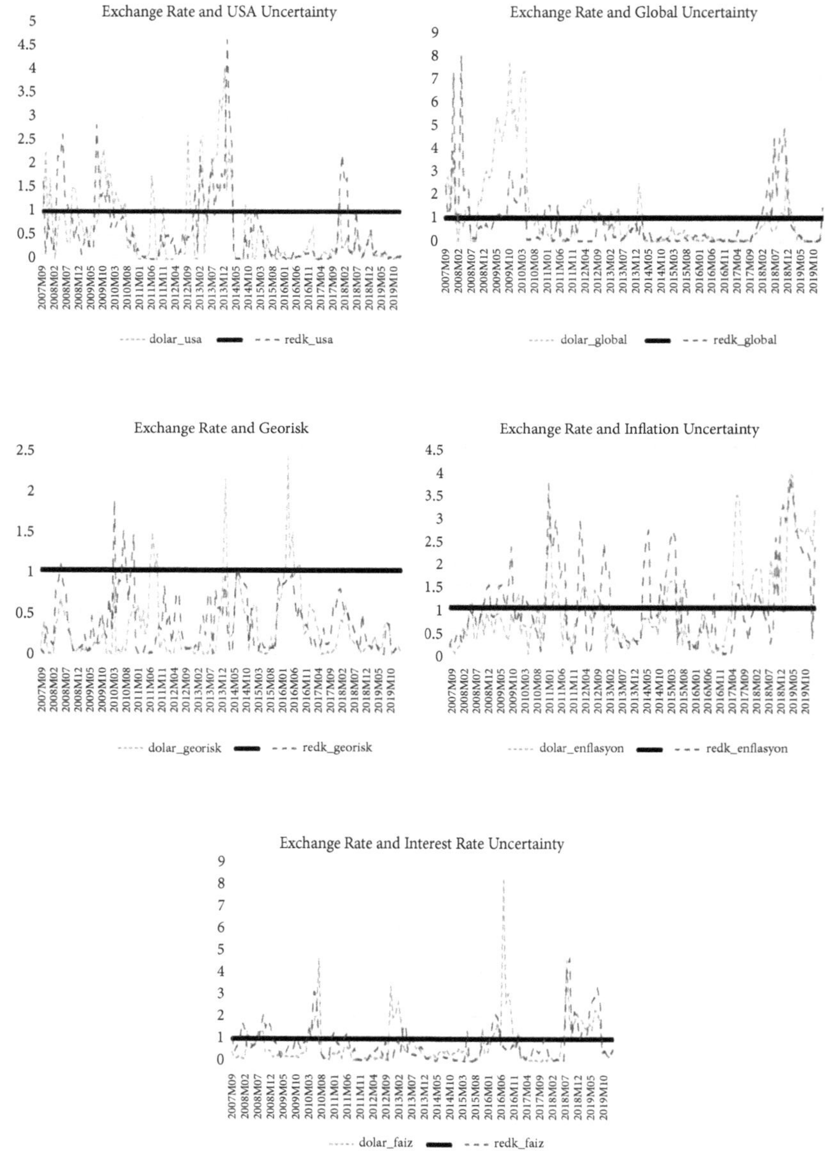

Fig. 3.1. Time Varying VAR Causality Test Results, Source: Author's own calculations

another local uncertainty, is the reason for the exchange rate throughout the sample. However supporting results were found only in certain periods of the sub-samples. Nevertheless, as in inflation uncertainty, a continuous causality relationship is observed between interest rate uncertainty and exchange rate.

When the time-varying causality relationships between the global uncertainties and the exchange rate are examined, first, besides a few sub-samples that can be considered as an exception, there could not be obtained a significant causality relationship between georisk, which defines geopolitical risk, and the exchange rate. In addition, the relationship between global risk and exchange rate clearly reflects the effects of the 2008 crisis. The causality relationship from global uncertainty to exchange rate is significant only during the 2008 crisis, except for 2018. So it is concluded that the exchange rate in Turkish economy is not affected by global uncertainty in normal conditions but in times of crisis. Finally, the effect of global uncertainty on the real effective exchange rate is longer when it is compared to the dollar. This result supports the view that real effective exchange rate is a more inclusive indicator.

5. Conclusion

This study investigates the causal relationship between the local and global uncertainties with the exchange rate in Turkey by applying the time-varying parameter causality test. The period between 2006 and 2020, since when Turkey has started to implement open economy inflation targeting regime, was selected as sample and monthly data were employed. The causality tests based on the VAR model for the whole period show that there is no causal relationship between global uncertainties and the exchange rate. It is concluded that there is a causal relationship between local uncertainties and the exchange rate. Accordingly, while there is a relationship between interest rate uncertainty and inflation uncertainty with exchange rate, the exchange rate appears to be the cause of inflation uncertainty as expected.

In the next step, time-based causality tests were applied since the causality relationship examined may change depending on the time during the period examined. Global or local structural changes and cyclical fluctuations, such as the 2008 global financial crisis in the period under review, can change the structure of the causality relationship. In this context, the sample was divided into 150 sequential sub-samples and the causality tests were repeated. As expected, the causality relationship has been observed to change over time. There are two main conclusions that can be summarized from the findings of time-dependent causality tests. According to the first of these, the causality relationship between inflation and interest rate uncertainty, which are local uncertainties, with the exchange rate, has been stable and explicitly continuing since 2017, when the high and volatile inflation period began. Secondly, it is noteworthy that there is a causal relationship from global uncertainties to the exchange rate especially in the period during the 2008 global crisis and immediately afterwards, where it has not been seen a casuality relationship between the variables in the whole sample. The causality relationship between global uncertainties and the exchange rate is more permanent in terms of real effective exchange rate.

References

Acaravcı, A., & Öztürk, İ. (2002). Döviz kurundaki değişkenliğin Türkiye ihracatı üzerine etkisi: ampirik bir çalışma. Review of Social, Economic and Business Studies, 2, 197–206.

Antonakakis, N., Chatziantoniou, I., & Filis, G. (2013). Dynamic co-movements of stock market returns, implied volatility and policy uncertainty. Economics Letters, 120(1), 87–92.

Baker, S., Bloom, N., & Davis, S. (2013). "Measuring economic policy uncertainty". Chicago Booth Research Paper (13–02).

Baker, S. R., Bloom, N., & Davis, S. J. (2016). Measuring economic policy uncertainty. The Quarterly Journal of Economics, 131(4), 1593–1636.

Balcılar, M., & Özdemir, Z. A. (2013). Asymmetric and timevarying causality between inflation and inflation uncertainty in G-7 countries. Scottish Journal of Political Economy, 60(1), 1–42.

Balcilar, M., Özdemir, Z. A., & Arslanturk, Y. (2010). Economic growth and energy consumption causal nexus viewed through a bootstrap rolling window. Energy Economics, 32(6), 1398–1410.

Ball, L. (1992). Why does high inflation raise inflation uncertainty?. Journal of Monetary Economics, 29(3), 371–388.

Beckmann, J., & Czudaj, R. (2017). Exchange rate expectations and economic policy uncertainty. European Journal of Political Economy, 47, 148–162.

Bekiros, S., Gupta, R., & Paccagnini, A. (2015). Oil price forecastability and economic uncertainty. Economics Letters, 132, 125–128.

Benigno, G., Benigno, P., & Nisticò, S. (2012). Risk, monetary policy, and the exchange rate. NBER Macroeconomics Annual, 26(1), 247–309.

Bloom, N. (2009). The impact of uncertainty shocks. Econometrica, 77(3), 623–685.

Bloom, N. (2014). Fluctuations in uncertainty. Journal of Economic Perspectives, 28(2), 153–176.

Brogaard, J., & Detzel, A. (2015). The asset-pricing implications of government economic policy uncertainty. Management Science, 61(1), 3–18.

Brooks, C., & Hinich, M. J. (1998). Episodic nonstationarity in exchange rates. Applied Economics Letters, 5(11), 719–722.

Caldara, D., & Iacoviello, M. (2017). "Measuring Geopolitical Risk," working paper, Board of Governors of the Federal Reserve Board, Retrieved from https://papers.ssrn.com/sol3/papers.cfm?abstract_id=3117773 (12.09. 2020).

Çevik, E. İ., Uygurtürk, H., & Korkmaz, T. (2016). Enflasyon Belirsizliği İle Pay Senedi Getirisi Ve Volatilitesi Arasındaki İlişki: Türkiye Örneği. International Journal of Management Economics and Business, 30, 159–172.

Ceylan, F., Tüzün, O., Ekinci, R., & Ceylan, I. E. (2018). The Casual relationship between inflatıon uncertaınty and interest rate in Turkey: Rollıng wındow causalıty test. Journal of Mehmet Akif Ersoy University Economics and Administrative Sciences Faculty, 5(3), 977–990.

Colombo, V. (2013). Economic policy uncertainty in the US: Does it matter for the Euro area?. Economics Letters, 121(1), 39–42.

Cukierman, A., & Meltzer, A. H. (1986). A theory of ambiguity, credibility, and inflation under discretion and asymmetric information. Econometrica: Journal of the Econometric Society, 54(5), 1099–1128.

Davis, S. J. (2016). An index of global economic policy uncertainty (No. w22740). National Bureau of Economic Research https://www.nber.org/papers/w22740 Erişim Tarihi: 12 September 2020.

Doğru, B. (2013). Farklı para politikası rejimlerinde enflasyon belirsizliği ve enflasyon ilişkisi. BDDK Bankacilik ve Finansal Piyasalar, 7(2), 77–99.

Dzielinski, M. (2012). Measuring economic uncertainty and its impact on the stock market. Finance Research Letters, 9(3), 167–175.

Economic Policy Uncertainty Index, Retrieved from www.policyuncertainty.com (12.09.2020).

Erkam, S. (2008). Enflasyon ve Enflasyon Belirsizliği: Türkiye Örneği. Journal of Sosyoekonomi, 7(7), 157–174.

Esen, Ö. (2012). Türkiye'de döviz kuru belirsizliğinin ihracat üzerine etkisi. Journal of Finans, Politik & Ekonomik Yorumlar, 49(568), 87–97.

Friedman, M. (1977). Nobel lecture: Inflation and unemployment. Journal of Political Economy, 85(3), 451–472.

Jirasavetakul, L. B. F., & Spilimbergo, M. A. (2018). Economic policy uncertainty in Turkey. International Monetary Fund.

Jurado, K., Ludvigson, S. C., & Ng, S. (2015). Measuring uncertainty. American Economic Review, 105(3), 1177–1216.

Kang, W., & Ratti, R. A. (2013). Oil shocks, policy uncertainty and stock market return. Journal of International Financial Markets, Institutions and Money, 26, 305–318.

Karahan, Ö. (2012). The relationship between inflation and inflation uncertainty: Evidence from the Turkish economy. Procedia Economics and Finance, 1, 219–228.

Koç, H., & Değer, M. K. (2010). Döviz Kuru Belirsizliği Ve Yurtiçi Yatırımlar: Türkiye Ekonomisi Üzerine Nedensellik Testleri (1988–2007). Ataturk University Journal of Economics & Administrative Sciences, 24(3), 79–93.

Korap, L. (2009). On the links between inflation, output growth and uncertainty: System-GARCH evidence from the Turkish economy. MPRA Paper No. 19054, Retrieved from https://mpra.ub.uni-muenchen.de/19054/1/MPRA_paper_19054.pdf (12.09.2020).

Krol, R. (2014). Economic policy uncertainty and exchange rate volatility. International Finance, 17(2), 241–256.

Leduc, S., & Liu, Z. (2014). "Uncertainty shocks are aggregate demand shocks". Working Paper Series Federal Reserve Bank of San Francisco, 2012–10, Retrieved from https://www.frbsf.org/economic-research/files/wp12-10bk.pdf (12.09.2020).

Nasr, A. B., Balcilar, M., Ajmi, A. N., Aye, G. C., Gupta, R., & Van Eyden, R. (2015). Causality between inflation and inflation uncertainty in South Africa: Evidence from a Markov-switching vector autoregressive model. Emerging Markets Review, 24, 46–68.

Nelson, S. C., & Katzenstein, P. J. (2014). Uncertainty, risk, and the financial crisis of 2008. International Organization, 68(2), 361–392.

Öksüzler, O., & Ekinci, M. F. (2013). Döviz Kuru Belirsizliğinin Özel Sabit Sermaye Yatırımlarına Etkisi: Türkiye Örneği. Journal of Management and Economics Research, 11(20), 32–42.

Oltulular, A. G. S., & Terzi, H. (2006). Yüksek Enflasyon Enflasyon Belirsizliğini Artırıyor Mu?. E-journal of Econometrics and Statistics, (3), 1–22.

Özdemir, Z. A., & Fisunoğlu, M. (2008). On the inflation-uncertainty hypothesis in Jordan, Philippines and Turkey: A long memory approach. International Review of Economics & Finance, 17(1), 1–12.

Özer, O. O. (2012). Türkiye'nin Tarım Ürünleri İhracat Fonksiyonu ve Döviz Kuru Belirsizliğinin İhracatta Olan Etkileri. Journal of Selçuk Agriculture Sciences, 26(2), 63–69.

Özoğuz, A. (2009). Good times or bad times? Investors' uncertainty and stock returns. The Review of Financial Studies, 22(11), 4377–4422.

Saatçioğlu, C., & Karaca, O. (2011). Döviz kuru belirsizliğinin ihracata etkisi: Türkiye örneği. Doğuş Üniversitesi Dergisi, 5(2), 183–195.

Şahin, İ., & Sekmen, F. (2013). Türkiye'de Döviz Kuru Belirsizliğinin Hisse Senedi Getirilerine Etkisi. Dumlupınar University, Journal of Social Sciences, (36), 149–156.

Şahinöz, S., & Coşar, E. (2018). Economic policy uncertainty and economic activity in Turkey. Applied Economics Letters, 25(21), 1517–1520.

Sarıoğlu, S. E. (2013). Reel Döviz Kuru Belirsizliğinin Türkiye'nin İhracatına Etkisi: Farklı Sektörler Üzerine Bir Analiz. Anadolu University Journal of Social Sciences, 13(1), 77–92.

Sever, E. (2012). Türkiye'de Dolarizasyon Süreci ve Döviz Kuru Belirsizliği İlişkisi. Sosyoekonomi, 17(1), 203–222.

Sever, E., & Demir, M. (2008). Enflasyon hedeflemesi sürecinde enflasyon ve enflasyon belirsizliği ilişkisinin analizi. Journal of Management and Economics Research, 24(1), 41–63.

Su, C. W., Yu, H., Chang, H. L., & Li, X. L. (2017). How does inflation determine inflation uncertainty? A Chinese perspective. Quality & Quantity, 51(3), 1417–1434.

Tari, R., & Yildirim, D. Ç. (2009). Döviz Kuru Belirsizliğinin İhracata Etkisi: Türkiye İçin Bir Uygulama. Journal of Management & Economics, 16(2), 95–105.

The Central Bank of Turkey, Electronic Data Delivery System, Retrieved from https://evds2.tcmb.gov.tr/ (12.09.2020).

Tiryaki, H. N., & Tiryaki, A. (2019). Determinants of Turkish stock returns under the impact of economic policy uncertainty. International Journal of Economics and Administrative Studies, (22), 147–162.

Trung, N. B. (2019). The spillover effect of the US uncertainty on emerging economies: A panel VAR approach. Applied Economics Letters, 26(3), 210–216.

Yilanci, V., & Bozoklu, Ş. (2014). Türk sermaye piyasasında fiyat ve işlem hacmi ilişkisi: Zamanla Değişen Asimetrik Nedensellik Analizi. Ege Academic Review, 14(2), 211–220.

Yıldırım, H., & Alkan, B. (2018). Türkiye için bir makroekonomik belirsizlik endeksi önerisi. The Banks Association of Turkey Journal of Banking, 104, 6–24.

Zhang, B. (2019). Economic policy uncertainty and investor sentiment: Linear and nonlinear causality analysis. Applied Economics Letters, 26(15), 1264–1268.

Ayça Özekin[1]

Chapter 4 Modeling of the Complex Adaptive System of the International Trade between Developed and Developing Countries

Abstract: The dynamic and complex structure of economic events has led to their modeling and analysis with complex adaptive systems in recent years. International trade by definition is also a topic, which is appropriate to be expressed with complex adaptive systems through both the complex relations created by trade network connections of many countries in the world and through the dynamic structures that carries adaptive features at the point that it produces a new strategy for the highest benefit of the country in every period by sticking to the international agreements. In this study, it is aimed to model international trade as a complex adaptive system. An agent-based modeling, in which countries are represented as agents, will be conducted for the analysis of the complex adaptive system. The network topology that is suitable for this model is called Small World Networks, one of the complex network models believed to be able to reflect real world conditions well. In addition, the required adaptability feature for the formation and sustainability of the trade links on the network is provided by adding the evolutionary strategies to the model. Thus, the agents who need finite features and rules that govern their behavior and decision making ability can realize these features and rules through evolutionary strategies. Evolutionary strategies have been used in the simulation of the model and in the calculation of the pay-off matrix of the prisoner's dilemma game, which is used to express trade relations with its structure that allows cooperation. The pay-off matrix values will be created to reflect the argument of the Prebisch-Singer hypothesis, which is used to explain trade between developed and developing countries, and whose discussions are still ongoing. The results show that countries tend to make and maintain trade agreements regardless of the country's strategy and that cumulative gain between country groups begin to open only after 20 years. While this explains the appearance of the emerging markets, it displays that countries, which can change their production structure or provide product diversity (within the first 20 years) in line with

1 This study is produced from Ayça Özekin's PhD thesis named "Agent-Based Network Modelling within the Framework of Evolutionary Game Theory in the Examination of the International Trade Between Developed and Developing Countries: The Case of Prebisch-Singer Hypothesis" submitted to the Marmara University in 2017.

the suggestions of Prebish and Singer, have the opportunity to make gain from trade as well as developed countries.

Keywords: Complex Adaptive Systems, Agent-Based Modeling, Evolutionary Game Theory, Small World Networks, Prebisch-Singer Hypothesis

1. Introduction

Theoretical developments in the experimental knowledge based on sciences such as mathematics, physics and biology, which have increased in the last century, have led to the emergence of new research fields in the other disciplines along with the technologic advances. This situation, combined with the process of criticizing the limiting assumptions particularly in the science of economics, gave birth to new research fields. The new economics, which emerged from the criticism that started with the abandonment of the assumptions, has become the mainstream in economics nowadays. While the schools of thought, that emerged both with the effect of other sciences and the combination of the criticisms of the assumptions that existed until today, is called heterodox economics, classical and neoclassical economics are called orthodox economics, representing the view existed and belief until that day. There are also studies in heterodox economics that are based on other sciences, however there are also other studies that are considered heterodox only because they criticize or do not accept the assumptions of neoclassical economics. According to the separation made by Colander, Holt and Rosser (2003), Davis and Sent (2006) and Eren (2013), studies that only criticize the assumptions without breaking away from the neoclassical economics axis are considered as mainstream heterodox economics, and studies that completely include innovative approaches based on other sciences are called new heterodox economics.

In the context of the new heterodox economics, the use of chaos and complexity concepts, which play an important role through the effects of physics on the other sciences and the dynamic and complex structure of economic events, have increased the number of studies that develop complex adaptive systems for these events. Agent-based modeling studies have also gained speed in terms of providing a computable method to model the complexity and evolutionary thought of complex adaptive systems.

Agent-based modeling reflects the evolutionary thought of complex adaptive systems to the model with evolutionary rules of conduct. One of the rules of conduct used for this purpose is the evolutionary game theory. The game theory, suggested by Von Neumann and Morgenstern (1944) and developed by the studies of Nash (1950a, 1950b, 1950c), has been the subject of the critical studies simultaneously with economics due to the assumptions of economics based on rational and fully informed homogeneous individual (Krugman, 1991; Fisher, 1989; Shapiro, 1989; Harsanyi, 1967). In line with the criticisms brought to the game theory, the evolutionary game theory, which evolves based on evolutionary biology, has been able to offer complementary applications for new heterodox economics schools by providing bounded rationality and heterogeneous features to individuals considered purely rational in classical game theory and incorporating the concept of learning into the strategies it contains. Thus, the game theory, which was reshaped with the emergence of new heterodox economics schools, became an evolutionary game theory and became usable in the analysis of its evolutionary structures such as the analysis of complex adaptive systems.

2. Modeling International Trade as a Complex Adaptive System

International trade by its definition shows a dynamic structure, which is adapted with the complex relations created both by the fact that many countries around the world are connected to each other with commercial networks, and by developing a new strategy for the highest benefit of the country in every period through adhesion to the international agreements. This dynamic structure causes a change in the product structure in which countries have comparative advantage via factor endowment. In this context, it is observed that underdeveloped countries mostly suffer from capital scarcity against their rich population potential, and therefore they are forced to export labor-intensive goods. Therefore, they aim to become a developed country by exporting high technology and capital intensive goods in the long run with a fast industrialization (Masça, t.y.). In developed countries that have achieved this goal by industrializion, agriculture has been substituted by industry, and technological development has enabled foreign trade to increase worldwide. While the developed countries that have completed their economic transformation are only concerned with economic growth, this process continues to be an issue to be investigated for the developing countries that has not completed it (Dulupçu, 2002: 38). However, initially static, then time series, cross-sectional and dynamic panel data studies are found to be insufficient in explaining the trade, particularly between developed and developing countries.

In this study, it is aimed to model international trade as a complex adaptive system due to its dynamic nature. In this context, the argument of the

Prebisch-Singer hypothesis, which is the symbol of the structuralist development approach from heterodox economics schools, will be discussed especially in order to examine the effect of cross-country development differences on trade. The Prebisch-Singer hypothesis basically states that in developing countries producing primary goods, export items will shrink proportionally, while import items will not change or increase. As a result of this situation, the terms of foreign trade, which are constantly upgrading against developing countries, have been expressed as the reason that makes developed countries more profitable from trade in the long term (Prebisch, 1950; Singer, 1950). To overcome this problem, the Prebisch-Singer hypothesis suggests developing countries to adopt specific export policies for them by changing the import substitution policies and the primary goods production structure. The validity of the hypothesis has become a subject that has been discussed especially with the financial liberalization process after the 1980s. Today, there is an argument that the hypothesis' shape has changed and remained valid through the decrease in the terms of trade in developed countries and the occurrence of developing countries such as *emerging markets* within the changing trade structures with the financial liberalization process after 1980s (Sarkar and Singer, 1991; Arrighi, Silver and Brewer, 2003; Witkowska, 2016).

Based on this argument, under the assumption that the gains in the Prebisch-Singer hypothesis exist with the simulation of the complex adaptive systems, an idea can be produced related to the trade structure that will occur, and related to how the decisions of the countries in favor or against cooperation with each other will end up.

3. Method and Methodology

The effect of development differences between countries in international trade, which constitutes the main economic subject of the study, will be examined through the agent-based modeling as a complex adaptive system. The rules of conduct in the network topology chosen for the placement of the agents in the agent-based model to be used for this will be determined by the tit-fot-tat strategy, which is an evolutionary strategy. The agent-based network model to be created will enable inferences to be made with an alternative analysis method for trade relations between developed and developing countries.

3.1. Setting of an Agent-Based Model

Agents set: Characteristics of agents, which are determined as countries should be finite, definable, autonomous, heterogeneous.

Fig. 4.1: Regular Ring Topology, Source: Author's own construction

Agent relationships and interaction methods set: The physical topology that indicates to the placement of agents in the agents set has been determined as the appropriate network topology to model the trade issue. Small World Networks, one of the complex network models used particularly for modeling complex relations, have become appropriate to be used in trade issues with the expression of the globalization and on the other side regionalization of the world trade networks, and with the tendency to sustain cooperatively the transnational economic links after Newman and Watts' shortcut addition method.

The system will start with the regular network topology in the shape of the ring given in Fig. 4.1. In this regular ring topology, the node degree, which represents the number of nodes to which each node is connected, has been determined as $k = 2$. Every country (agent) is the main input for trade. In other words, each node initially forms a connectivity cluster by being naturally[2] connected with its neighbor on the right and left.

2 Starting from the previous studies' point of view, the network model based on the opinion that the fact that countries have borders to each other will increase the trade and encourage the economic cooperation between these countries, is included. This assumption is accepted in the foreign trade studies considered in heterodox economics such as the gravity model on the basis of *low transportation costs* (Frankel, Stein & Wei, 1997; Golovko, 2009; Atik, 2006).

However, the characteristics of regular networks, which include uniformly distributed node degree distribution and zero entropy that shows randomness level, prevents the analysis of issues such as trade involving complex relationships with such networks. For this reason, such issues are handled with complex network models that express complex relationships. At this point, new links will be added to the simulation that started with regular ring topology with n nodes using the Newman-Watts method[3], starting from a randomly selected link. Thus, by increasing the randomness rate, the small world network structure will be determined at the point of the number of links giving the shortest average path length without changing the cluster coefficient much. These links added in the Newman-Watts method are called shortcuts. Shortcuts will symbolize the decision to trade between the two players. When the small world network is reached, the system will be simulated without adding 100 period shortcuts to fit the market structure and the obtained results will be interpreted.

Rules of conduct of agents: In the game theory, prisonner's dilemma is considered as the best representative for trade with the studies of Conybeare (1984,1987), Krugman (1991) and Samuelson and Nordhaus (1992), however Axelrod (1984)'s tit-for-tat strategy, which is thought as giving the best results for iterative situations in prisoner's dilemma will be used as rule of conduct. Since the trade between countries is not a phenomenon that is not performed once and again, the game in question is played as iterative among countries in the real world.

Each player on the network will have two strategies. *Being cooperative* symbolizes all of the behaviors suggested by the World Trade Organization in general, such as following the moderate policies in trade, and following existing trade agreements. *Being non-cooperative* symbolizes the whole of aggressive attitudes such as violations of the trade agreements, unnecessary and high taxation. Although the first round starts with cooperative behavior, it will be continued with the adoption of the strategy (cooperative or non-cooperative) of the players who are linked in the ongoing rounds, with the highest gain in the previous round.

At this point, it becomes crucial to calculate how the gains that a country, which is only linked with the countries to its right and left, will take into account

---

3 p=M/(NN-12) Since the Newman-Watts method link adding process will not allow to the unlinked country in the model, it will also ensure that the average path length is never ∞.

Tab. 4.1. Prisoner's Dilemma Game Payoff Matrix According to the Prebisch-Singer Hypothesis, Source: Author's own calculations

Country B	Country A		
	Strategies	Cooperate	Defect
	Cooperate	*0,6; 1*	*0; 1,1*
	Defect	*1,1; 0*	*0,3; 0,3*

Note: While country A indicates the developed country, country B implies the developing country. The payoff matrix values were determined by the author to meet the constraints of T> V> Y> Z and V> (T + Z) / 2, which Flood (1952) stated for the Prisoner's dilemma game.

the implementation of the tit-for-tat strategy in the complex structure that emerges with the expansion of the commercial networks in the ongoing stages. The assumption that countries can obtain different gains from the relations with their border in addition to their trade with the rest of the world reveals the gains of the two-person prisoner's dilemma game from their trade with the right and left countries. To implement the tit-for-tat strategy, first determinant of the total payoff, which express the value that will be taken into consideration, is the gain calculated according to the two-person prisoner dilemma game with the neighbors to the right and left as shown in Tab. 4.1.

Another determinant will be the income that each country will gain from the trade it will do with all the countries in the network. This value essentially symbolizes the general welfare increase that the country will gain from trade. This value will also be calculated from the prisoner's dilemma game payoff matrix, however since it is a multiplayer, it will be calculated using the payoff function developed by Alexander (2007) for the multiplayer prisoner's dilemma game.

$$w_i = mp + c_i \quad \textbf{(1)}$$

$$w_i = mp + d_i \quad \textbf{(2)}$$

The Equation 1 formulize the payoff of the player that cooperate in the multiplayer prisoner dilemma game, and the Equation 2 the payoff of the non-cooperative player, where i = 1. . ..n. In addition, p denotes the increase rate of the rising payoff in both the cooperative and non-cooperative players according to the ratio of the cooperative players in the m group, c_i shows the payoff limit of the player who will cooperate when the ratio of the cooperative players in the group is 0, and d_i indicates non-cooperative payoff limit when the ratio of the cooperative players in the group is equal to 0.

Oh (2015) mentioned that the curve for increasing gains in these equations may vary. This variability causes increasing gain curves to yield different results for different payoff functions. Therefore, the equations given by Alexander (2007) are weighted as in the Equations 3 and 4 by the coefficient taken from the concept of increasing returns in economics.

$$w = \frac{1}{2.5} e^{mp} + c_i \tag{3}$$

$$w = \frac{1}{2.5} e^{mp} + d_i \tag{4}$$

In case of increasing returns on the economic issue, Oh (2015)'s payoff functions for the multiplayer prisoner's dilemma game give better results.

In addition to the parameters in the payoff function, the mutation rate and the number of agents in the network must be determined in order to simulate the established agent-based network model. At this point, Yang, Abbass and Sarker (2006) studied with 80 population size and 1 % mutation rate, which they thought that would yield ideal simulation results. After the proof of 80-population size as ideal number that has become widespread in the field, it was also used in the multi-agent modeling study of Lee, Park and Cho (2010) for international trade markets. However, Lee et al. (2010) state that the mutation rate should be 5 % for international trade markets. The ratio of 1 % means that each unit in the population will change strategy with a probability of 1 %. This situation is seen as the reason for long-term stagnation since it means changing a strategy in an average of 100 periods.

Agent's environment: Within the scope of the study, there will be no change of location in the environment to which the agents belong. Only new trade links will be created in the dynamic process.

3.2. Empirical Findings

The agent-based model created will be simulated through program coding in the Python programming language. Being a programming language, not a package program makes Phyton more flexible to use the concepts employed in this study together with the game theory, evolutionary algorithm, network theory, over its equivelants such as Netlogo, Swarm, TNGLab (Trade Network Game Laboratory), and Gams, where all these concepts can be limitedly analyzed, and this provides a more advantageous position to Phyton. Due to this flexible working structure, to be able to easily change the model is one of the main reasons to be preferred in this study.

Tab. 4.2 Model Parameters, Source: Author's own calculations

Parameter	**Value**	**Unit**
Population	80	Node, agent
Mutation rate	0.05	%5
c_i	0	lim-coop
d_i	0.25	lim-def
m	0.5	ratio-coop
p	Variable	ratio
Weight (w)	$\frac{1}{2.5}e$	

Starting from the regular network in the study, a shortcut addition process is applied to increase the randomness rate to determine the average path length and the number of links giving the cluster coefficient, reflecting the small world network feature. Each time the process starts when $p = 0$, 100 shortcuts in 100 periods are added and the average path length and cluster coefficient of the network are calculated for each shortcut. Then, the system is run without adding any links for a 100 periods for the settlement of the market structure and to observe the effects of the added links. The normalized values of the average path length and cluster coefficient are performed as 100 shortcuts addition and 100 periods waiting process until the point, where the average path length < the cluster coefficient[4]. At that point, the system stops the operation and records this number of links.

The histogram of the number of links obtained from the result of 10000 iteration performed in the way explained above is shown in the Fig. 4.2. As it can be seen from the histogram, the number of links showing the small world feature is between 200 and 350 and follows a normal distribution as expected. The tour numbers corresponding to these link numbers are 401–500, 501–600 and 601–700.

This range is quite wide to determine the number of links that give small world networks exactly. For this reason, in order to determine the number of tours that show the small world network feature, the average path length and cluster coefficient values of the link addition process were compared. From the

4 To calculate the average path length and cluster coefficient, standard program codes of the average path length and cluster coefficient formulas in the.Net C# Network Library are used.

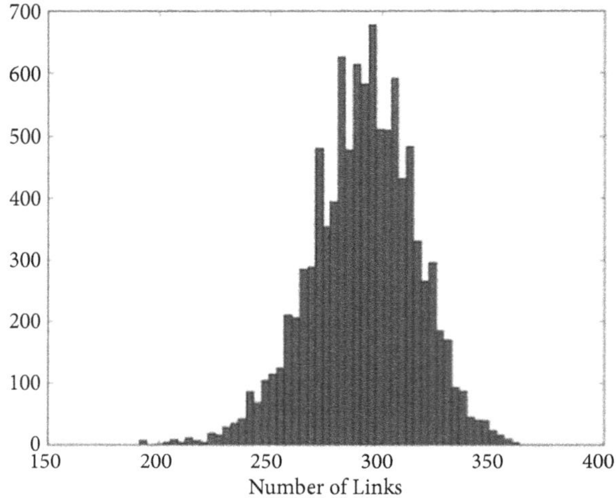

Fig. 4.2: Histogram of the Link Numbers Revealing Small World Network with 10000 Iterative Simulation Results, Source: Author's own calculation

third panel of the Fig. 4.3 where this comparison is given, it is seen that at the point where the average path length (apl) is smaller than the clustering coefficient (cc), the number of tours is 450. Accordingly, it is concluded that the number of links that give the small world network is between 201 and 300.

After determining the link range that gives the small world network, the cumulative payoff tables were obtained by collecting the two player and multiplayer prisoner's dilemma game payoffs for each tour between 201 and 300 links in accordance with the analysis steps. The two-player prisoner dilemma game payoffs are calculated from the Tab. 4.1, while the multiplayer prisoner dilemma game payoffss are calculated in accordance with the claim of the Prebish-Singer hypothesis using the Equations 3 and 4.

In the Fig. 4.4, the payoffs calculated for each tour are shown as cumulative for every 10 tours between 201 and 240 tours, since there is no difference in the system between 240 and 301 tours. The first remarkable point here is that although the differences in gains between developed and developing countries are reflected in the model, these differences do not create a distinction in the first 10 tours. At the end of the second 10-tour period, it is seen that some developed countries, even if in a small amount, can gain close to some developing countries. The difference between these two groups of countries is becoming more evident from the end of the 30th tour and gradually widening. Another important point

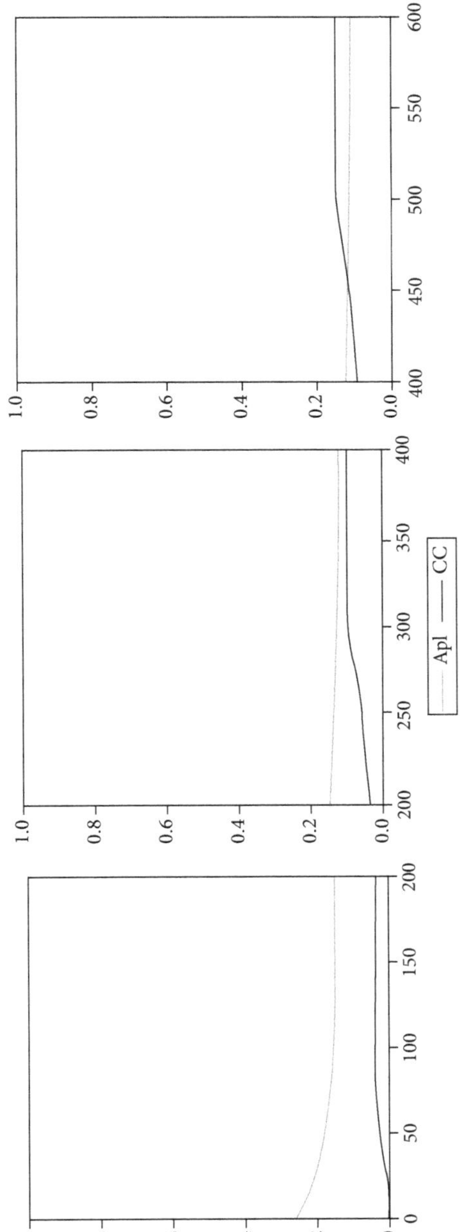

Fig. 4.3: Comparison of Average Path Length and Cluster Coefficient, Source: Author's own construction

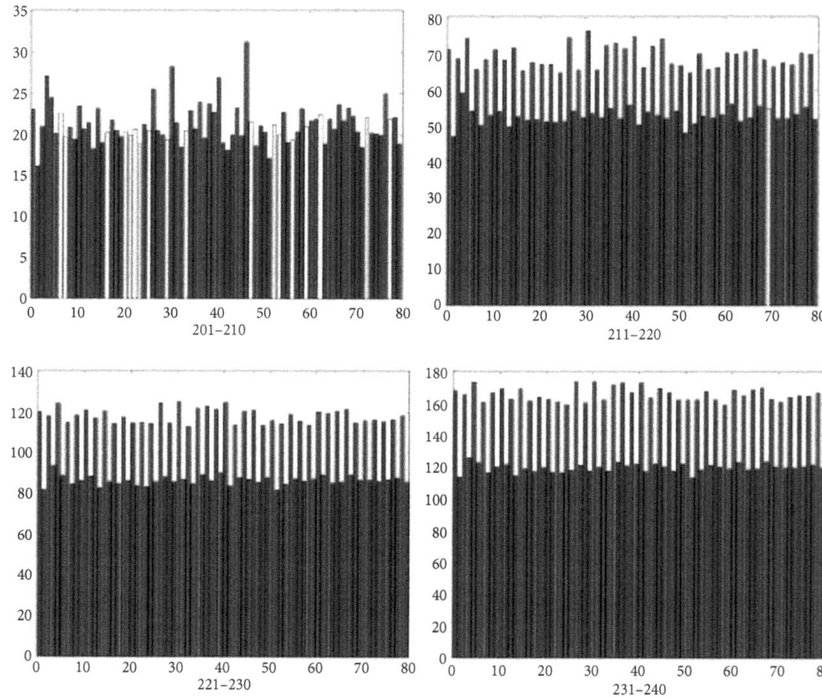

Fig. 4.4: Cumulative Payoff Values Between 201 and 240 Links, Source: Author's own calculations. Not: The players in the non-cooperative strategy are expressed in white, and the players in the cooperative strategy in black.

is that the cooperative strategy is dominant in the link range that has the feature of the small world network. The reason for this is basically that the system allows developing countries, which in some cases have a cooperative strategy, to earn more from their neighbors who choose the cooperative strategy, than their neighbors who choose the non-cooperative strategy. As a result of this situation, the non-cooperative strategy cannot easily find the opportunity to spread.

In the following step of the analysis, the system, which was shown to be a small world network after 300 links additive, was run without adding a 100 tours for the market structure settlement. The cumulative payoffs obtained as a result of this transaction are given in Fig. 4.5. It is observed that the difference between payoffs continues to widen with cooperate strategy dominance and without strategy transformation allowed.

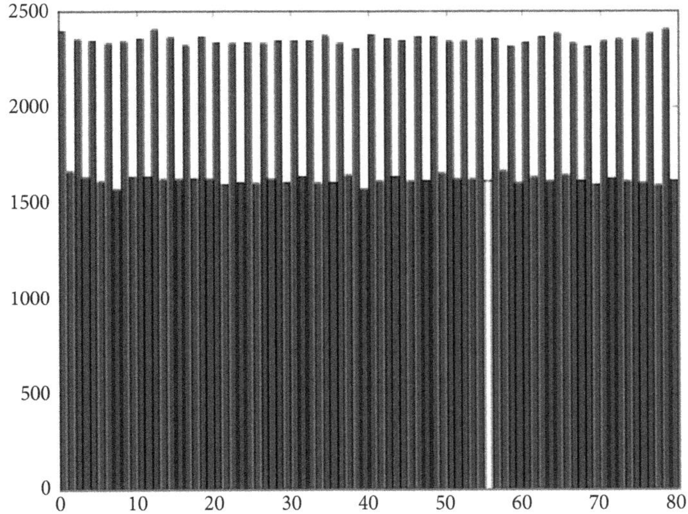

Fig. 4.5: Cumulative Payoff Values After 100 Tours in the Small World Network, Source: Author's own calculations

The result shows that countries tend to make and maintain trade agreements regardless of the country's strategy and those cumulative payoffs between the country-groups begin to open only after 20 years. While this explains the appearance of the emerging markets, it shows that countries, which can change their production structure or provide product diversity in line with the recommendations of Prebish and Singer (within the first 20 years), have the opportunity to gain as much income from trade as developed countries.

4. Conclusion

In the present study, the modern interpretation of the Prebisch-Singer hypothesis, which claims the trade advantage of developed countries over underdeveloped countries is simulated on an agent based model as developed countries gain more from trade than developing countries.

In the results obtained, it is first observed that the cooperative strategy is dominant where the system shows the features of the small world network. In other words, countries tend to make and maintain trade agreements regardless from their country's strategy. Subsequently, while adding a shortcut between 201 and 300, which shows the feature of a small world network, no significant differences are observed in the first 10 tours (201–210), the differences are seen at the end of the 20th tour (210–220). Here, developing countries, which are able to achieve the same level of cumulative payoffs with their developed neighbors, are found locally. This means, cumulative payoffs between the country groups start to be widen after 20 years. While this explains the emergence process of emerging markets, it confirms the claim that countries, which can change the current production structure or provide product diversity in line with the recommendations of Prebish and Singer will have the opportunity to gain as much profit from trade as developed countries. In today's world, if the view that emerging markets take the place of developed countries, which has decreasing terms of trade, it can be considered that trade between the emerging markets that express developing countries with high value added production and the developing countries producing low value added products will result in favor of emerging markets.

Simulations have become one of the main methods of studying complex adaptive systems. However, Colander (2008: 6) also emphasizes the limitations of what we can find through simulations and that many methodological studies should be done beforehand. Accordingly, this study includes the limitations of the simulation technique and the prisoner's dilemma game. In future studies, it is possible to examine different economic issues with similar algorithms in appropriate game types.

References

Alexander, J. M. (2007). *The Structural Evolution of Morality*. New York: Cambridge University Press.

Arrighi, G., B. J. Silver & B. D. Brewer. (2003). Industrial Convergence, Globalization and the Persistence of the North-South Divide. *Studies in Comparative International Development*, Spring, 3–31.

Atik, H. (2006). Tercihlerde Benzerlik Teorisi: Türkiye ve Bazı Komşu Ülkelerin Dış Ticareti Üzerine Bir Analiz. *Ankara Üniversitesi SBF Dergisi*, 61(2), 33–43.

Axelrod, R. (1984). *The Evolution of Cooperation*. New York: Basic Books.

Colander, D. (2008). Complexity and the History of Economic Though. *Middlebury College Economics Discussion Paper*, No.08–04.

Colander, D., R. Holt & B. Rosser. (2003). The Changing Face of Mainstream Economics. *Middleburry College Economics Discussion Paper*, No.03–27.

Conybeare, J. (1984). Public Goods, Prisoner's Dilemma and the International Political Economy. *International Studies Quarterly*, 28(5), 5–22.

Conybeare, J. (1987). *Trade Wars*. New York: Colombia University Press.

Davis, J. & E. M. Sent. (2006). Heterodoxy's Strategic Pluralism. *European History of Economics Society Meetings*. Porto, Portugal.

Dulupçu, M. A. (2002). Kalkınma İktisadı Üzerine Bazı Düşünceler. *Gazi Üniversitesi İ.İ.B.F. Dergisi*, 1/2002, 31-52.

Ercan, F. & Ö. Biçen. (2005). İktisat ve Kalkınma Ekonomisi: Kalkınma İdeolojisinin Sosyalizasyonu Olarak Kalkınma Ders Kitaplarının Eleştirisi. *Ekonomik Yaklaşım*, 16(57), 51–102.

Eren, E. (2013). Kompleksite İktisadı ve Ajan-Temelli Modelleme: Metodolojik Bir Yaklaşım. *Türkiye Ekonomik Kurumu Tartışma Metni*, 2013/3.

Fisher, F. M. (1989). Games Economists Play: A Noncooperative View. *Rand Journal of Economics*, 20(1), 113–124.

Flood, M. M. (1952). Some Experimental Games. *RAND Cooperation*. Santa Monica, California.

Frankel, J., E. Stein & S. J. Wei. (1997). *Regional Trading Blocs in the World Economic System*. U.S.A: Institute For International Economics.

Golovko, A. (17–19 Haziran 2009). Çekim Modeli: Avrasya Ülkelerinin Dış Ticareti. *Anadolu Uluslararası İktisat Kongresi*, Eskişehir: Anadolu Üniversitesi.

Harsanyi, J. C. (1967). Games with Incomplete Information Played by "Bayesian" Player I–III. *Managment Science*, 14(3), 159–182.

Krugman, P. (1991). The Move toward Free Trade Zones. *Economic Review*, November/December, 5–25.

Lee, S. H., H. S. Park & S. B. Cho. (18–23 Temmuz, 2010). *Emprical Analysis of Internatioal Trade Market Using Evolutionary Multi-agent Modeling with Game Theory. IEEE Congress on Evolutionary Computation*. Spain: Centre Convencions Internacional Barcelona.

Masça, M. (t.y.). Uluslararası İktisat. *Afyon Kocatepe Üniversitesi Ders Notları*. http://blog.aku.edu.tr/mmasca/files/2016/12/Ulus_ikt_ders_notu_2011_2012.pdf adresinden alınmıştır (28.02.2017).

Nash, J. F. (1950a). Equilibrium Points in n-Person Games. *Proceedings of the National Academy of Sciences*, 36(1), 48–49.

Nash, J. F. (1950b). The Bargaining Problem. *Econometrica*, 18(2), 155–162.

Nash, J. F. (1950c). *Non-cooperative Games*. Princeton University, *PhD Dissertation*. University of Princeton. Retrieved from https://library.princeton.edu/special-collections/sites/default/files/Non-Cooperative_Games_Nash.pdf (09.10.2014).

Oh, Y. J. (2015). Agent-Based Network Modelling for the 2008 Financial Crisis and the Sluggish Recovery. *Yayınlanmamış Doktora Tezi*. Dallas: University of Texas.

Prebisch, R. (1950). The Economic Development of Latin America and Its Principle Problems. *United Nations Publications*, No.50.

Samuelson, P. A. & W. D. Nordhaus. (1992). *Economics*. New York: McGraw Hill.

Sarkar, P. & H. W. Singer. (1991). Manufactured Exports of Developing Countries and Their Terms of Trade Since 1965. *World Development*, 19(4), 333–340.

Shapiro, C. (1989). The Theory of Business Strategy. *RAND Journal of Economics*, 20(1), 125–137.

Singer, H. W. (1950). The Distribution of Gains between Investing and Borrowing Countries. *The American Economic Review*, 40(2), 473–485.

Von Neumann, J. & O. Morgenstern. (1944). *Theory of Game and Economic Behaviour*. Princeton: Princeton University Press.

Witkowska, E. A. (2016). Reconsideration of the Prebisch-Singer Hypothesis. *Real-World Economics Review*, 76, 95–108.

Yang, A., H. A. Abbass & R. Sarker. (2006). Land Combat Scenario Planning: A Multiobjective Approach. In T. D. Wang (Ed.), *Simulated Evolution and Learning 6th International Conference Proceedings* içinde, Almanya: Springer.

Aykut Karakaya, Melih Kutlu

Chapter 5 Dynamic Volatility Spillover between Stock Exchange and Interbank Market after the Global Crisis in Turkey

Abstract In this paper, we investigate the dynamic volatility spillover between Borsa İstanbul and interbank market for the period January 4, 2010, to December 31, 2019. In particular, we focus on the after financial crisis dynamic causality between Borsa Istanbul All Shares Index and interbank overnight rates. EGARCH model is used to estimate asymmetric volatility in the series. The Cross Correlation Function testing procedure is applied to research the causality-in-mean and causality-in-variance. Borsa Istanbul All Shares Index and overnight interest rate are asymmetrical and negative. There is a causality from Borsa Istanbul return to interest market return the next day.

Keywords: Dynamic Volatility Spillover, Cross Correlation Function Test, Borsa Istanbul, Interbank Market

1. Introduction

Investors evaluate alternative investments before making an investment decision. They consider both the risk and return of alternatives. They make the investment decision based on risk and return. Investment opportunities have increased even more with globalization. Thus, there is an increase in the number of alternatives in terms of financial instruments and markets for investors. This situation causes higher level of interactions between the markets compared to the past.

The interaction between the markets is important for developing economies. Along with financial liberalization, sensitivity among markets increased. In this context, the link between macroeconomic indicators and the stock market is important in investment decision. Among these, indicators such as inflation, interest, growth, exchange rate, foreign exchange reserve, employment, budget balance and current account deficit are observed.

Future changes in the interest rates affect the stocks negatively (Peiro, 2016; 293). The negative link among interest rates and stock markets can be explained in two ways. With the effect of the contractionary monetary policy, interest rates increase and investors turn to securities with fixed returns, so stock prices fall. As a result of the expansionary monetary policy, interest rates decrease and stock prices increase (Banerjee & Adhikary, 2009; 3).

The risk of investment in stocks is more than the risk of investment in bonds. The change in interest rates affects both the stock and bond value. Bond value causes stock demand to change. Changing the target interest rates of central banks also affects the value of stocks. Therefore, there is a negative relationship among the value of shares and interest rates. Beyond this negative relationship, there is also a negative causal relationship among interest rates and stock value. According to Jensen and Johnson (1995; 94) in the periods following the decrease of interest rates, stock returns higher than in the periods following the increase of interest rates. Federal funds ratio is the overnight borrowing rate of interbanks in the US. There are studies showing that there is a negative connection among federal fund rate and stock prices (Smirlock & Yawitz, 1985; Thorbecke & Alami, 1994; Thorbecke, 1997; Lobo, 2000; Lobo, 2002). Negative movements are more effective than positive movements in estimating volatility (Black, 1976). This situation is called leverage effect.

The interbank overnight money market is the last resort for banks at the end of the day, as well as providing unsecured borrowing opportunities. Overnight interest rates are affected by daily payment flows, central bank activities and open market policies. In addition, liquidity shocks are determinants of the overnight interest rate and reveal the risk of contagion. If the shocks that will occur in the market affect one or more bank balance sheets, this shock will affect other banks through the interbank interest rate (Green et al., 2016; 159).

The interaction between markets is important for developing economies and inter-market sentiment increased with financial liberalization. In addition banks and stock exchanges are the most important elements of financial markets. Interbank Money Market (IMM) is a market while the banks can transaction with themselves or the Central Bank of the Republic of Turkey (CBRT) in Turkey. Interbank enables banks that wish to benefit from short-term cash surpluses and those with short-term cash needs who do not wish to meet this need from their long-term assets. In IMM, the interest rate for these transactions is calculated overnight. Low interest rates indicate excess cash in the market and vice versa. Stock exchanges are another important element of the financial system. Stock exchanges are established in order to provide liquidity opportunity to the holders of savings and to establish an organized structure. The high volatility in the markets adversely affects price formations. Therefore, the CBRT may reduce the borrowing limits in IMM for smooth of the markets. This decrease means a reduction in liquidity and this may increase the interest rates. Liquidity decrease is a negative situation for investors. The increase in interest rates has an impact on the market value of banks directly and indirectly from real sector firms. On the other hand, during the banking crises, central banks use interbank interest rates to reduce threats to the banking system (Freixas et al., 2011; 2659). The aim of this study is to investigate the spillover and causality between interbank money market interest rate and Borsa Istanbul after the 2008 Global Financial Crisis. This aim is accomplished with asymmetric diagnostic tests, conditional heteroscedasticity test including the leverage effect and the causality test.

2. Theory

Macroeconomic factors such as interest rates, inflation and level of production systematically affect stock returns (Chen et al., 1986; 383). Changes in interest rates affect future cash flows and the discount rate that reduces these cash flows to present value. Thus, asset prices are also affected (Chen et al., 1999; 898). Stock prices and interest rates are moving at the same time. Industrial production affects stock prices by one year lag. Both variables are important in determining stock returns (Peiro, 2016; 294).

Stock market returns should be negatively correlated with expected inflation and this relationship is established through short-term interest rates as a proxy (Fama, 1981). It can be said that the interest rate factor consists of unexpected inflation and real interest rate changes. With this statement, various mechanisms can be held responsible for the liquidity effect. These mechanisms are priced by market participants. In addition, stock sensitivity is priced against interest rate change (Sweney & Warga, 1986, 406).

There may be increases in the short-term interest rates, spontaneously or due to a positive shock in stock prices. Shocks arising from stock are long-term due to the persistence of volatility. These shocks direct the interest rate in the same direction. For these reasons, positive covariance occurs among stock prices and interest rates in the long term. In the opposite case, if the shock originates from the interest rate, it will create a negative effect and a negative correlation between the stock and interest rates (Rigobon & Sack, 2003; 2).

Expansionary monetary policies, which include shocks of the federal funding rate, have a large and significant positive effect on stock returns; and contractionary monetary policies, which include shocks of the federal funding rate, have a large and significant negative effect on stock returns (Thorbecke, 1997, 640).

According to Lobo (2002; 73), unexpected decreases in the target of federal funds rate significantly rise the stock prices. Increasing the federal fund rate target value decreases the stock prices and decreasing the federal fund target increases the stock prices. This change proves the liquidity effect (Thorbecke & Alami, 1994; 13: Smirlock & Yawitz, 1985). The interest rate and liquidity effects are interrelated.

On the other hand, new information on interest rates affected stock returns. When monetary policy makers change their targets, this is perceived as new information by the stock exchange. New information has a significant impact on stock returns. Risk averse investors are more sensitive to new information (Lobo, 2000; 139).

3. Literature

There are studies examining the relationship between stocks and interest rates. Alaganar and Bhar (2003) examined the causal relationship among interest rates and financial sector returns in the G7 countries. Cheung and Ng (1996) used this analysis as their research method. As a result of the study, a feedback mechanism is determined between the financial sector returns and interest rates. Najand and Noronha (1998) concluded that interest rates negatively affect stock returns in Japan. There is a negative causal relationship from interest rates to stock prices in Colombo Stock Exchange (Amarasinghe, 2015; 96). According to Tripathy (2011) there is a bidirectional causality relationship between the BSE index and three month treasury bill interest rates. Gjerde and Saettem (1999) found that the change in interest rates negatively affects stock returns in Norway. On the other hand, Hussain et al. (2014) could not determine the causal relationship between Karachi index stock prices and interest rates. Poyraz and Tepeli (2015) found a bidirectional negative relationship between BIST index and treasury bill interest rates. According to Coşkun et al. (2016), shocks in BIST and interest rates affect each other bidirectional and balance is reached at the end of a certain period. Yılmaz et al. (2006), on the other hand, determined a one-way causality relationship from interest rates to BIST. The change in the interest rate negatively affects BIST. In addition, besides BIST's own shocks, the shock that affects BIST the most is the interest rate shock.

Durukan (1999) examine the relationship between Borsa Istanbul 100 Index (BIST) return and macroeconomic variables. He used the Least Squares Method in his research between 1986 and 1998. The results of the research show that the most effective explanatory macroeconomic indicator for stock returns is deposit interest. The relationship between stock prices and deposit interest rate is negative. Demir and Yağcılar (2009) analyzed the factors affecting the returns of bank stocks traded on Borsa Istanbul. Arbitrage Pricing Model is used in the study where monthly interest rate of Treasury bills is used between 2000 and 2006. The existence of a negative relationship between treasury bill interest rates and bank stocks is partially determined.

Sayılgan and Süslü (2011) investigated the relationship between macroeconomic factors and stock return in Turkey, and developing countries. Panel data analysis is used in the study between 1996 and 2006. According to the results, no significant relationship is found between the deposit interest rate and stock returns. Özer et al. (2011) used the Least Squares Estimation Method, Johansen-Juselius Cointegration Test, Granger Causality Test and VEC models in their studies in which they investigated the relationship between stock prices and macroeconomic indicators. The study period is between 1996 and 2009. According to the Least Squares Estimation Method, a significant relationship is found between BIST and interest rate. According to Johansen-Juselius Cointegration Test, there is a long-term relationship between interest rates and stock exchange index. According to the causality test, one-way causality from the interest rates to the stock market index is found.

Kasman et al. (2011) investigated the effects of interest rate and exchange rate on Turkish banking stock returns with the Least Squares and GARCH models. The exchange rate is the dollar and Euro basket rate, and the interest rate is a two-year treasury bond yield. The research period covers 1999–2009 for ten banks, 2000–2009 for one bank, 2004--2009 for another bank and 2005–2009 for another bank. In the study, it is assume that the interest rate and exchange rate negatively affect the bank's conditional returns. Aktaş and Akdağ (2013) investigated the effect on Turkey's BIST 100 index of basic macroeconomic indicators. Deposit interest rate has a significant effect on BIST 100 index in the 2008–2012 period. There is a mutual causality between deposit interest rates and BIST100.

Sevinç (2014) investigated the effects of macroeconomic variables on stock returns with the Arbitrage Pricing Model. In the study carried out with data between 2003 and 2013, Borsa Istanbul 30 index stocks are used. In the study, it is concluded that as deposit interest rates increase, stock returns decrease. Şentürk and Dücan (2014) used Unit Root Tests, VAR analyzes and Granger causality analysis in their studies, in which they investigated the effect of interest rate and exchange rate on the Borsa Istanbul return. The study covers between the years 1997–2013. According to the results, deposit rates negatively affect the return of BIST 100 index for about three months. In addition, deposit rates affect more than the dollar rate.

Uzun and Güngör (2017) used the panel data analysis in their study, where they examined the relationship between stock market indexes and macroeconomic indicators. The study period covers the years 2004–2013. In the study, 25 developed countries and 23 developing countries datasets are used. Turkey is consideres as a developing country in the data sets. No long-term relationship is determined between the interest rate between banks and the stock market index. In the short term, a moderate causality relationship from the stock market index to the interbank interest rate and a strong causality relationship from the interbank interest rate to the stock exchange index have been identified.

Sadeghzadeh and Elmas (2018) investigated macroeconomic factors affecting stock returns. The research covers the years 2000–2017. Multiple Structural Break Unit Root Test, Panel Unit Root Tests and Panel ARDL methods are used in the study. It is concluded that the increases in interest rates applied by banks to time deposits reduced the returns of stocks, especially in the short term. Taştan and Güngör (2019), analyzed the relationship between Turkey's long-term slow-moving stock market volatility and macroeconomic variables. The study covers the period between the years 2011–2019. GARCH-MIDAS and ARDL are used as methods. According to the findings, a positive correlation is observed between the interest rate, CDS risk premium and S&P 500 volatility and the long-term volatility of the BIST 100 Index.

Durmuş et al. (2019) investigated the relationship between the returns of BIST Bank Index and BIST Financial Index with mean deposit interest rate, dollar rate, euro rate, inflation rate and gold prices. VAR method is used in the study that analyzed data between the years 2006 and 2018. As a result of a shock in the deposit interest rate, BIST Bank and BIST Financial indices are affected negatively in the first, fourth, fifth, sixth and seventh periods, and positively in other periods.

According to the findings of the studies examined above, there is a negative link among interest rates and stock returns in general. Only in the study of Taştan and Güngör (2019), a positive correlation is found between interbank interest rate volatility and long-term volatility of BIST100 index. This shows that to investigate the causality relationship between interest rate volatility and Borsa Istanbul volatility has a research gap. We aim to provide to the literature by research the causality among interbank interest rate and stocks.

4. Data and Methodology

4.1. Data

In the study, after the 2008 financial crisis, daily Borsa Istanbul All Shares Index return (ΔBIST) and interbank overnight interest rate change (ΔIOI) are used between the years 2010–2019. Considering the studies in the literature section, BIST100 Index is generally taken as data. In order to consider the value of all public company, the Borsa Istanbul All Shares Index is taken in this study. BIST100 index represents only a certain part. The time series of data consisting of 2473 frequencies are shown in the Figs. 5.1 and 5.2, respectively. According to the Fig. 5.1, there is a volatility cluster in the all BIST index that lasted from May to June 2010, in June 2013, and from May 2018 to the end of 2018. It is thought that the volatility cluster that took place in 2010 is due to the efforts to increase the number of companies listed on the Borsa Istanbul. Gezi Park events may have caused the volatility cluster that emerged in 2013. In the year 2018, it can be said that the resulting volatility clustering effect of fluctuations are due to the challenges posed by the trade wars and elections in Turkey. In the change of the overnight interest rate shown in the Fig. 5.2, volatility cluster is observed in the first quarter of 2011. Since 2009, interest rates, especially housing interest rates, started to decrease. These rates have increased since the first quarter of 2011. This change in interest rates can be shown as the reason for the volatility cluster in interest rates.

Descriptive statistics for the data are shown in the Tab. 5.1. As of the period analyzed, Borsa Istanbul mean return is negative. The mean change in the overnight interest rate is positive. The fact that the overnight interest rate mean and median values are close to zero showed that the central trend measures of the

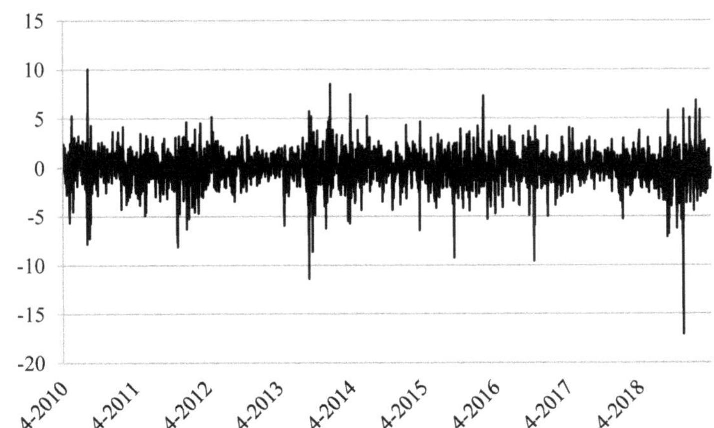

Fig. 5.1. ΔBİST All Shares Index (ΔBİST), Source: Finnet Database

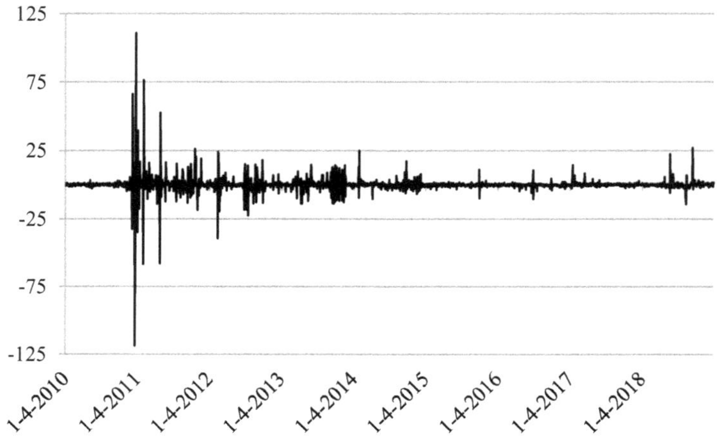

Fig. 5.2. ΔInterbank Overnight Interest (ΔIOI), Source: Finnet Database

Tab. 5.1. Variables Descriptive Statistics, Source: Authors' own calculations

	ΔBIST	**ΔIOI**
Mean	-0.020715	0.029259
Median	0.028433	0.000000
Maximum	10.04259	110.6123
Minimum	-17.09738	-118.7146
Std. Deviation	1.801432	5.652453
Skewness	-0.863754	0.404143
Kurtosis	9.888575	177.3111
Jarque-Bera (JB)	5197.087	313092.0
JB Prob.	0.0000	0.000000
Observations	2473	2473

series are not in the direction that earned or lost investors during the examination period.

The skewness coefficient shows how far the series moves away from symmetry, and the kurtosis shows how different the series is from its normal height. According to the skewness coefficients shown in the Tab. 5.1, ΔBIST series is left-skewed (asymmetry is negative) and ΔIOI series is right-skewed (asymmetry is positive). According to the kurtosis findings, the height of the distribution of the series is more pointed than the height of the standard normal distribution. These findings related to flatness for both series are called leptocurtic distribution (fat tail). The leptocurtic distribution corresponds to the points of extreme movements in the financial series and there are high volatile periods due to extreme values. Jargue-Bera normal distribution test also shows that there is non- normal distribution in the series.

4.2. Methodology

Interbank money market interest rate and Borsa Istanbul Index are financial time series. Financial time series show the volatility cluster, leverage effect and excessive. The emergence of these features causes the variance to change and testing cannot be performed with fixed variance-based time series models. The Autoregressive Conditional Heteroskedasticity (ARCH) of Engle (1982) and The Generalized Autoregressive Conditional Heteroskedasticity (GARCH) models of Bollerslev (1990) emerged for the volatility modeling of stock returns. Together with the model of Engle (1982), both the conditional mean and the conditional variance of a series can be calculated simultaneously. In ARCH and GARCH models, the effect of positive and negative shocks on volatility is the same.

Nelson (1991) developed the Exponential GARCH (EGARCH) model, which assumes that the negative and positive movements (asymmetry) that may occur in the series have a different effect on the prediction of volatility. In the EGARCH model, the Logarithmic Conditional Variance gives information about the asymmetric information, and the use of standardized error terms gives information about the magnitude of the shock. Cheung and Ng (1996) developed a test that investigates the mutual causality of conditional variances of financial asset prices. This test consists of two stages. The first stage includes a univariate time series analysis. The second stage consists of standardizing the residual squares of the series with conditional variances.

In order to avoid spurious regression problem in the test phase of the study, the stationary tests of the return and change series are performed in the first phase. Augmented Dickey–Fuller (ADF-1979), Phillips–Perron (PP-1988) and Kwiatkowski, Phillips, Schmidt, Shin (KPSS-1992) unit root tests, which are widely used in stationary analysis of time series, are used in the study of stationarity. After the stationary analysis, the existence of serial correlation and conditional variance variance problems are investigated in the return and change series. For this, Ljung and Box (1978) Q test (ARCH effect test) and ARCH test are performed with LM test, which is widely used in econometrics with the work of Breusch and Pagan (1980).

In the second stage, asymmetry diagnostic tests recommended by Engle and Ng (1993) are performed to determine whether volatility has an asymmetrical structure in returns and change series. The diagnostic indicators of the sign asymmetry, negative value asymmetry, positive value asymmetry and the sum of compound asymmetry proposed by Engle and Ng (1993) for the purpose of determining the volatility asymmetry are calculated by the following regression equations:

$$\text{SignBias} \quad \varepsilon_{i,t}^2 = \alpha + bS_{i,t-1}^- + u_{i,t} \tag{1}$$

$$\text{NegativeSizeBias} \quad \varepsilon_{i,t}^2 = \alpha + bS_{i,t-1}^- \varepsilon_{i,t-1} + u_{i,t} \tag{2}$$

$$\text{PositiveSizeBias} \quad \varepsilon_{i,t}^2 = \alpha + bS_{i,t-1}^+ \varepsilon_{i,t-1} + u_{i,t} \tag{3}$$

$$\text{Joint} \quad \varepsilon_{i,t}^2 = \alpha + b_1 S_{i,t-1}^- + b_2 S_{i,t-1}^- \varepsilon_{i,t-1} + b_3 S_{i,t-1}^+ \varepsilon_{i,t-1} + u_{i,t} \tag{4}$$

$\varepsilon_{i,t-1}$ is the error term of the series in t -1. $S_{i,t-1}^-$ is a dummy variable that is equal to 1 if $\varepsilon_{i,t-1} < 0$, if not 0. $S_{i,t-1}^+$ is a dummy variables that is equal to 1, if $\varepsilon_{i,t-1} > 0$, 1, if not 0. In the first three asymmetry tests given above, the test value t and the statistical significance of the coefficient *b* are reported. In the Joint Asymmetry Test in the Equation (4), the value and statistical significance of the F test, b_1 b_2 and b_3 are all reported to be zero (Patterson, 2000: 729).

The sign asymmetry test examines the effect of positive and negative shocks (good and bad news) only on volatility. In particular, if the response of volatility to shocks is asymmetrical, the t value of the term sign asymmetry is statistically significant. In addition, the size of the shock is also important in the spread of volatility. Therefore, the negative value asymmetry takes into account the effects of large and small negative shocks (bad news) on volatility. In addition, positive value asymmetry focuses on the effects of large and small positive shocks (good news) on volatility. The compound asymmetry Test takes into account both the sign and magnitude of the shocks and the total effects of volatility (Jin, 2015:345).

In the third stage, as a result of Asymmetry Diagnostic tests, the exponential GARCH (EGARCH) model is used to estimate asymmetric volatility in the series, In the Equations (5) and (6) below, the mean and variance formulas of the EGARCH model are given:

$$x_t = \omega_0 + \sum_{i=1}^{k} \omega_i + u_t, \; E_{t-1}(u_t) = 0, \; E_{t-1}\left(u_t^2\right) = h_t \tag{5}$$

$$log(h_t) = \alpha_0 + \sum_{j=1}^{p} \beta_j log(h_{t-j}) + \sum_{i=1}^{q} \alpha_i \frac{|u_{t-i}|}{\sqrt{h_{t-i}}} + \sum_{i=1}^{q} \gamma_i \frac{u_{t-i}}{\sqrt{h_{t-i}}} \quad (6)$$

In the equation number 6, the natural logarithm of the conditional variance uses the standardized error term ($\frac{|u_{t-i}|}{\sqrt{h_{t-i}}}$) instead of its own lagged values. β_j and α_i are the ARCH and GARCH parameters, respectively. The parameter γ_i shows asymmetric leverage effect in volatility. If the a value is not equal to zero, there is an asymmetrical effect. Being less than zero indicates leverage effect.

Based on the standardized error terms obtained by the EGARCH method, CCF test developed by Cheung and Ng (1996) is used in the analysis of causality between ΔBIST and ΔIOI in the fourth stage in terms of mean and variance. Thus, the Cross-Correlation Function (CCF) of ΔBIST and ΔIOI standardized residues are used to test the null hypothesis claiming that there is no causality on mean and the CCF of standardized square residues suggesting no causality in variance.

CCF calculation steps for causality between the means (returns) of two stationary series are as follows (Cheung and Ng, 1996):

1. The standardized errors obtained from the ARCH or GARCH conditional mean (return) model of both stationary series are calculated,
2. Lags (such as -1, -2 and -3) and leads (such as +1, +2 and +3) cross correlations between the standardized errors of the Conditional Mean (return) Model of the two series are calculated.
3. Cross correlations calculated between two series are squared. After averaging these squares, they are multiplied by the total length of time (number of observations). The statistic obtained is the S statistic expressing the magnitude, significantness of the cross correlations between the averages (returns) of the two series. The S statistic is subtracted from the length used in the cross correlations, and the AR length in the return equation is subtracted and tested against the null hypothesis that an added degree of freedom is less than the Chi-Square (X^2) table value. If S>X^2, cross correlations are significant, if S<X^2 is not significant. This means that there is a causality between the returns of the two series respectively or not. The above processes are also applied for volatility, and for causality between the squares of the standardized errors of the two series, respectively.

The two-step calculation process of the causality test proposed by Cheung and Ng (1996) is summarized below. First, it is assumed that the ΔBIST (X) and ΔIOI (Y) series are stationary and there are three sets of information shown below:

$$I_{1t} = \left(X_{t-j}; j \geq 0\right) \tag{7}$$

$$I_{2t} = \left(Y_{t-j}; j \geq 0\right) \tag{8}$$

$$I_{3t} = \left(X_{t-j}\ ,\ Y_{t-j}; j \geq 0\right) \tag{9}$$

If $E[X_t \,|I_{1t-1}] \neq E[X_t \,|I_{t-1}]$ in the mean equation, Y_t is the cause of X_t. Similarly if $E[Y_{2t} \,|I_{2t-1}] \neq E[Y_t \,|I_{t-1}]$ in the mean equation X_t is the cause of Y_t (Toyoshima ve Hamori, 2012:851). If Y_t causes X_t and X_t causes Y_t in the mean equation, there is a causal relationship feedback in the mean equation. On the other hand, if $E[(X_t - \mu_{x,t})^2 \,|I_{1t-1}] \neq E[(X_t - \mu_{x,t})^2 X_t \,|I_{t-1}]$in the variance equation, Y_t is the cause of X_t. $\mu_{x,t}$ is the conditional mean of the X_t series relative to I_{1t-1}. Similarly if $E[(Y_t - \mu_{y,t})^2 \,|I_{2t-1}] \neq E[\left(Y - \mu_{y,t}\right)^2 Y_t \,|I_{t-1}]$ in the variance equation, X_t is the cause of Y_t. $\mu_{y,t}$ is the conditional mean of the Y_t series relative to I_{2t-1} (Bhar ve Hamori, 2008: 276). If Y_t causes X_t and X_t causes Y_t in the variance equation, there is a causal relationship feedback in the variance equation. The presence of causality in the variance equation means that there is a volatility spill-over between two different markets. Additional explanations of the conceptually defined causality process in terms of implementation are given below.

ε_t of X and ς_t of Y are non-observable standardized error terms derived from model EGARCH model. ε_t and ς_t are used in testing causality in terms of mean. For the consistent estimate of causality between X and Y in terms of mean, the formula for the cross correlation $r_{\varepsilon,\varsigma}\,(k)$ coefficient calculated in the k lag is as follows (Xu ve Hamori, 2012: 347):

$$r_{\varepsilon,\varsigma} = \frac{Covariance_{\varepsilon,\varsigma}\,(k)}{\sqrt{Variance_{\varepsilon\varepsilon}\,(0)\ Variance_{\varsigma\varsigma}\,(0)}} \tag{10}$$

$$Covariance_{\varepsilon,\varsigma} = \begin{cases} \frac{1}{T}\sum\limits_{t=1}^{T-k} \left(\hat{\varepsilon}_t - \bar{\varepsilon}\right)\left(\hat{\varsigma}_{t+k} - \bar{\varsigma}\right)\ for\ k = 0,\ 1,\ 2, \ldots \\ \frac{1}{T}\sum\limits_{t=1}^{T+k} \left(\hat{\varepsilon}_{t-k} - \bar{\varepsilon}\right)\left(\hat{\varsigma}_t - \bar{\varsigma}\right)\ for\ k = 0, -1 - 2 \ldots \end{cases} \tag{11}$$

In the causality test of the mean between X and Y, the significance levels of the $r_{\varepsilon,\varsigma}\,(k)$ coefficients of the standardized errors calculated by the CCF process are tested with the equation below (Cheung ve Ng, 1996: 37):

$$S_1 = T\sum_{i=j}^{k} r^2_{\varepsilon,\varsigma}\ i = 1, 2, \ldots m \tag{12}$$

The value of S_1 is compared with the chi-square table value at $k - j + 1$ degrees of freedom. If S_1 is greater than the table value as a result of comparison, the null hypothesis suggesting that there is no causality-in-mean is rejected.

The causal relationship between the two series in terms of variance equation, namely volatility, is calculated as follows by applying it to standardized error terms. υ_t of X and ν_t of Y are non-observable squares of standardized error terms derived from the GARCH model. For the consistent estimate of causality between X and Y in terms of variance, the formula for the cross correlation $r_{\upsilon,\nu}(k)$ coefficient calculated in the k lag is below (Xu ve Hamori, 2012: 347):

$$r_{\upsilon,\nu} = \frac{Covariance_{\upsilon,\nu}(k)}{\sqrt{Variance_{\upsilon\upsilon}(0)\, Variance_{\nu\nu}(0)}} \quad (13)$$

$$Covariance_{\upsilon,\nu} = \begin{cases} \frac{1}{T}\sum_{t=1}^{T-k} (\hat{\upsilon}_t - \upsilon)(\hat{\nu}_{t+k} - \bar{\nu}) \; for\; k = 0,\ 1,\ 2, \ldots \\ \frac{1}{T}\sum_{t=1}^{T+k} (\hat{\upsilon}_{t-k} - \bar{\upsilon})(\hat{\nu}_t - \bar{\nu}) \; for\; k = 0, -1 - 2 \ldots \end{cases} \quad (14)$$

In the test of causality-in- variance between X and Y, the significance levels of the $r_{\upsilon,\nu}(k)$ coefficients of the standardized error term squares calculated by the CCF process are tested by the following equation (Cheung and Ng, 1996: 37):

$$S_2 = T\sum_{i=j}^{k} r^2_{\upsilon,\nu}\; i = 1, 2, \ldots m \quad (15)$$

The value of S_2 is compared with the chi-square table value at $k - j + 1$ degrees of freedom. If S_2 is greater than the table value as a result of comparison, the null hypothesis suggesting that there is no causality-in-variance is rejected. Thus, the existence and direction of volatility spillover between the two markets is determined.

More detailed information about the existence and direction of causality can be obtained by calculating the S statistic for each space according to the normal distribution with 1-degree of freedom in the following formula (Giannellis et al., 2010:434):

$$\mathrm{CCF_m - statistic} = \sqrt{\mathrm{T}} * \mathrm{r}_{\varepsilon,\zeta(\mathrm{k})} \quad (16)$$

$$CCF_v - statistic = \sqrt{T} * r_{U,V}(k) \quad (17)$$

5. Findings

According to the unit root test results given in the Tab. 5.2, the series are stationary at the level. According to the ARCH effect tests (Q test), it is observed that there are serial correlations in both error series and error square series. Series correlation is found in ΔBIST and ΔIOI errors, and error square series; and ARCH effect is detected in error series with ARCH-LM test. Thus, ARCH effect is provided in ΔBIST and ΔIOI volatility estimation, and asymmetric diagnostic tests are conducted to determine which of the symmetric and asymmetric ARCH models are suitable for volatility estimates. According to the results of the asymmetric diagnostic tests, the significant indication of Sign Asymmetry in the ΔBIST series shows that the shock size in this series is effective in volatility. The negative value and positive value asymmetry test of the ΔIOI series is significant. These results showed the necessity to analyze volatility in series with an ARCH type asymmetric model.

EGARCH test results, which is an asymmetric model, are given in the Tab. 5.3. In the mean equation, parameters for ΔBIST and ΔIOI are significant. In

Tab. 5.2. Unit Root, ARCH Effect, and Asymmetric Diagnostic Tests, Source: Authors' own calculations

	ΔBIST	**ΔIOI**
Unit Root Tests		
ADF	-17.489**	-45.171**
PP	-84.798**	-45.135**
KPSS	0.048	0.049
ARCH Effect Tests		
Q (10)	30.865**	425.65**
Q (20)	39.657**	489.28**
Q^2 (10)	246.45**	706.34**
Q^2 (20)	260.45**	725.18**
ARCH LM Testi	215.527**	698.158**
Asymmetric Diagnostic Tests		
Sign Bias	3.063**	0.875
Negative Size Bias	-13.012**	-32.105**
Positive Size Bias	-2.026*	0.153
Joint	54.206**	382.423**

* and ** refer to significance levels of 5 %, and 1 %, respectively

the variance equation, the term leverage in ΔBIST and ΔIOI series is significant. It is also not equal to zero or less than zero. This result shows the existence of both asymmetric effect and leverage effect in the series. According to Ljung and Box (1978) Q test and ARCH-LM tests, where serial correlation and conditional variance problems are investigated, there is no serial correlation or heteroskedasticity.

For the CCF Test, the lead-serie ΔIOI (t = 0, +1, +2 and +3) and the lag-serie ΔBIST (t = 0, -1, -2 and -3) are taken. In the Tab. 5.4, CCF results of causality relationship between ΔBIST and ΔIOI in causailty-in-mean and causality-in-variance models are presented. The causal relationship between the stock market in Turkey interbank interest rate is found to be one-way to the stock market. These findings showed that the return on the stock market in Turkey affects the interbank interest rate. Considering the conditional variance model, no causality-in-variance relationship is found between ΔBIST volatility and ΔIOI volatility. In Turkey, there is non-causal link between interest rates and

Tab. 5.3: EGARCH Test Results, Source: Authors' own calculations

	$\Delta BIST_t$	ΔIOI_t
Mean Equation		
ω_0	0.028	0.040*
ω_1	0.119**	
ω_1		0.031*
Variance Equation		
α_0	0.041*	0.051**
β_j	0.945**	0.926**
α_i	0.058**	0.050**
γ_i	-0.106**	-0.102**
Skewness	-0.520	-0.858
Kurtosis	6.195	44.648
Log Likelihood	-4783.667	-4529.638
Q (10)	5.0791	22.582
Q (20)	11.628	38.092
Q^2(10)	3.005	1.047
Q^2(20)	9.280	15.953
ARCH LM Test	2.112	0.694

* and ** refer to significance levels of 5 %, and 1 %, respectively.

stock market volatility. In the return, it is found to be one-way from the stock market to the interest market. Thus, it is observed that it affects the stock market return on interest returns in Turkey. It is concluded that the reverse effect is not in question.

The lead-serie (+1, +2 and +3) of the cross correlations in the Tab. 5.5 shows the quantity and direction of causality from ΔIOI to ΔBIST. In contrast, lag-serie of Cross Correlations (-1, -2 and -3) expresses the quantity and direction of causality from ΔBIST to the ΔIOI. Similarly, the lead (+1, +2, and +3) of the S with CCF test statistics reveals the statistical significance of causality from ΔIOI to ΔBIST.

Causality from ΔIOI to ΔBIST is not significant in causality-in-means CCF lead. CCF test statistics S lags (-1, -2 and -3) show statistical significance of causality from ΔBIST to ΔIOI. CCF in lag (1) is -0.054 and statistically significant from Borsa Istanbul Return to the Interbank Interest Rate (S = -2.217 and

Tab. 5.4: CCF Test between ΔBIST and ΔIOI, Source: Authors' calculations

Direction of Causality	S Statistic	Result
Causalty-in-Mean		
ΔBIST → ΔIOI	**5.914****	Causality
ΔIOI → ΔBIST	1.612	No Causality
Causalty-in-Variance		
ΔBIST → ΔIOI	0.883	No Causality
ΔIOI → ΔBIST	0.745	No Causality

* and ** refer to significance levels of 5 %, and 1 %, respectively.

Tab. 5.5: Cross Correlations Tests

	Causalty-in-Mean		Causalty-in-Variance	
Lag/Lead	**Cross Correlation**	**S Statistic**	**Cross Correlation**	**S Statistic**
-3	0.022	1.112	-0.011	-0.536
-2	-0.014	-0.652	-0.012	-0.596
-1	**-0.054**	**-2.217****	-0.008	-0.363
0	-0.000	-0.001	0.003	0.118
+1	0.007	0.318	-0.008	-0.343
+2	-0.014	-0.649	-0.012	-0.587
+3	0.021	1.096	-0.011	-0.534

* and ** refer to significance levels of 5 %, and 1 %, respectively.

$p < 0.05$). Thus, the return in the Borsa Istanbul led to an interest market return the next day. However, there is no effect from interest to the stock market's return. When looking at volatility, it is determined that CCF test statistics are not statistically significant in leads and lags. Based on this finding, it is observed that there is only one-way causality between ΔBIST and ΔIOI from ΔBIST to ΔIOI causality-in-mean. In terms of volatility, no causal relationship is found between ΔBIST and ΔIOI. For Turkey, in terms of whether there is a relationship between the ΔIOI and ΔBIST or not, whereas it has reached that there is no causality relationship in variance.

6. Conclusion

Causality-in-mean and causality-in-variance between interest rate and the stock return in Turkey are examined in this study. EGARCH model is used to estimate asymmetric volatility in the series. The main research objective of this study is to test dynamic volatility spillover between the stock index and interbank market for Turkey after the global crisis.

Economic and political events cause fluctuations (shock) in stock indexes and interest rates. Volatility cluster occurs as a result of these fluctuations and negative shocks are more effective than positive shocks. In this study, it is observed that the volatility shocks that occurred in Borsa Istanbul and overnight interest rate have asymmetrical and leverage effects. It is also observed that the impact of shocks is more effective for Borsa Istanbul volatility than for the overnight interest rate. In addition, there is a causality from Borsa Istanbul return to the next day interest market return. However, there is no such effect from interest rate to stock exchange. Uzun and Güngör (2017) and Taştan and Güngör (2019) results are different from this study. For Durmuş et al. (2019) similar results have been reached. Chen et al. (1986), Sweney and Warga (1986) and Peiro (2016) argue that macroeconomic factors affect stock returns. In this study, causality between the return on the stock market and interest rate market in Turkey (causality-in-mean) has been shown to exist. Therefore, this study supports the theory.

In terms of investors and depositors in Turkey, there are usually two alternatives for speculative purposes. The first is to earn interest by buying bonds or creating deposits at the bank, and the second is to get returns by purchasing stocks. There is a negative relationship between interest and stock market investments. Stock market investments are more risky and profit-oriented investments. Interest investments are more protective. According to the results obtained from this study, it is concluded that investors should take into consideration Borsa Istanbul return on interest in their investments.

While evaluating the results of the study, it should be kept in mind that it is based on Borsa Istanbul All Index and overnight interest rate. Inter-market causations can be elaborated by examining different stock indices and periods. In the period after the global crisis, stock market returns are determinant in the interest market return. The study provides useful information for academics and decision makers by understanding the relationship between the stock market and the interest market.

References

Aktaş M., & Akdağ, S. (2013). The Research on the Relation of Economic Factors and Stock Prices in Turkey. *International Journal Social Science Research*, 2(2), 50–67.

Alaganar V.T., & Bhar, R. (2003). An International Study of Causality-in-Variance: Interest Rate and Financial Sector Returns. *Journal of Economics and Finance*, 27, 1, 39–55.

Amarasinghe, A.A.M.D. (2015). Dynamic Relationship between Interest Rate and Stock Price: Empirical Evidence from Colombo Stock Exchange. *International Journal of Business and Social Science*, 6, 4, 92–97.

Banerjee, P. K., & Adhikary, K. B. (2009). Dynamic effects of changes in interest rates and exchange rates on the stock market return in Bangladesh. *Ritsumeikan Journal of Asia Pacific Studies*, 25, 119–133. Retrieved from http://en.apu.ac.jp/rcaps/uploads/fckeditor/publications/journal/RJAPS_V25_Banerjee_Adhikary.pdf (15.11.2020).

Bhar, R., & Hamori, S. (2008). Information Content of Commodity Futures Prices for Monetary Policy. *Economic Modelling* 25, 274–283.

Black, F. (1976). Studies of Stock Price Volatility Changes. *Proceedings of the 1976 Meeting of the Business and Economic Statistics, American Statistical Association*, Washington DC, 177–181.

Bollerslev, T. (1990). Modelling the Coherence in Short-Run Nominal Exchange Rates: A Multivariate Generalized ARCH Model. *The Review of Economics and Statistics*, 72(3), 498–505.

Breusch, T. S., & Pagan, A. R. (1980). The Lagrange Multiplier Test and Its Applications to Model Specification in Econometrics. *Review of Economic Studies*, 47(1), 239–253.

Chen, C. R., Mohan, N. J., & Steiner, T. L. (1999). Discount Rate Changes, Stock Market Returns, Volatility, and Trading Volume: Evidence from Intraday Data and Implications for Market Efficiency. *Journal of Banking & Finance*, 23, 897–924.

Chen, N. F., Roll, R., & Ross, S. A. (1986). Economic Forces and the Stock Market. *The Journal of Business*, 59(3), 383–403.

Cheung, Y-W., & Ng, L. K. (1996). A Causality-in-Variance Test and Its Application to Financial Market Prices. *Journal of Econometrics*, 72, 33–48.

Coşkun, M., Kiracı, K., & Muhammed, U. (2016). Relationship between Stock Prices and Selected Macroeconomic Variables: An Empirical Study. *Finance, Politics and Economics Reviews*, 53(616), 61–74.

Demir, Y., & Yağcılar, G. G. (2009). Determining the Factors Effecting Banks' Stock Returns Trading in Imkb by Arbitrage Pricing Model. *Alanya İşletme Fakültesi Dergisi*, 1(2), 36–51.

Dickey, D. A., & Fuller, W. A. (1979). Distribution of the Estimators for Autoregressive Time Series with a Unit Root. *Journal of the American Statistical Association*, 74(366), 427–431.

Durmuş, S., Yılmaz, T., & Şahin, D. (2019). The Effect of Macro Economic Indicators on Index Revenues: BIST Example. *Avrasya Uluslararası Araştırmalar Dergisi*, 7(16), 870–886.

Durukan, B. (1999). İstanbul Menkul Kıymetler Borsasında Makroekonomik Değişkenlerin Hisse Senedi Fiyatlarına Etkisi. *İMKB Dergisi*, 3(11), 19–47.

Engle, R. F. (1982). Autoregressive Conditional Heteroskedasticity with Estimates of the Variance of U.K. Inflation. *Econometrica*, 50, 987–1008.

Engle, R. F., & Ng, V. K. (1993). Measuring and Testing the Impact of News on Volatility. *Journal of Finance*, 5, 1749–1778.

Fama, E. F. (1981). Stock Returns, Real Activity, Inflation, and Money. *The American Economic Review*, 71(4), 545–565.

Freixas, X., Martin, A., & Skeie, D. (2011). Bank Liquidity, Interbank Markets, and Monetary Policy. *The Review of Financial Studies*, 24(8), 2656–2692.

Giannellis, N., Kanas, A., & Papadopoulos, A. (2010). Asymmetric Volatility Spillovers between Stock Market and Real Activity: Evidence from the UK and the US. *Panaeconomicus*, 4, 429–445.

Gjerde, Ø., & Sættem, F. (1999). Causal Relations among Stock Returns and Macroeconomic Variables in a Small, Open Economy. *Journal of International Financial Markets*, 9, 61–74.

Green, C., Bai, Y., Murinde, V., Ngoka, K., Maana, I., & Tiriongo, S. (2016). Overnight Interbank Markets and the Determination of the Interbank Rate: A Selective Survey. *International Review of Financial Analysis*, 44, 149–161.

Hussain, A., Gohar, Z., & Baloch, Q. B. (2014). The Causal Relationshıp of Interest Rate and Stock Prices: Empirical Evidence from Pakistani Market. *City University Research Journal*, 4(2), 147–155.

Jensen, G. R., & Johnson, R. R. (1995). Discount Rate Changes and Security Returns in the U.S., 1962–1991. *Journal of Banking & Finance*, 19, 79–95.

Jin, X. (2015). Asymmetry in Return and Volatility Spillover between China's Interbank and Exchange T-Bond Markets. *International Review of Economics and Finance*, 37, 340–353.

Kasman, S., Vardar, G., & Tunç, G. (2011). The Impact of Interest Rate and Exchange Rate Volatility on Banks' Stock Returns and Volatility: Evidence from Turkey. *Economic Modelling*, 28, 1328–1334.

Kwiatkowski, D., Phillips, P. C. B., Schmidt, P., & Shin, Y. (1992). Testing the Null Hypothesis of Stationarity Against the Alternative of a Unit Root: How Sure Are We That Economic Time Series Have a Unit Root? *Journal of Econometrics*, 54, 159–178.

Ljung, G. M., & Box, G. E. P. (1978). On a Measure of Lack of Fit in Time Series Models. *Biometrika*, 65, 297–303.

Lobo, B. J. (2000). Interest Rate Surprises and Stock Prices. *The Financial Review*, 37, 73–92.

Lobo, B. J. (2002). Asymmetric Effects of Interest Rate Changes on Stock Prices. *The Financial Review*, 35, 125–144.

Najand, M., & Noronha, G. (1998). Causal Relations among Stock Returns, Inflation, Real Activity, and Interest Rates: Evidence from Japan. *Global Finance Journal*, 9(1), 71–80.

Nelson, D. B. (1991). Conditional Heteroscedasticity in Asset Returns: A New Approach. *Econometrica*, 59(2), 347–370.

Özer, A., Kaya, A., & Özer, N. (2011). Interaction of Macroeconomic Variables with Stock Prices. *Dokuz Eylul University Faculty of Economics and Administrative Sciences Journal*, 26(1), 163–182.

Patterson, K. (2000). *An Introduction to Applied Econometrics.* Bristol: McMillian Press.

Peiro, A. (2016). Stock Prices and Macroeconomic Factors: Some European Evidence. *International Review of Economics and Finance*, 41, 287–294.

Phillips, P. C. B., & Perron, P. (1988). Testing for a Unit Root in Time Series Regressions. *Biometrika*, 75, 335–346.

Poyraz, E., & Tepeli, Y. (2015). Analysis of the Impact of Selected Macroeconomic Indicators on Istanbul Stock Exchange Xu100 Index. *Paradoks Economics, Sociology and Policy Journal*, 11(2), 102–128.

Rigobon, R., & Sack, B. (2003). Spillovers across U.S. Financial Markets. *NBER Working Paper*, 9640, 1–21.

Sadeghzadeh, K., & Elmas, B. (2018). The Effect of Macroeconomic Factors on Stock Returns: An Application in Stock Exchange Istanbul. *The Journal of Accounting and Finance*, 205–230. Retrieved from http://www.journal.mufad.org.tr/attachments/article/968/12.pdf (15.11.2020).

Sayılgan, G., & Süslü, C. (2011). The Effect of Macroeconomic Factors on Stock Returns: A Study of Turkey and Emerging Markets. *BDDK Bankacılık ve Finansal Piyasalar Dergisi,* 5(1), 73–96.

Şentürk, M., & Dücan E. (2014). The Relationship between Exchange Rate-Interest Rate and Stock Return in Turkey: An Empirical Analysis, *Business and Economics Research Journal*, 5 (3), 67–80.

Sevinç, E. (2014). Determination of the Impact of Macroeconomic Variables on Stock Returns Traded on Bist-30 by Using Arbitrage Pricing Theory. *Istanbul University Journal of the School of Business*, 43(2), 271–292.

Smirlock, M., & Yawitz, J. (1985). Asset Returns, Discount Rate Changes, and Market Efficiency. *The Journal of Finance*, 40(4), 1141–1158.

Sweney, R. J., & Warga, A. D. (1986). The Pricing of Interest-Rate Risk: Evidence from the Stock Market. *Journal of Finance,* 41(2), 393–409.

Taştan, H., & Güngör, A. (2019). Macroeconomic Fundamentals of Turkey Stock Market Volatility. *Business and Economics Research Journal*, 10(4), 823–832.

Thorbecke, W. (1997). On Stock Market Returns and Monetary Policy. *Journal of Finance*, 52(2), 635–654.

Thorbecke, W., & Alami, T. (1994). The Effect of Changes in the Federal Funds Rate Target on Stock Prices in the 1970s. Journal of Economics and Business, 46, 13–19.

Toyoshima, Y., & Hamori, S. (2012). Volatility transmission of swap spreads among the US, Japan and the UK: A cross-correlation function approach. *Applied Financial Economics*, 22, 849–862.

Tripathy, N. (2011). Causal Relationship between Macro-Economic Indicators and Stock Market in India. *Asian Journal of Finance & Accounting*, 3(1), 208–226.

Uzun, U., & Güngör, B. (2017). Investigation of the Relationship between Stock Market Indices and Selected Macroeconomics Indicators at International Level. *AİBÜ Sosyal Bilimler Enstitüsü Dergisi*, 17(4), 1–30.

Xu, H., & Hamori, S. (2012). Dynamic Linkages of Stock Prices between the BRICs and the United States: Effects of the 2008–09 Financial Crisis. *Journal of Asian Economics*, 23, 344–352.

Yılmaz, Ö., Güngör B., & Kaya V. (2006). Hisse Senedi Fiyatları Ve Makro Ekonomik Değişkenler Arasındaki Eşbütünleşme Ve Nedensellik, İMKB Dergisi, 9(34), 1–16.

Coşkun AKDENİZ, Ali İLHAN

Chapter 6 The Validity of the Real Interest Differential Model for Turkey with Markov Regime Switching

Abstract: Factors driving the fluctuations in exchange rates have always been on the agenda of economists. For this purpose, many theories have been developed to find the determinants of exchange rate movements. One of the best known of these theories is Frankel's (1979) Real Interest Differential (RID) Model, which explains exchange rate movements with a monetarist approach. RID model is an approach that tries to explain exchange rate changes among countries by the differences between money supplies, income levels, interest rates and expected inflation rates. Although this monetary model is useful in explaining long-term relationships, it has been considered as inadequate to explain the mutual dynamic interactions between monetary fundamentals and exchange rates that change over time. The nonlinear relationship between exchange rates and monetary fundamentals has led to the analysis of theoretical models to explain exchange rate movements with nonlinear methods. Accordingly, in this study the validity of Frankel's (1979) RID model is tested for Turkey during the 1990:01–2018:12 period by performing the Markov Regime Switching (MS) method. Findings show that there are two regimes reflecting; specifically the periods of decrease in exchange rates (first regime) and the periods of increase (second regime) throughout the analyzed period. According to the MS estimation results, while all the explanatory variables other than the relative interest rate are statistically significant in the first regime, the effect of relative income on the exchange rate is positive and contrary to expectations. In the second regime, all the explanatory variables except the relative income level are statistically significant and the coefficient signs are consistent with the predictions of the RID model. In this context, it is possible to state that the RID model helps to understand the movements in the USD/TL exchange rate in certain periods.

Keywords: Exchange Rate, Monetary Exchange Rate Model, Real Interest Differential Model, Markov Regime Switching, Turkish Economy

1. Introduction

In the 1970s, following the collapse of the Bretton Woods system, where a system similar to the fixed exchange rate regime, many countries, particularly developed countries, allow their exchange rates to float. In an environment where the flexible exchange rate regime is implemented, the increasing integration between financial markets and the removal of obstacles to capital movements has further increased the volatility in exchange rates. In parallel with the increase in volatility, many theoretical models have been developed to understand the movements in exchange rates.

Monetary exchange rate models are theoretical models created to establish the determinants of the movements in exchange rates. In monetary exchange rate models, it is claimed that nominal exchange rates and monetary fundamentals are related to each other. According to models, exchange rate is the price of a nation's currency in terms of another currency and is determined by the relative supply and demand of domestic money stocks (Taşkın, 1995: 69). The fact that money supply and money demand are at the center of the analysis means that real variables, which are the determinants of money demand, as well as money supply, can have an effect on exchange rates (Yay, 2012: 154).

There are various types of monetary models depending on the elasticity of prices in the economy. These are flexible-price monetary models developed by Frenkel (1976) and Bilson (1978), and sticky-price monetary models by Dornbusch (1976) and Frankel (1979). In the models, as the way exchange rates can be associated with different monetary fundamentals, the expected effects of monetary fundamentals on exchange rates may also differ.

Monetary models are simple and useful for analyzing long-term relationships among variables. However, it is difficult to state that the models fully capture the mutual dynamic interactions between macroeconomic variables and exchange rates. The change of macroeconomic fundamentals over time makes their relations with exchange rates quite unstable. This weakens the explanatory power of linear models in the analysis of these relationships (Frömmel et al., 2005: 486–489; Bacchetta and van Wincoop, 2013: 18). In this respect, it is seen that nonlinear analysis such as regime switching approach is used to capture the dynamic course of exchange rates under the time-varying structure of macroeconomic fundamentals.

Turkey abolished the controls on capital movements in 1989 and has made its domestic currency convertible. Since then, in Turkey, where have occurred sharp fluctuations in exchange rates and even these fluctuations ended up with severe economic crises, understating of the movements in exchange rates has been always at the center stage. In this context, the aim of this study is to test Frankel (1979)'s Real Interest Differential (RID) model, which is one of the sticky-price monetary models for Turkish economy. In this direction, the

RID model for the United States Dollar/Turkish Lira (USD/TL) exchange rate[1] is analyzed by employing the Markov Regime Switching (MS) method for the period 1990:01–2018:12.

The chapter consists of six sections. In the second part following the introduction, the theoretical background of the monetary exchange rate models and Frankel's (1979) RID model are explained. In the third part, empirical studies examining the movements in the exchange rate through monetary exchange rate models, primarily the RID model, are summarized. While the data set and methodology are described in the fourth section, the empirical findings obtained in the study are included in the fifth part. The chapter ends with the conclusion section where empirical findings are evaluated.

2. Monetary Exchange Rate Models: Real Interest Differential Model

The RID model is a monetary model developed to explain the movements in exchange rates. The model is formed as a combination of two approaches that provide different explanations for the relationship between interest rates and exchange rates. The first of these is the Chicago Theory, which argues that prices are perfectly elastic. According to the theory, nominal interest rates reflect the change in expected inflation rates in the long run. When the domestic interest rate exceeds the foreign interest rates, it is likely that the domestic currency will depreciate in the near future and the general level of prices will rise. The exchange rate depreciates instantly over the decline in relative demand of the domestic currency. Therefore, there is a positive relationship between the nominal interest rate differential and the exchange rate. The second approach is the Keynesian Theory, which assumes that prices are sticky, at least in the short run. According to the theory, the increase in the domestic interest rate compared to the foreign interest rate causes the capital inflows to accelerate due to the sticky prices. The domestic currency appreciates against the increase in capital inflows. In other words, in the Keynesian theory, the increase in the nominal interest rate causes the nominal exchange rate to fall. In this context, in the RID model, if the nominal interest rate differential rises due to the tightening of the monetary policy stance, the nominal exchange rate falls below the equilibrium value. On the other hand, if the only reason for the increase in nominal

1 In this study, exchange rate is taken as the price of domestic currency in terms of foreign currency. In other words, USD/TL exchange rates indicate TL price of 1 USD.

interest rate differential is the high expected inflation difference, the exchange rate equilibrium value increases over time as much as the differentiation in the inflation rate (Frankel, 1979: 610–611).

In monetary exchange rate models, it is assumed that there is no restriction on the capital movements between countries. Power purchasing parity (PPP) and uncovered[2] interest rate parity (UIP) are used to define the equilibrium conditions. In addition to this, money demand functions for countries are assumed to be stable.

Equilibrium conditions in money markets depend on real income and price level in logarithmic form and nominal interest rates. Money market equilibriums for both domestic and foreign countries are as follows (Civcir, 2004: 86–87):

$$m_t = p_t + \delta y_t - \lambda i_t \tag{1}$$

$$m_t^* = p_t^* + \delta^* y_t^* - \lambda^* i_t^* \tag{2}$$

In the equations above, m_t implies the domestic money supply, p_t the domestic price level, y_t the national real income and i_t the domestic nominal interest rate. δ indicates the income elasticity of the demand for money, while λ represents the semi-elasticity of the interest rate. These variables and coefficients for the foreign country are shown with the notation (*).

The second building block of the model is PPP. In case the currency of two countries is expressed in a single currency, PPP states that the price level in the two countries should be the same. Accordingly PPP:

$$e_t = \alpha + p_t - p_t^* \tag{3}$$

α refers to the constant term, while e_t implies the nominal exchange rate, which is the domestic price of the foreign currency. In the flexible-price versions of monetary exchange rate models, PPP is assumed to be valid continuously. When we rearrange the equations (1) and (2) for price levels and substitute them in the Equation (3), the nominal exchange rate is obtained as follows:

$$e_t = \alpha + \beta (m_t - m_t^*) + \delta (y_t - y_t^*) + \lambda (i_t - i_t^*) \tag{4}$$

2 Uncovered term means that investors carry out transactions by spot exchange rates instead of protecting themselves by forward contracts against the fluctuations in exchange rates (Yay, 2012: 144).

It is possible to write the nominal interest rate in the Equation (4) as follows according to Fisher's equation:

$$i_t = r_t + \pi_t^e \tag{5}$$

$$i_t^* = r_t^* + \pi_t^{e^*} \tag{6}$$

r_t denotes the real interest rate and π_t^e expresses the expected inflation rate.

$$i_t - i_t^* = \pi_t^e - \pi_t^{e^*} \tag{7}$$

Assuming the same real interest rate for both countries in line with UIP, the equation (7) is achieved. When the Equation (4) is rewritten considering the equation above, the flexible-price model of the Chicago Theory is obtained as follows:

$$e_t = \alpha + \beta\,(m_t - m_t^*) + \delta\,(y_t - y_t^*) + \lambda\left(\pi_t^e - \pi_t^{e^*}\right) \tag{8}$$

According to the flexible price model, the parameter β is expected to be equal to 1, δ to be negative and λ to be positive. An increase in the domestic money supply causes the domestic currency to depreciate by raising the general level of prices at the same rate whereas an increase in income or a decrease in expected inflation causes the domestic currency to appreciate.

The sticky-price versions of the monetary model assume that PPP is valid only in the long run (Chinn, 2012: 48). The RID model developed by Frankel (1979), which is a monetary model with a sticky price, includes the short-term interest rate in addition to the variables in the flexible-price models. In this respect, the RID model explains the direct effects of monetary expansion, the liquidity-driven effects of interest rates, capital movements and exchange rates, and the indirect effects of expected inflation (Zakaria and Ahmad, 2009: 134).

The RID model starts with two basic assumptions. The first of these is UIP, which means that the expected returns of bonds issued by countries are the same when expressed in a single currency. According to UIP, the bonds of different countries are the perfect substitute of each other and the opportunity for interest arbitrage disappears. Despite the differentiation in interest rates, the depreciation of the exchange rate equates the bond returns (Frankel, 1979: 611–613):

$$d_t = i_t - i_t^* \tag{9}$$

The d in equation (9) reflects the expected depreciation at the nominal exchange rate. The second assumption of the model is that d is a function of the difference between the current spot exchange rate and the equilibrium exchange rate, and the expected long-term inflation difference between countries:

$$d_t = -\vartheta\left(e_t - \bar{e}_t\right) + \pi_t^e - \pi_t^{e^*} \tag{10}$$

The parameter ϑ indicates the adjustment speed of the current exchange rate towards the long-term equilibrium value. $\bar{e}_t$ symbolizes the long-term equilibrium exchange rate. According to the Equation (10), the current exchange rate is expected to reach its long-term equilibrium at the rate of ϑ coefficient. As a result of the combination of the Equations (9) and (10), it is possible to express the difference between the current exchange rate and the long-term equilibrium exchange rate as follows:

$$e_t - \bar{e}_t = -\frac{1}{\vartheta}\left[\left(i_t - \pi_t^e\right) - \left(i_t^* - \pi_t^{e^*}\right)\right] \tag{11}$$

Frankel (1979) states that the part in square brackets in the equation above can be defined as the real interest rate differential between countries. In addition to this, under the presence of UIP and relative PPP conditions, when $e_t = \bar{e}_t$ in the long run leads to $\bar{i}_t - \bar{i}_t^* = \pi_t^e - \pi_t^{e^*}$. Therefore, it becomes possible to write the part of the Equation (11) shown in square brackets in the form as follows:

$$\left[\left(i_t - i_t^*\right) - \left(\bar{i}_t - \bar{i}_t^*\right)\right] \tag{12}$$

Accordingly, a tightening of the monetary policy stance increases the capital inflows and appreciated the currency by causing the nominal interest rates to exceed the long-term equilibrium value.

Under the combination of UIP and relative PPP conditions, the equation (4) can be written as:

$$\bar{e}_t = \alpha + \beta\left(\bar{m}_t - \bar{m}_t^*\right) + \delta\left(\bar{y}_t - \bar{y}_t^*\right) + \lambda\left(\pi_t^e - \pi_t^{e^*}\right) \tag{13}$$

When we substitute the equation (13) into the equation (11), which shows the short-run condition, and assume that the current equilibriums of money supplies and income levels are equal to their actual values, we arrive to the final equation:

$$e_t = \alpha + \beta(m_t - m_t^*) + \delta(y_t - y_t^*) - \frac{1}{\vartheta}(i_t - i_t^*) + \left(\frac{1}{\vartheta} + \lambda\right)\left(\pi_t^e - \pi_t^{e^*}\right) \quad (14)$$

When we add the error term and rearrange the equation, Frankel's (1979) RID model can be tested as follows:

$$e_t = \alpha + \beta(m_t - m_t^*) + \delta(y_t - y_t^*) + \theta(i_t - i_t^*) + \omega\left(\pi_t^e - \pi_t^{e^*}\right) + \varepsilon_t \quad (15)$$

According to the model, it is expected β to be equal to one[3], δ and $\theta\ (= -1/\vartheta)$ to be negative, and the coefficient $\omega\ \ (= 1/\ \vartheta + \lambda)$ to be positive.

3. Literature Review

There are many studies in the literature that analyze the determinants of exchange rates with monetary models. In these studies, it is possible to state that while linear methods are preferred intensively, the number of studies in which nonlinear methods are used has increased significantly[4]. Moreover, among nonlinear methods, the MS method seems to be more suitable for the analysis of the said relationship due to its advantages.

Frömmel et al. (2005) tested the validity of the RID model by using MS for Germany, United Kingdom and Japan covering the period 1974:01–2000:10. In the study where the determined two different regimes are differentiated permanently, one of the regimes verifies the coefficient signs predicted by the RID model for a certain period of time. Wu (2015) analyzed the validity of the RID model with both linear methods and MS for 6 Asia-Pacific countries in the period 2000:01–2011:12. When compared with linear methods, it has been observed that MS gives more consistent results with the expectations of the

---

3 In the regression analysis performed by Frankel (1979) using the model above, the parameter β is fixed to 1. However, in many studies in the literature, the fact that β equals to 1 has been interpreted as the parameter being greater than zero and the coefficient β has also been estimated. Similarly, in this study, the coefficient -a priori expectation positive- was estimated.

4 Qi and Wu (2003), Frömmel et al. (2005), De Grauwe and Vansteenkiste (2007), Junttila and Korhonen (2011), Bacchetta and van Wincoop (2013), Tang and Zhou (2013), Zhang (2014), Wu (2015) and Hadian and Sajedianfard (2018) are among the studies, which use nonlinear methods in the analysis of the relationship between exchange rates and monetary fundamentals.

RID model in terms of the significance and signs of the coefficients. Hadian and Sajedianfard (2018) examined the RID model for Iran with Time-Varying Transition Probabilities in the period 1990:02–2014:03. According to the empirical findings, it was determined that the RID model failed to explain the exchange rate movements in Iran.

There are several studies that investigate the exchange rate movements with the monetary exchange rate models for Turkey. It is seen that the findings regarding the validity of monetary models differ in the studies where linear methods are predominantly preferred. Taşkın (1995), examining the movements of exchange rates between TL and USD, and TL and Deutsche Mark (DM) for the period 1988:08–1993:04 by using cointegration analysis with monetary models, determined a relationship for the TL/DM rate in line with the expectations of the monetary model whereas she could not achieve a similar relationship for the TL/USD rate. Dülger and Cin (2002) tested the validity of the monetary exchange rate model by using the cointegration method in determining the nominal exchange rate for the period 1986:01–1999:12. According to the findings, the existence of a long-term relationship between the variables in the model and the exchange rate was determined. In addition, the estimation results regarding to the coefficient signs confirmed the expectations of the monetary model. Civcir (2004) who extended the monetary exchange rate model for TL/USD rate with the relative prices of tradable and non-tradable goods found a long-term relationship between exchange rate, monetary fundamentals and relative prices. Pazarlıoğlu and Güloğlu (2007) examined the relationship between nominal exchange rate and monetary fundamentals by using the cointegration method. Besides the long-term relationship determined between monetary fundamentals and the exchange rate, the estimated coefficient signs (except the money supply) support the predictions of the RID model. Investigating the relationship between exchange rates and economic indicators for the fragile five countries for the period between 1980 and 2012 by employing the cointegration analysis, Uçan et al. (2014) did not obtain consistent results neither with flexible-price nor with sticky-price monetary models. Uğur et al. (2014) analyzed the relationship between the nominal exchange rate and monetary fundamentals in Turkey by using the flexible-price monetary model for the period 1998:01–2011:02. Accordingly, no relationship was found between monetary fundamentals and nominal exchange rate. Öruç (2016), who examined the relationship between TL/USD exchange rate and the monetary fundamentals for the period 1988Q1–2015Q2 found that RID model is more appropriate for Turkish economy in terms of determining the exchange rates. Korap (2020), analyzing the determinants of the TL/USD rate for the period 2005Q4–2018Q3, obtained findings consistent with the predictions of the sticky-price monetary model in his study.

4. Data Set and Methodology

In this study, the RID model for Turkish economy is estimated by employing the MS method. The analysis period is taken as 1990:01–2018:12. For the dependent variable USD/TL exchange rate (e_t), similar to the study of Wu (2015), exchange rate volatility is preferred. While the industrial production index, which is also an indicator of economic activity, is used as the proxy of domestic income (y_t), the broadest-based money supply (M3) as the proxy of the domestic money supply (m_t)[5]. Discount rates in both countries are used for nominal interest rates (i_t). Annual percentage changes of consumer price indices are employed for expected inflation rates (π_t^e)[6]. In the study, in which the logarithms of all variables except inflation and interest rate series are taken, estimation is made over the standardized data to eliminate the level difference between the series. All variables used in the study were obtained from the Federal Reserve Bank of St. Louis (FRED) economic database.

Business cycles in a nonlinear structure by the Markov switching model were first presented by Hamilton (1989). Krolzig (1997) developed various Markov switching definitions allowing changes in the mean, constant and residual variance between regimes over the unknown state variable. In this context, the Markov Regime Switching Intercept Autoregressive Heteroskedasticity (MSIAH) model allows full parameter changes and takes into account the changes in the variance of residuals throughout the system state (Çatık and Önder, 2011: 127). When the time series are subject to regime changes, the MS method can be considered as a general regime-switching model since it is not appropriate to use models with constant parameter. The underlying idea of the regime-switching model is that the observed time series vector y_t depends upon the unobservable regime variable s_t, reflecting different regime possibilities. Let $s_t \in \{1, \ldots, M\}$, the transition probabilities of the Markov stochastic process are expressed as follows:

$$p_{ij} = Pr\left(s_{t+1} = j \,|\, s_t = i\right) \quad \sum_{j=1}^{M} p_{ij} = 1 \quad \forall i, j \in \{1, \ldots, M\} \qquad (16)$$

5 Zhang et al. (2007), Zakaria and Ahmad (2009), Uğur et al. (2014) and Öruç (2016) used M1 as a proxy of the money supply, whereas Civcir (2003), Frömmel et al. (2005), Ekong and Onye (2013) M2, Sichei et al. (2005) and Korap (2020) M3.

6 It is seen in the literature that different proxies are used for the expected inflation rate variable. Frömmel et al. (2005), Wu (2015) used the long-term interest rates as the proxy of the expected inflation rate variable whereas Zhang et al. (2007), Pazarlıoğlu and Güloğlu (2007), Zakaria and Ahmad (2009), Ekong and Onye (2013), Korap (2020) the consumer price indices, Sichei et al. (2005) the actual inflation rates, and Öruç (2016) GDP deflator.

To put it more clearly, under the assumption that s_t follows an irreducible ergodic M state Markov process, P transition matrix is defined as follows:

$$= \begin{bmatrix} p_{1M} \; p_{1M} \cdots \; p_{1M} \\ p_{2M} \; p_{2M} \cdots \; p_{2M} \\ \vdots \quad \vdots \quad \ddots \quad \vdots \\ p_{1M} \; p_{1M} \cdots \; p_{1M} \end{bmatrix} \tag{17}$$

Here, $p_{iM} = 1 - p_{i1} - \ldots - p_{i,M-1}$ for $i = 1, \ldots, M$ (Krolzig, 1997: 11–16). MS model for M regime and pth order can generally be defined as follows:

$$y_t - \mu(s_t) = \beta_1(s_t)(y_{t-1} - \mu(s_{t-1})) + \ldots + \beta_p(s_t)\left(y_{t-p} - \mu\left(s_{t-p}\right)\right) + \varepsilon_t \tag{18}$$

In the Equation 18 $\varepsilon_t \sim IID(0, \Sigma(s_t))$, and $\mu(s_t)$, $\beta_p(s_t)$ and $\Sigma(s_t)$ are parameter shift functions describing the dependence of the parameters μ, $\beta_1, \ldots, \beta_p$ and Σ respectively on the realized regime s_t. These shift functions can be expressed as follows (Krolzig, 1997: 11–12):

$$(s_t) = \begin{cases} \mu_1 & s_t = 1, \\ \vdots & \\ \mu_M & s_t = M. \end{cases} \tag{19}$$

After an immediate change in the mean $\mu(s_t)$, a regime change occurs. It becomes more plausible to assume a smooth transition approach from one state to another. In such a case, the model with a regime-dependent intercept term $c(s_t)$ can be used:

$$y_t = c(s_t) + \beta_1(s_t)\, y_{t-1} + \ldots + \beta_p(s_t)\, y_{t-p} + \varepsilon_t \tag{20}$$

Within this theoretical framework, Frankel (1979)'s RID model that is estimated for Turkish economy can be expressed as follows in the MSIAH form:

$$\begin{aligned} e_t = (s_t) + \beta(s_t)\left(m_t - m_t^*\right) + \delta(s_t)\left(y_t - y_t^*\right) \\ + \theta(s_t)\left(i_t - i_t^*\right) + \omega(s_t)\left(\pi_t^e - \pi_t^{e^*}\right) + \varepsilon_t \end{aligned} \tag{21}$$

5. Empirical Findings

In this study where the changes in the exchange rate are discussed over two different regimes, Regime-1 indicates the periods of decreasing in the exchange

Tab. 6.1: Transition Probabilities of the MS Model, Source: Authors' own calculations

	Regime-1	**Regime-2**
Regime-1	0.9770	0.0230
Regime-2	0.0317	0.9683

rate and Regime-2 shows the increasing periods. In the Tab. 6.1, the transition probabilities of the regimes corresponding to the periods of decreasing and rising are given.

While the exchange rate is in the period of decreasing, the probability of the following period to decreasing again is 97.70 %. On the other hand, when the exchange rate is in the rising period, the probability of staying on the rise again is 96.83 %. In addition, the probability of the exchange rate transition from the decreasing period to the rising period is 2.30 % whereas the probability of transition from the rising period to the decreasing period is 3.17 %. The regime probabilities of the MS model are shown in Fig. 6.1.

The USD/TL exchange rate witnessed sharp fluctuations and even in the periods when these fluctuations resulted in economic crises. When the periods of increase in exchange rates, which can be seen as the Regime-2 in Fig. 6.1, are analyzed, it is seen that the first increasing period started before the 1994 crisis and continued throughout the crisis[7]. The exchange rate, which continued its moderate course in the second half of the 1990s, increased sharply with the November 2000 and February 2001 crises. The exchange rate, which repeated its sharp rise during the global financial crisis, entered a downtrend in the post-crisis period with the abundance of global liquidity created by the expansionary policies of developed countries. The exchange rate started to rise again after the Federal Reserve (FED) announcement that included signals that monetary expansion would be terminated in May 2013. Although it was tried to be kept under control with interest rate increases and foreign exchange market interventions, exchange rate increased sharply in the second half of 2018 and once more passed to high exchange rate regime era. In this context, it is possible to state that the volatile course of exchange rate movements indicates the existence of different regimes in the analyzed period.

MS model estimation results for different regimes are included in the Tab. 6.2. The linearity test results should be mentioned before proceeding with the

7 The regime dates of the MS model are given in detail in the Appendix.

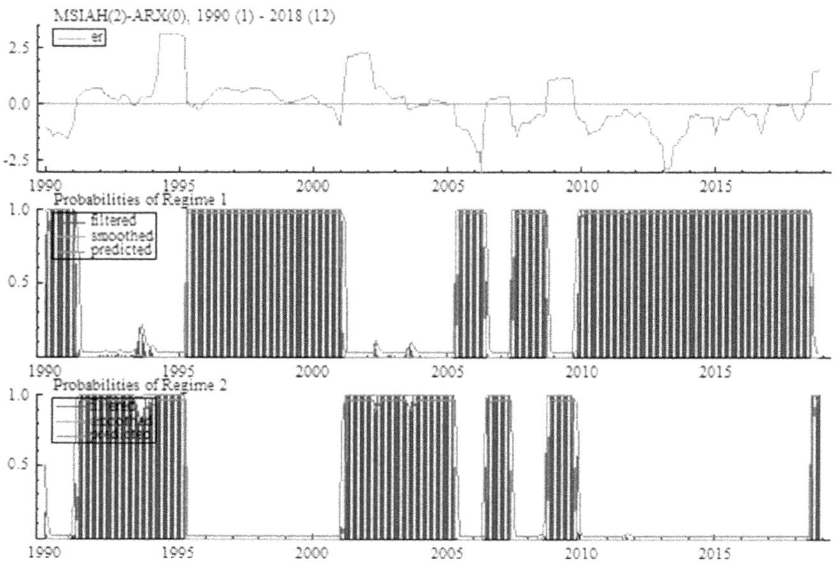

Fig. 6.1: Regime Probabilities of the MS Model, Source: Authors' own calculations

estimation results. In the study, the validity of the linear model was tested using the Log Likelihood-Ratio (LR) test. According to the results of LR linearity test statistics, it is concluded that the linear model is not valid, in other words, it is appropriate to use regime-switching models.

According to the coefficient results of Regime-1, which reflects the periods of decrease in the exchange rate, it is seen that all the explanatory variables are statistically significant except the relative interest rate. In addition to this, with the exception of the domestic income coefficient, the coefficient signs of the variables that are statistically significant are consistent with the predictions of the RID model. Accordingly, it is seen that the rises in the relative money supply and the expected inflation rate differentials increase the exchange rate. Contrary to the expectations, the effect of the growth in the domestic income differential on the exchange rate is positive.

In Regime-2, which expresses the periods of increase in the exchange rate, different from Regime-1, all explanatory variables except the relative income level are statistically significant. The coefficient signs of all statistically significant variables are compatible with the expectations in the RID model. Accordingly, the increase in the relative money supply and the expected inflation differential has a positive effect on the exchange rate. The increase in relative interest rate decreases the exchange rate.

Tab. 6.2: Estimation Results of the MS Model, Source: Authors' own calculations

Regime-1 (n:218.1, Prob: 0.578)			
Variable	**Coefficient**	**Standard Error**	**t-value**
α	-0.658	0.051	-12.838***
m_t	0.590	0.116	5.052***
y_t	0.358	0.114	3.146***
i_t	0.192	0.140	1.367
π_t^e	0.876	0.112	7.796***
Standard Error (Regime-1): 0.472			
Regime-2 (n:129.9, Prob: 0.421)			
Variable	Coefficient	Standard Error	t-value
α	0.671	0.040	16.625***
m_t	1.212	0.068	17.694***
y_t	0.064	0.120	0.537
i_t	-0.272	0.107	-2.536***
π_t^e	1.432	0.064	22.262***
Standard Error (Regime-2): 0.386			
LR Linearity Test: 324.4375	Chi (6) = (0.000)***	Chi (8) = (0.000)***	

Note: ***, **, * indicate that null hypotheses are rejected at 1 %, 5 % and 10 % significance levels, respectively.

6. Conclusion

In this chapter, Frankel's (1979) RID model, one of the monetary approaches developed for the determinants of nominal exchange rate changes; is analyzed for Turkish economy covering the period 1990:01–2018:12 by employing MS method. The validity of the RID model is determined by using the MS model since the series subject to analysis during the estimation period are nonlinear.

According to the empirical findings obtained, there are two different regimes reflecting the periods of decrease and increase in the exchange rate. In the regime where the exchange rate is low, it is seen that all explanatory variables except for the relative interest rate are statistically significant. In other words, changes in interest rates have no effect on the exchange rate during the periods when the domestic currency appreciates. On the other hand, the effect of domestic income on exchange rate is found to be positive contrary to the predictions of the RID model. In monetary exchange rate models, it is predicted that the price-lowering effect of increasing national income will decrease the nominal exchange rate through PPP. However, in the Mundell-Fleming approach, the rising income level worsens the trade balance by increasing import expenditures and requires the nominal exchange rate to increase for the restore of the balance (Civcir, 2004). In the study, the positive effect of domestic income on nominal exchange rate is consistent with the predictions of the Mundell-Fleming approach. In other words, during periods when the domestic currency appreciated in Turkey, it can be stated that domestic income growths fuel the import expenditures, and this amplifies the current account deficit and has effect to increase the nominal exchange rate.

In the high exchange rate regime, all the estimated variables are statistically significant and consistent with the expectations of the RID model, except for the relative income level. In the past thirty years, even though different exchange rate regimes have been implemented officially in Turkey, it is seen that in practice managed floating regime has been prominent. Even if the monetary authorities have not been *de jure*, they have tried to keep the exchange rate at certain levels *de facto* and in this direction, they used short-term interest rates as well as international reserves. Furthermore, it is observed that monetary authorities intervened in the foreign exchange market mostly during the periods when the nominal exchange rate rose due to reasons such as the distorting effects of the fluctuations in the exchange rate on the financial sector's balance sheets and the exchange rate pass-through effect. According to the empirical findings, the fact that the relative interest rate, which is not significant in the low regime, is significant in the high regime, and the coefficient sign is in line with the expectations of the RID model coincides with the efforts of monetary authorities to affect exchange rates with short-term interest rates.

In the study, it is seen that the findings obtained under low and high exchange rate regimes differ. This supports the preference of a nonlinear method in the analysis of the period in question. Moreover, the coefficient estimates are largely in line with theoretical expectations. In this context, it is possible to state that the RID model helps to understand the movements in the USD/TL exchange rate in certain periods. For the future researches, the analyses by employing different non-linear methods with different samples and different proxies are expected to contribute to the literature about the determinants of the exchange rate movements in Turkey.

References

Bacchetta, P., & van Wincoop, E. (2013). On the Unstable Relationship between Exchange Rates and Macroeconomic Fundamentals, *Journal of International Economics,* 91, 18–26, doi: 10.1016/j.jinteco.2013.06.001.

Bilson, J. F. O. (1978). The Monetary Approach to the Exchange Rate: Some Empirical Evidence, *IMF Staff Papers,* 25(1), 48--75.

Chinn, M. D. (2012). Macro Approaches to Foreign Exchange Determination, In *Handbook of Exchange Rates,* Eds. J. James, I. W. Marsh & L. Sarno, New Jersey: John Wiley&Sons, doi: 10.1002/9781118445785.ch2.

Civcir, I. (2003). The Monetary Model of the Exchange Rate under High Inflation: The Case of the Turkish Lira/US Dollar, *Czech Journal of Economics and Finance,* 53(3–4), 113–129.

Civcir, I. (2004). The Long-Run Validity of the Monetary Exchange Rate Model for a High Inflation Country and Misalignment: The Case of Turkey, *Emerging Markets Finance and Trade,* 40(4), 84–100, doi: 10.1080/1540496X.2004.11052575.

Çatık, A. N., & Önder, A. Ö. (2011). Inflationary Effects of Oil Prices in Turkey: A Regime-Switching Approach, *Emerging Markets Finance and Trade,* 47(5), 125–140, doi:10.2753/REE1540-496X470506.

De Grauwe, P., & Vansteenkiste, I. (2007). Exchange Rates and Fundamentals: A Non-Linear Relationship?, *International Journal of Finance and Economics,* 12, 37–54, doi: 10.1002/ijfe.310.

Dornbusch, R. (1976). Expectations and Exchange Rate Dynamics, *The Journal of Political Economy,* 84(6), 1161–1176.

Dülger, F., & Cin, M. F. (2002). Türkiye'de döviz kuru dinamiklerinin belirlenmesinde parasalcı yaklaşım ve eşbütünleşme yöntemiyle sınama, *ODTÜ Gelişme Dergisi,* 29(1–2), 47–68.

Ekong, C. N., & Onye, K. U. (2013). The Failure of the Monetary Exchange Rate Model for the Naira-Dollar, *MPRA Paper,* 88238, Retrieved from: https://mpra.ub.uni-muenchen.de/88238/. (01.10.2020)

Frankel, J. A. (1979). A Theory of Floating Exchange Rates Based on Real Interest Differentials, *The American Economic Review,* 69(4), 610–622.

Frenkel, J. A. (1976). A Monetary Approach to the Exchange Rate: Doctrinal Aspects and Empirical Evidence, *The Scandinavian Journal of Economics,* 78(2), 200–224.

Frömmel, M., MacDonald, R., & Menkhoff, L. (2005), Markov Switching Regimes in a Monetary Exchange Rate Model, *Economic Modelling,* 22, 485–502, doi: 10.1016/j.econmod.2004.07.001.

Hadian, E., & Sajedianfard, N. (2018). Monetary Fundamental-Based Exchange Rate Model in Iran: Applying a MS-TVTP Approach, *Iran Economic Review,* 22(2), 557–578.

Hamilton, J. D. (1989). A New Approach to the Economic Analysis of Nonstationary Time Series and the Business Cycle, *Econometrica,* 57(2), 357–384, doi: 10.2307/1912559.

Junttila, J., & Korhonen, M. (2011). Nonlinearity and Time-variation in the Monetary Model of Exchange Rates, *Journal of Macroeconomics,* 33, doi: 10.1016/j.jmacro.2010.10.001

Korap, L. (2020). TL/ABD Doları Döviz Kuru Belirlenme Modeli: ARDL Sınır Testi Uygulaması, *Optimum Ekonomi ve Yönetim Bilimleri Dergisi,* 7(1), 201–214, doi: 10.17541/optimum.533921.

Krolzig, H.-M. (1997). *Markov-Switching Vector Autoregressions: Modelling, Statistical Inference, and Application to Business Cycle Analysis,* Lecture Notes in Economic and Mathematical Systems (Book 454), Berlin: Springer.

Öruç, E. (2016). Döviz Kurlarının Belirlenmesinde Parasalcı Yaklaşım: Türkiye Örneği, *Kocaeli Üniversitesi Sosyal Bilimler Dergisi,* 32, 101–122.

Pazarlıoğlu, M. V., & Güloğlu, S. (2007). Türkiye'nin Döviz Kurunun Belirlenmesinde Monetarist Yaklaşım, *Süleyman Demirel Üniversitesi İktisadi ve İdari Bilimler Fakültesi Dergisi,* 12(3), 19–34.

Qi, M., & Wu, Y. (2003). Nonlinear Prediction of Exchange Rates with Monetary Fundamentals, *Journal of Empirical Finance,* 10, 623–640, doi:10.1016/S0927-5398(03)00008-2.

Sichei, M. M., Tewodros, G. G., & Olusegun, A. A. (2005). An Econometric Model of the Rand-US Dollar Nominal Exchange Rate, *University of Pretoria Department of Economics Working Paper Series,* 14, Retrieved from: https://www.up.ac.za/media/shared/61/WP/wp-14.zp39540.pdf. (01.10.2020)

Tang, X. & Zhou, J. (2013). Nonlinear Relationship between the Real Exchange Rate and Economic Fundamentals: Evidence from China and Korea, *Journal of International Money and Finance,* 32, 304–323, doi: 10.1016/j.jimonfin.2012.04.010.

Taşkın, F. (1995). Döviz Kuru Belirlenmesinde "Parasalcı" Yaklaşım Modeli: Türkiye'deki Döviz Kurları Üzerine Bir Uygulama, *Ekonomik Yaklaşım,* 6(18–19), 67–87.

Uçan, O., Akın, C. S., & Aytun, C. (2014). Exchange Rate Determination in High Fragile Emerging Countries, *European Scientific Journal,* 1, 361–368.

Uğur, A., Akbas, Y. E., & Senturk, M. (2014). Long Term Validity of Monetary Exchange Rate Model: Evidence from Turkey, *The Romanian Economic Journal,* XVII(51), 111–136.

Wu, J.-T. (2015). Markov Regimes Switching with Monetary Fundamental-Based Exchange Rate Model, *Asia Pacific Management Review,* 20, 79–89, doi: 10.1016/j.apmrv.2014.12.009.

Yay, G. G. (2012). *Para ve Finans Teori-Politika,* 1 Baskı, İstanbul: İstanbul Bilgi Üniversitesi Yayınları.

Zakaria, M., & Ahmad, E. (2009). Testing the Monetary Models of Exchange Rate Determination: Some New Evidence from Modern Float, *Chulalongkorn Journal of Economics,* 21(3), 125–145.

Zhang, G. (2014). Exchange Rates and Monetary Fundamentals: What Do We Learn from Linear and Nonlinear Regressions?, *Hindawi Publishing Corporation Economics Research International,* doi: 10.1155/2014/746956.

Zhang, S., Lowinger, T. C., & Tang, J. (2007). The Monetary Exchange Rate Model: Long-run, Short-run, and Forecasting Performance, *Journal of Economic Integration,* 22(2), 397–406.

Appendix

Tab. 6.A1: Regime Dates of the MS Model, Source: Authors' own construction

Regime-1	Regime-2
1990:01–1991:02	1991:03–1995:03
1995:04–2001:01	2001:02–2005:04
2005:05–2006:05	2006:06–2007:05
2007:06–2008:09	2008:10–2009:10
2009:11–2018:07	2018:08–2018:12

Metin Tetik, Reşat Ceylan, Hakan Ulucan, Bilgin Bari

Chapter 7 Conclusions of Cooperative and Noncooperative Interaction between Monetary and Fiscal Policies in Small Scale Open Economy[1]

Abstract: Interactions between the monetary and fiscal policy are analyzed in a game-theoretical framework on the base of the new-Keynesian model. The interactions between policymakers are modeled by using a dynamic stochastic equilibrium model (DSGE) for a small-scale open economy. From this point of view, the interactions between policymakers are evaluated in two different hypothetical scenarios. Optimal policy rules for a small-scale open economy are derived by using Nash Solution (a non-cooperative solution) and cooperative equilibrium. The performances of the derived policy rules are evaluated by comparing counter-factual experiments via dynamic simulation. The model parameters are calibrated for the Turkish economy. Then, the policy mix providing the minimum social loss is obtained. The main finding of dynamic simulations is that cooperative interaction shows better performance in the Turkish economy than non-cooperative interaction.

Keywords: Game Theory, Nash Solution, Cooperative Equilibrium, New Keynesian Model, Dynamic Stochastic Equilibrium Model

1. Introduction

In today's World, there is a consensus on implementing economic policies by obeying certain rules to ensure macroeconomic stability. The reason is that the arbitrary implementation of monetary and fiscal policies in an incompatible manner creates a reliability problem for the future. Unreliability problem created by the arbitrary implementation of the policies leads to lower welfare by moving the economy from the equilibrium committed by policymakers (Kydland and Prescot, 1977). Rule-based policies, on the other hand, result in

1 This study is made from Metin Tetik's Ph.D Thesis, which was accepted at Pamukkale University Institute of Social Sciences, "A Game Theoretical Approach to the Interaction Between Monetary and Fiscal Policies in The New Keynesian Model Framework: The Case Of Turkey".

better outcomes than arbitrary policies with respect to macroeconomic stability (Barro and Gordon, 1983a, 1983b). One of the popular policy rules is Taylor rule, which is developed when the rule-based policies gain more importance. Taylor's rule, a monetary policy rule, indicates the required policy rule in order to hit the target, and there are lots of studies in the literature that gives emphasis on Taylor's rule.

In this perspective, deriving the optimal policy rule gains importance for policymakers. However, monetary and fiscal policies having strong effects on the macroeconomy can have contradicting distinct goals. The contradiction between policymakers moves the economy from stability and efficiency. There is a need for effective coordination between policymakers for this reason. However, it should also be noted that two policymakers have independent and different authorities in the policy design process. Fiscal policy is under the Government's control, while the monetary policy is the responsibility of the central bank. Each policy maker can implement expansionary or contractionary policies. Expansionary fiscal policy means lower tax rates and higher government expenditure. This can reduce unemployment at the expense of higher inflation. Expansionary monetary policy means lower interest rates and easier borrowing, with a risk of higher inflation too (Blinder, 1983).

The leading problems due to the lack of coordination between policymakers are inflation, divergence from the potential output, and budget deficit, reducing the social welfare. In this sense, the offer of an optimal policy rule is important to solve the problem of lack of coordination between policymakers. This study analyzes the interaction between policymakers by following Keynesian modes as a base under the framework of game theory. The strategic interactions between policymakers are analyzed for a small-scale open economy by using the Dynamic Stochastic General Equilibrium (DSGE) model. The strategic interaction is examined under two hypothetic scenarios. Non-cooperative and cooperative equilibrium are derived for a small-scale open economy. Based on the derived varying policy rules from this step, the performance of the policy rule is evaluated by using the data from the Turkish Economy. The corresponding social welfares of the alternative policy rules are compared to find out the optimal policy rule for the economy of Turkey.

The study is designed as follows: In the first section, the principal equations constructed by following the new-Keynesian framework to evaluate alternative interactions between policymakers are introduced. In the second section, these interactions are reconsidered under a game theoretical framework. Then, the non-cooperative Nash equilibrium is calibrated from a game in which both policymakers follow their own interest. The following scenario is the corporation between policymakers, providing cooperative monetary and fiscal policy rules. In the third section, the numerical analysis of the models derived in the previous sections is conducted. In this framework, DSGE model parameters are calibrated, and each scenario is simulated by using the data from the 2007–2017 period in Turkey. In the light of counterfactual experiments, social welfare based on different simulations are compared. In the last section, the suggestion of an optimal policy strategy is presented and evaluated.

2. Basic Model: New Keynesian Macroeconomic Model

The new-Keynesian macroeconomic model suggests that the aggregate demand is the main key determinant of economic activity due to short-run price rigidities. In this manner, monetary policy has strong effects on the real economy (Goodfriend & King, 1997). The reason for the choice of this model in the study is that the model shows the effects of the macroeconomic policies by placing the price and wage rigidities at the center of economic fluctuations. Clarida et al. (1999) explain this perspective by stating that firms in the good market are reluctant to respond to adjust their prices in the cases of increasing demand to their commodities and costs. Then, the economy's response to shocks is slow. Thus, the existence of price and nominal wage rigidities of the firms operating in an imperfectly competitive market allows the policies to have real effects. However, these effects disappear in the long run.

The new-Keynesian macroeconomic model is constituted by a supply equation, also known as the new-Keynesian Philips curve, and forward-looking aggregate demand equation, also known as the IS curve. Besides, there is an intertemporal budget constraint equation that includes optimal policy rules and interaction between policymakers. In this framework, the Keynesian model is constructed on three blocks: (1) aggregate demand block: Intertemporal IS equation, (2) aggregate supply block: New-Keynesian Philip's curve equation (3) Government Budget: ıntertemporal budget constraint equation

These three equations used by this study presents the principal Dynamics of the economy as well as its constraints. Alternative monetary and fiscal rules, on the other hand, are derived by analyzing the interactions between policymakers in a game-theoretic framework. Therefore, a policy blocky is added to the Keynesian model by the study.

2.1. A Small-Scale Open Economy

The studies by Gali and Monacelli (2004, 2005 and 2008), and Çebi (2012) are followed to construct the representative economy from which the policy rules are from the interaction between monetary and fiscal policymakers. The domestic decisions in each economy are assumed to have no effect on the rest of the World. Besides, each economy has the same preferences and market structures; then the economies are exposed to shocks. Such an economy consists of households, the firms from monopolistic competition, the government, and the central bank.

The Keynesian Philips curve for an open small scale economy is represented below:

$$\pi_{H,t} = \beta E_t \{\pi_{H,t+1}\} + \kappa \tilde{y}_t - \sigma_\alpha \tilde{g}_t \tag{1}$$

$\pi_{H,t}$ denotes the domestic inflation rate showing the change in the prices of domestic goods price index, which is the consumer price index. $\tilde{y}_t$ shows the output gap. The domestic output gap ($\tilde{y}_t \equiv y_t - y_t^N$) is defined as the deviation of realized output (y_t) from the natural level of output (y_t^N). $\tilde{g}_t$ represents the fiscal gap and shows the difference between its realized value and optimal value when there is no nominal contributions ($\tilde{g}_t \equiv g_t - g_t^N$). Parameter κ shows the slope of new Keynesian Philips curve[2].

IS equation for an open small-scale economy is represented by the equation below:

$$\tilde{y}_t = E_t \{\tilde{y}_{t+1}\} - \frac{1}{\sigma_a} \left(r_t - E_t \{\tilde{\pi}_{H,t+1}\} - r_t^N\right) - E_t \{\Delta \tilde{g}_{t+1}\} \tag{2}$$

2 κ parameter in its explicit form is, $\kappa \equiv \lambda(\sigma_\alpha + \varphi)$. It is represented by $\lambda \equiv \frac{(1-\beta\theta)(1-\theta)}{\theta}$ and $\sigma_\alpha \equiv \frac{\sigma}{1+\alpha(\omega-1)}$ from the equation. φ and β parameters Show slope elasticity of supply of labor and discount reta defining the intertemporal preference rate between the periods, respectively. θ parameter shows the level of price rigidity, σ shows the level of intertemporal substitution elasticity, α denotes the openess level. ω parameter in its explicit form is $\omega \equiv \sigma\gamma + (1-\alpha)(\sigma\eta - 1)$. γ parameter in this identity shows the substitution elasticity of the goods produced in different countries. η parameter shows the elasticity of substitution between domestic and foreign goods.

In Equation 2 $r_t^N = \sigma_\alpha(E_t\{y_{t+1}^N\} - y_t^N) - \alpha(\omega - 1)(\rho_{c^*} - 1)c_t^*$ is the nominal natural interest rate. This rate can be written in terms of natural productivity level and World output shocks by changing potential output level[3]:

$$r_t^N = \frac{\sigma_\alpha(1+\varphi)(\rho_a - 1)}{(\sigma_\alpha + \varphi)} a_t + \frac{\varphi\alpha(\omega - 1)}{(\sigma_\alpha + \varphi)}(\rho_{c^*} - 1)c_t^*$$

In the equation above, natural productivity level and output shocks are determined exogenously, and two variables are assumed to follow AR (1) process.

In an economy under flexible prices, government expenditures and tax incomes are assumed to be zero. This means that equilibrium under flexible prices, there is no budget deficit or surplus. Çebi (2012), Fragetta and Kirsanova (2010) assumes $\pi_{H,t+1}^N = g_{t+1}^N = 0$ for the natural level of government expenditure and natural level of inflation. Thus, we can write down, $\tilde{g}_{t+1} = g_{t+1}$ and $\tilde{\pi}_{H,t+1} = \pi_{H,t+1}$.

The interaction between the monetary and fiscal policies stems from the effects of the intertemporal budget constraint. A fiscal policy move that increases the nominal budget constraint is financed by an increase in the future tax income or a rise in the other government liabilities like monetary supply regarded as nominal. This is called as "unpleasant monetarist arithmetic" by Sargent and Wallace (1984) in the literature. Thus the model used in this study is completed by a fiscal constraint. Fragetta and Kirsanova (2010) states the linearized government debt payment constraint (fiscal constraint) as follows[4]:

$$\tilde{b}_{t+1} = (r_t - r_t^N) + \frac{1}{\beta}(\tilde{b}_t - \pi_{H,t} + \frac{\bar{C}}{\bar{B}}\tilde{g}_t + \frac{1 - \bar{C} - \tau}{\bar{B}}\tilde{y}_t) \tag{3}$$

In the Equation 3, $b_t = \log\left(\frac{B_t}{P_{H,t+1}}\right)$ and B are nominal debt stocks. $\bar{B}$ and $\bar{C}$ are respectively steady-state debt/GDP and steady-state consumption/GDP ratios.

The borders of a hypothetic economy required for modeling the strategic interactions between the monetary and fiscal policymakers are drawn by equations 1, 2, and 3, which base on the New Keynesian macroeconomic model. The optimal policy rules of monetary and fiscal policymakers are derived by depending on these equations.

3 In the equation representing the natural interest rate, ρ_a parameter shows AR coefficient of natural productivity level, and ρ_{c^*} denotes the AR coefficient of World output.

4 Since natural inflation rate is assumed to be zero, $\pi_{H,t}^N = 0$k, $\pi_t$symbol is used instead in the equation of the budget constraint.

3. Derivation of Optimal Interest Rate with Game Theoretical Approach

In this section, a policy rule for each policymaker is derived depending on the structure of the interaction between the monetary and fiscal policymakers. Firstly, a non-cooperative model is considered in a framework of a game simultaneously played by players. The equilibrium derived at this stage is a Nash Equilibrium. In the other scenario, the relationship between the policymakers are evaluated as a cooperative to find the cooperative equilibrium.

The main goal of each policymaker is to minimize the loss function corresponding to the equilibrium condition of the economy. Policymakers solve their optimization problems by committing on their policy rules. This approach is used since it ensures consistency with the desired equilibrium and time. The Lagrangian technique used by Gioanni and Woodford (2002a), Gioanni and Woodford (2002b) and Saulo et al. (2013) is used in this study to solve the optimization problem. This approach is widely used in the literature on monetary policy. The consistency of the solutions belonging to every scenario is checked by using the packaged software Maple 11. The objective and constraint functions of policymakers are represented in this sub-section before derivation of policy rules.

It is stated in the previous sections that the game between monetary and fiscal policymakers are based on the behavior of each policymaker to minimize the loss functions. If we add a time dimension to these equations[5]:

The objective (loss) function of monetary policymaker:

$$L_t^M = \gamma_\pi \pi_t^2 + \gamma_y \tilde{y}_t^2 + \gamma_r (r_t - r^*)^2 \tag{4}$$

The objective (loss) function of fiscal policymaker:

$$L_t^F = \rho_\pi \pi_t^2 + \rho_y \tilde{y}_t^2 + \rho_g \tilde{g}_t^2 \tag{5}$$

These functions denote the objective functions of two policymakers. γ_π and ρ_π with positive weights show the deviation from inflation rate target, γ_y and ρ_y parameters Show the deviation from the output gap, γ_r parameter shows the deviation from the optimal interest rate, and, lastly, ρ_g parameter shows the deviation from the optimal government spending.

5 Since natural inflation rate is assumed to be zero, $\pi_{H,t}^N = 0$k, $\pi_{H,t}^2$ and $\pi_{H,t}$ symbols are used instead of $\tilde{\pi}_{H,t}^2$ ve $\tilde{\pi}_{H,t}$ in the e.

The aggregate supply curve is shown by equation 1, aggregate demand equation denoted by equation 2, and government budget equation represented by equation 3 from the first section, in which definitions are given for a small-scale open economy, are used for constraint equations.

3.1 Solutions for the First Scenerio: Non-cooperative Nash Equilibrium

3.1.1. Optimal Interest Rate Rule in the Framework of Non-cooperative Nash Game

Monetary policymaker aims to minimize loss function represented by Equation (4) which corresponds to the equilibrium condition of the economy. In this way, monetary policymaker implements the optimal policy rule where the players simultaneously move. Parameters, γ_π, γ_x and γ_i, respectively shows the weights on the square of the deviation of nominal inflation from the inflation target, the square of the output gap, and the deviation of interest rate from the real interest rate. The main goal of the monetary policymaker is to solve the following problem under the constraints of the economy.

$$\min E_0 \left\{ \frac{1}{2} \sum_{t=0}^{\infty} \beta^t \left(L_t^M \right) \right\}$$ [6]

Equations below are the constraint equations 1 and 2 respectively:

$$\pi_{H,t} = \beta E_t \left\{ \pi_{H,t+1} \right\} + \kappa \tilde{y}_t - \sigma_\alpha \tilde{g}_t + \varepsilon_t^\pi$$

$$\tilde{y}_t = E_t \left\{ \tilde{y}_{t+1} \right\} - \frac{1}{\sigma_a} \left(r_t - E_t \left\{ \pi_{H,t+1} \right\} - r_t^N \right) - E_t \left\{ \tilde{g}_{t+1} \right\} + \tilde{g}_t$$

These problems are solved by constructing the lagrangian equation following Woodford (2003). Then, we get the optimal interest rate rule ($\hat{r}_t^{NCN}$) from the first-order condition of it, where NCN corresponds to Non-Cooperative Nash. The Lagrange structure of the problem is given as below:

$$\mathrm{L} = E_0 \left\{ \sum_{t=0}^{\infty} \beta^t \left(\begin{array}{c} \frac{1}{2}\gamma_\pi \pi_{H,t}^2 + \frac{1}{2}\gamma_y \tilde{y}_t^2 + \frac{1}{2}\gamma_r (r_t - r^*)^2 \\ +\Lambda_{1,t} \left(\tilde{y}_t - \tilde{y}_{t+1} + \frac{1}{\sigma_a} \left((r_t - r_t^N) - \pi_{H,t+1} \right) + \tilde{g}_{t+1} - \tilde{g}_t \right) \\ +\Lambda_{2,t} \left(\pi_{H,t} - \beta \pi_{H,t+1} - \kappa \tilde{y}_t + \sigma_\alpha \tilde{g}_t - \varepsilon_t^\pi \right) \end{array} \right) \right\}$$

6 1/2 constant in this equation is a scaling term, which has no effect on optimality, but simplifies the solution process.

The derivatives with respect to $(r_t - r^*)$ and the state variables in this equation are derived, in order to derive the first-order conditions. Before moving further, we should think about how to evaluate the expectation terms. Since this is a policy under a commitment, subtracting the expectation term means for policymakers to choose an old rule to be followed in the future. Because of this, the expectation operators on inflation, output gap, and government expenditure are removed. To illustrate, policy authority can optimize both at the same time, when the inflation rate determined by the policymaker can affect both the nominal and expected inflation rate (Saulo et al. 2013). A similar process is followed to derive the other optimal rules. The first-order conditions in this framework are:

$$\frac{dL}{d\pi_{H,t}} = \gamma_\pi \pi_{H,t} - \beta^{-1}\sigma_\alpha^{-1}\Lambda_{1,t-1} + \Lambda_{2,t} - \beta^{-1}\beta\Lambda_{2,t-1} = 0$$

$$\frac{dL}{d\tilde{y}_t} = \gamma_y \tilde{y}_t + \Lambda_{1,t} - \beta^{-1}\Lambda_{1,t-1} - \kappa\Lambda_{2,t} = 0$$

$$\frac{dL}{d\left(r_t - r^*\right)} = \gamma_r\left(r_t - r^*\right) + \sigma_\alpha^{-1}\Lambda_{1,t} = 0$$

Based on the Lagrangian multipliers, $\Lambda_{1,t} = -\sigma_\alpha\gamma_r\left(r_t - r^*\right)$ and $\Lambda_{1,t-1} = -\sigma_\alpha\gamma_r(r_{t-1} - r^*)$ are derived. An optimal policy rule is derived as follows by the required substitution process:

$$r_t^{NCN} = \Theta_{r,1}r_{t-1} - \Theta_{r,2}r_{t-2} + \Theta_{\pi,0}\pi_{H,t} + \Theta_{y,0}\tilde{y}_t - \Theta_{y,1}\tilde{y}_{t-1} - \Theta_{r^*}r^* \quad (6)$$

where, $\Theta_{r,1} = \frac{(\sigma_\alpha\kappa+\beta+1)}{\beta}$, $\Theta_{r,2} = \frac{1}{\beta}$, $\Theta_{\pi,0} = \frac{\gamma_\pi\kappa}{\gamma_r\sigma_\alpha}$, $\Theta_{y,1} = \Theta_{y,0} = \frac{\gamma_y}{\gamma_r\sigma_\alpha}$ ve $\Theta_{r^*} = \frac{\sigma_\alpha\kappa}{\beta}$

Equation 6 is the policy rule on which the monetary policymaker is committed, and this rule can be called as a non-cooperative nash interest rate rule. Non-cooperative nash interest rate rule is simultaneously determined with the inflation rate, whereas it shows a simultaneous or a lagged response to the output gap. Besides, it includes history dependency since it depends on previous interest rates.

3.1.2 *Optimal Government Spending Rule in a Non-cooperative Nash Game*

Fiscal policymaker aims to minimize the loss function represented by Equation (5) which corresponds to the equilibrium condition of the economy. Thus, the fiscal policymaker obeys the optimal policy rule in the simultaneous move case. ρ_π, ρ_y and ρ_g parameters sequentially represent the wights on the square of the deviation of inflation rate target from realized inflation rate, the square of the output gap, and the deviation of government spending from its equilibrium level. The principal problem of the fiscal policymaker is to solve the following problem by taking into accounts the constraints:

$$\min E_0 \left\{ \frac{1}{2} \sum_{t=0}^{\infty} \beta^t \left(L_t^F \right) \right\}$$

Equation (1), (2), and (3) are constraint functions respectively:

$$\pi_{H,t} = \beta E_t \left\{ \pi_{H,t+1} \right\} + \kappa \tilde{y}_t - \sigma_\alpha \tilde{g}_t + \varepsilon_t^\pi$$

$$\tilde{y}_t = E_t \left\{ \tilde{y}_{t+1} \right\} - \frac{1}{\sigma_a} \left(r_t - E_t \left\{ \pi_{H,t+1} \right\} - r_t^N \right) - E_t \left\{ \tilde{g}_{t+1} \right\} + \tilde{g}_t$$

$$\tilde{b}_{t+1} = (r_t - r_t^N) + \frac{1}{\beta} (\tilde{b}_t - \pi_{H,t} + \frac{\bar{C}}{\bar{B}} \tilde{g}_t + \frac{1 - \bar{C} - \tau}{\bar{B}} \tilde{y}_t) + \varepsilon_t^b$$

We hold the optimal government spending rule, $\tilde{g}_t^{NCN}$, by writing these equations and then by solving their first-order conditions. The lagrangian structure of the problem is given as below:

$$\mathrm{L} = E_0 \left\{ \sum_{t=0}^{\infty} \beta^t \left(\begin{array}{c} \frac{1}{2} \rho_\pi \tilde{\pi}_{H,t}^2 + \frac{1}{2} \rho_y \tilde{y}_t^2 + \frac{1}{2} \rho_g \tilde{g}^2 \\ + \Lambda_{1,t} \left(\tilde{y}_t - \tilde{y}_{t+1} + \frac{1}{\sigma_a} \left(r_t - \pi_{H,t+1} - r_t^N \right) + \tilde{g}_{t+1} - \tilde{g}_t \right) \\ + \Lambda_{2,t} \left(\pi_{H,t} - \beta \pi_{H,t+1} - \kappa \tilde{y}_t + \sigma_\alpha \tilde{g}_t - \varepsilon_t^\pi \right) \\ + \Lambda_{3,t} \left(\tilde{b}_{t+1} - (r_t - r_t^N) - \frac{1}{\beta} (\tilde{b}_t - \tilde{\pi}_{H,t} + \frac{\bar{C}}{\bar{B}} \tilde{g}_t \right. \\ \left. + \frac{1 - \bar{C} - \tau}{\bar{B}} \tilde{y}_t) - \varepsilon_t^b \right) \end{array} \right) \right\}$$

First-order conditions in this analysis:

$$\frac{dL}{d\pi_{H,t}} = \rho_\pi \pi_{H,t} - \beta^{-1}\sigma_\alpha^{-1}\Lambda_{1,t-1} + \Lambda_{2,t} - \beta^{-1}\beta\Lambda_{2,t-1} + \beta^{-1}\Lambda_{3,t} = 0$$

$$\frac{dL}{d\tilde{y}_t} = \rho_y \tilde{y}_t + \Lambda_{1,t} - \beta^{-1}\Lambda_{1,t-1} - \kappa\Lambda_{2,t} - \beta^{-1}\frac{1-\bar{C}-\tau}{\bar{B}}\Lambda_{3,t} = 0$$

$$\frac{dL}{d\tilde{g}_t} = \rho_g \tilde{g}_t + \beta^{-1}\Lambda_{1,t-1} - \Lambda_{1,t} + \sigma_\alpha\Lambda_{2,t} - \beta^{-1}\frac{\bar{C}}{\bar{B}}\Lambda_{3,t} = 0$$

$$\frac{dL}{d\tilde{b}_t} = \beta^{-1}\Lambda_{3,t-1} - \beta^{-1}\Lambda_{3,t} = 0$$

By moving from the Lagrange multipliers, Firstly $\Lambda_{3,t} = \Lambda_{3,t-1}$ is derived. In this case, depending on the fact that $\Lambda_{3,t}$ the parameter is independent of the time dimension, we construct the identity $\Lambda_{3,t} = \Lambda_{3,t-1} = \alpha$. α The parameter has no effect on the optimal policy rules. In light of this information, we can derive $\Lambda_{2,t}$, as $\Lambda_{2,t} = -\frac{\rho_y \tilde{y}_t \bar{B} \rho_g \tilde{g}_t \bar{B} - \alpha + \alpha\tau}{\bar{B}(\sigma_\alpha + \kappa)}$. By defining $\Lambda_{2,t-1} = -\frac{\rho_y \tilde{y}_{t-1} \bar{B} \rho_g \tilde{g}_{t-1} \bar{B} - \alpha + \alpha\tau}{\bar{B}(\sigma_\alpha + \kappa)}$, we hold $\Lambda_{1,t-1}$ in the next equation. Then by adjusting $\Lambda_{1,t-1}$ due to time, $\Lambda_{1,t}$ is held. As a result of the required substitution process, the optimal nominal government spending rule is derived as follows:

$$\begin{aligned} \tilde{g}_t^{NCN} &= -sabit + \Psi_{g,+1}E_t\{\tilde{g}_{t+1}\} + \\ &\Psi_{g,1}\tilde{g}_{t-1} + \Psi_{y,+1}E_t\{\tilde{y}_{t+1}\} - \\ &\Psi_{y,0}\tilde{y}_t + \Psi_{y,1}\tilde{y}_{t-1} - \Psi_{\pi,+1}E_t\{\pi_{H,t+1}\} + \Psi_{\pi,0}\pi_{H,t} \end{aligned} \tag{7}$$

Equation 7 respectively includes, $\Psi_{g,+1} = \frac{\beta\sigma_\alpha}{D}$, $\Psi_{g,1} = \frac{\sigma_\alpha}{D}$, $\Psi_{y,+1} = \frac{\beta\sigma_\alpha\rho_y}{\rho_g D}$, $\Psi_{y,0} = \frac{\rho_y\sigma_\alpha(\beta+2)}{\rho_g D}$, $\Psi_{y,1} = \frac{\rho_y\sigma_\alpha}{\rho_g D}$, $\Psi_{\pi,+1} = \frac{\beta\sigma_\alpha\rho_\pi(\sigma_\alpha-\kappa)}{\rho_g D}$, $\Psi_{\pi,0} = \frac{\sigma_\alpha\rho_\pi(\sigma_\alpha-\kappa)}{\rho_g D}$ and $cons =$ lastly constant is $\frac{\alpha(-\sigma_\alpha+\bar{C}\sigma_\alpha-\bar{C}\kappa+\tau\sigma_\alpha-\bar{B}\sigma_\alpha{}^2+\bar{B}\sigma_\alpha\kappa+\bar{B}\beta\sigma_\alpha{}^2-\bar{B}\beta\sigma_\alpha\kappa)}{\bar{B}\beta\rho_g D}$.

Additionally, the definition, $D = \beta\sigma_\alpha + \sigma_\alpha + \kappa$, made for simplicity.

Equation 7 shows the policy rule that fiscal policymaker committed on, and this rule can be called as non-cooperative Nash government spending rule. This rule is the function of expected and current inflation rate, expected and the current previous output gap, and expected and previous government expenditures. Since the spending, rule responds to previous and future government expenditures, it includes forward-looking and backward-looking dependency.

3.2. Cooperative Equilibrium Solutions

3.2.1. Optimal Interest and Government Spending Rule in Cooperative Game Framework

This section analyzes the derivation of policy rules of monetary and fiscal policymakers cooperating for a common goal. In this case, each policymaker will take into account the other's response function. As stated in the previous section, the policy derived from a policymaker in a non-cooperative situation does not take into account the action of the other policymaker.

In the case of cooperation, the monetary and fiscal policymaker aims to minimize the social loss function corresponding to the economic equilibrium condition. The social loss function is a function that depends on the loss functions of money and fiscal policymakers in numbers 4 and 5 and is defined as the sum of the loss functions of each policymaker.

$$L_t^S = L_t^M + L_t^F$$

$$L_t^S = \gamma_\pi \pi_{H,t}^2 + \gamma_y \tilde{y}_t^2 + \gamma_r (r_t - r^*)^2 + \rho_\pi \pi_{H,t}^2 + \rho_y \tilde{y}_t^2 + \rho_g \tilde{g}_t^2$$

$$L_t^S = \delta_\pi \pi_{H,t}^2 + \delta_y \tilde{y}_t^2 + \delta_r (r_t - r^*)^2 + \delta_g \tilde{g}_t^2 \tag{8}$$

In the equation number 8, $\delta_\pi = \gamma_\pi + \rho_\pi$, $\delta_y = \gamma_y + \rho_y$, $\delta_r = \gamma_r$ and $\delta_g = \rho_g$. In this case, we will state the common problem of policy makers as Lagrange equation. Then we will solve the first order conditions and obtain the optimal interest rate rule (r_t^{CE}) and the government spending rule ($\tilde{g}_t^{CE}$).

$$L = E_0 \left\{ \sum_{t=0}^{\infty} \beta^t \left(\begin{array}{c} \frac{1}{2}\delta_\pi \pi_{H,t}^2 + \frac{1}{2}\delta_y \tilde{y}_t^2 + \frac{1}{2}\delta_r (r_t - r^*)^2 + \frac{1}{2}\delta_g \tilde{g}_t^2 \\ +\Lambda_{1,t}\left(\tilde{y}_t - \tilde{y}_{t+1} + \frac{1}{\sigma_a}\left(r_t - \pi_{H,t+1} - r_t^N\right) + \tilde{g}_{t+1} - \tilde{g}_t\right) \\ +\Lambda_{2,t}\left(\pi_{H,t} - \beta \pi_{H,t+1} - \kappa \tilde{y}_t + \sigma_\alpha \tilde{g}_t - \varepsilon_t^\pi\right) \\ +\Lambda_{3,t}(\tilde{b}_{t+1} - (r_t - r_t^N) - \frac{1}{\beta}\left(\tilde{b}_t - \tilde{\pi}_{H,t}\right. \\ \left. + \frac{\bar{C}}{\bar{B}}\tilde{g}_t + \frac{1-\bar{C}-\tau}{\bar{B}}\tilde{y}_t) - \varepsilon_t^b\right) \end{array} \right) \right\}$$

In this framework, first order conditions are:

$$\frac{dL}{d\pi_{H,t}} = \delta_\pi \pi_{H,t} - \beta^{-1}\sigma_\alpha^{-1}\Lambda_{1,t-1} + \Lambda_{2,t} - \beta^{-1}\beta\Lambda_{2,t-1} + \beta^{-1}\Lambda_{3,t} = 0$$

$$\frac{dL}{d\tilde{y}_t} = \delta_y \tilde{y}_t + \Lambda_{1,t} - \beta^{-1}\Lambda_{1,t-1} - \kappa\Lambda_{2,t} - \beta^{-1}\frac{1-\bar{C}-\tau}{\bar{B}}\Lambda_{3,t} = 0$$

$$\frac{dL}{d\left(r_t - r^*\right)} = \delta_r\left(r_t - r^*\right) + \sigma_\alpha^{-1}\Lambda_{1,t} - \Lambda_{3,t} = 0$$

$$\frac{dL}{d\tilde{g}_t} = \delta_g \tilde{g}_t + \beta^{-1}\Lambda_{1,t-1} - \Lambda_{1,t} + \sigma_\alpha\Lambda_{2,t} - \beta^{-1}\frac{\bar{C}}{\bar{B}}\Lambda_{3,t} = 0$$

Based on the Lagrange multipliers, in the last equation $\Lambda_{2,t}$, $\Lambda_{3,t}$, and $\Lambda_{1,t}$ are obtained respectively.
where, $\Lambda_{2,t} = -\frac{\rho_y\tilde{y}_t\bar{B}\beta+\rho_g\tilde{g}_t\bar{B}\beta-\Lambda_{3,t}+\Lambda_{3,t}\tau}{\beta\bar{B}(\sigma_\alpha+\kappa)}$, $\Lambda_{2,t-1} = -\frac{\rho_y\tilde{y}_{t-1}\bar{B}\beta+\rho_g\tilde{g}_{t-1}\bar{B}\beta-\Lambda_{3,t}+\Lambda_{3,t}\tau}{\beta\bar{B}(\sigma_\alpha+\kappa)}$.
As a result of the necessary replacement and separation process, the cooperative optimal interest rule is obtained as follows[7];

$$\begin{aligned} r_t^{CE} &= \Phi_{r,1}r_{t-1} - \Phi_{r,2}r_{t-2} - \Phi_{g,0}\tilde{g}_t + \Phi_{g,1}\tilde{g}_{t-1} \\ &\quad - \Phi_{g,2}\tilde{g}_{t-2} - \Phi_{y,0}\tilde{y}_t + \Phi_{y,1}\tilde{y}_{t-1} - \Phi_{y,2}\tilde{y}_{t-2} \\ &\quad + \Phi_{\pi,0}\pi_{H,t} - \Phi_{\pi,1}\pi_{H,t-1} - \Phi_{r^*}r^* \end{aligned} \tag{9}$$

In the equation number 9 described above, respectively:

$$\Phi_{r,1} = \frac{\sigma_\alpha\bar{B}\kappa+2\tau\sigma_\alpha+\bar{C}\sigma_\alpha-\bar{C}\kappa-2\sigma_\alpha+\sigma_\alpha\tau\beta-\beta\sigma_\alpha-\sigma_\alpha{}^2\bar{B}}{\sigma_\alpha\beta F},\ \Phi_{r,2} = \frac{(-1+\tau)}{\beta F},$$

$$\Phi_{g,0} = \frac{\delta_g(-1+\bar{B}\kappa+\tau+\bar{B}\beta\sigma_\alpha+\bar{C})}{\sigma_\alpha\delta_r F},\ \Phi_{g,1} = \frac{\delta_g(\bar{B}\kappa-1+\bar{C}+\bar{B}\beta\sigma_\alpha+\sigma_\alpha\bar{B}+\tau)}{\sigma_\alpha\delta_r F},\ \Phi_{g,2} = \frac{\bar{B}\delta_g}{\delta_r F},$$

$$\Phi_{y,0} = \frac{\delta_y(\bar{B}\beta\sigma_\alpha+\bar{C}+\sigma_\alpha\bar{B})}{\sigma_\alpha\delta_r F},\ \Phi_{y,1} = \frac{\delta_y(\bar{C}+2\sigma_\alpha\bar{B}+\bar{B}\beta\sigma_\alpha)}{\sigma_\alpha\delta_r F},\ \Phi_{y,2} = \frac{\delta_y\bar{B}}{\delta_r F},$$

$$\Phi_{\pi,0} = \frac{\delta_\pi(\bar{C}\sigma_\alpha-\sigma_\alpha+\tau\sigma_\alpha+\sigma_\alpha{}^2\beta\bar{B}-\sigma_\alpha\beta\bar{B}\kappa-\bar{C}\kappa)}{\sigma_\alpha\delta_r F},\ \Phi_{\pi,1} = \frac{\bar{B}\delta_\pi(\sigma_\alpha-\kappa)}{\delta_r F}\ \text{and}$$

7 The solution of the optimal interest rule within the framework of the cooperative game is obtained with Maple 11.

$\Phi_{r^*} = \frac{-\bar{C}\kappa-\sigma_\alpha-\bar{B}\sigma_\alpha{}^2+\bar{B}\sigma_\alpha\kappa+\sigma_\alpha\tau+\bar{C}\sigma_\alpha\bar{B}\beta\sigma_\alpha{}^2-\bar{B}\beta\sigma_\alpha\kappa}{\sigma_\alpha\beta F}$ where to keep it simple F defined as $F = -\sigma_\alpha\bar{B} - 1 + \bar{B}\kappa + \tau$.

Based on the Lagrange multipliers and as a result of the replacement and separation process, for the cooperative optimal government spending rule, the cooperative optimal government spending rule is obtained as follows[8];

$$\tilde{g}_t^{CE} = \Omega_{r,0}\,(r_t - r^*) + \Omega_{r,1}\,(r_{t-1} - r^*) - \Omega_{r,2}\,(r_{t-2} - r^*) + \Omega_{g,1}\tilde{g}_{t-1} - \Omega_{g,2}\tilde{g}_{t-2} - \Omega_{y,0}\tilde{y}_t + \Omega_{y,1}\tilde{y}_{t-1} - \Omega_{y,2}\tilde{y}_{t-2} + \Omega_{\pi,0}\pi_{H,0} - \Omega_{\pi,1}\pi_{H,t-1} \tag{10}$$

In the equation number 10 described above, respectively:

$\Omega_{r,0} = \frac{\sigma_\alpha\delta_r(1+\bar{B}\sigma_\alpha-\tau-\bar{B}\kappa)}{\delta_g T}$,

$\Omega_{r,1} = \frac{\delta_r(2\tau\sigma_\alpha-\sigma_\alpha{}^2\bar{B}-2\sigma_\alpha+\sigma_\alpha\tau\beta+\sigma_\alpha\bar{B}\kappa-\beta\sigma_\alpha+\bar{C}\sigma_\alpha-\bar{C}\kappa)}{\delta_g\beta T}$, $\Omega_{r,2} = \frac{\sigma_\alpha\delta_r(1+\tau)}{\delta_g\beta T}$,

$\Omega_{g,1} = \frac{T+\bar{B}\sigma_\alpha}{T}$, $\Omega_{g,2} = \frac{\sigma_\alpha\bar{B}}{T}$, $\Omega_{y,0} = \frac{\delta_y(\beta\bar{B}\sigma_\alpha+\bar{B}\sigma_\alpha+\bar{C})}{\delta_g T}$, $\Omega_{y,1} = \frac{\delta_y(\beta\bar{B}\sigma_\alpha+\bar{C}+2\bar{B}\sigma_\alpha)}{\delta_g T}$

$\Omega_{y,2} = \frac{\sigma_\alpha\delta_y\bar{B}}{\delta_g T}$, $\Omega_{\pi,0} = \frac{\delta_\pi(-\sigma_\alpha-\bar{C}\kappa+\sigma_\alpha{}^2\beta\bar{B}+\tau\sigma_\alpha+\bar{C}\sigma_\alpha+\sigma_\alpha\beta\bar{B}\kappa)}{\delta_g T}$, $\Omega_{\pi,1} = \frac{\sigma_\alpha\bar{B}\delta_\pi(\sigma_\alpha-\kappa)}{\delta_g T}$

where to keep it simple T defined as $T = \beta\bar{B}\sigma_\alpha - 1 + \tau + \bar{B}\kappa + \bar{C}$.

The policy rules derived from the scenario in which policy makers cooperated are similar to the rules achieved with non-cooperative Nash solution. However, both policy rules in this scenario have simultaneous reactions to the other policy instrument. The optimal nominal interest rule responds to the current government spending rule, while the optimal government spending rule responds to the current interest rate. Cooperation is thought to occur through these simultaneous cross-reactions.

Equation number 9, the cooperative equilibrium interest rule, is based on current and past inflation, output gap, government spending and balance and past interest rates. But the cooperative government spending rule is based on current and past inflation, output gap and interest rates, and past government spending. Diversely from the non-cooperated Nash policy rules, the cooperative balance policy rules depend on the steady-state debt / GDP ratio ($\bar{B}$), the steady-state consumption / GDP ratio ($\bar{C}$) and the fixed income tax rate (τ).

8 The solution of the optimal government spending rule within the framework of the cooperative game is obtained with Maple 11.

4. Testing Alternative Scenarios: Dynamic Simulation

In this section, the stochastic simulation of the model derived for alternative scenarios among policymakers is performed. This is done to evaluate the performance of optimal monetary and fiscal policies derived for each scenario. As a result of the simulation, the responses of each scenario to exogenous shocks are analyzed by using impulse-response functions, and their effects on social loss are analyzed. Then, loss analysis is performed to find out which scenario caused the lowest social loss.

The performance of optimal monetary and fiscal policies for alternative scenarios is assessed by a simulation using the dynamic IS curve equation, the New Keynesian Phillips curve equation, the government budget constraint equation, and optimal monetary and fiscal policy rules. For this, the model needs to be calibrated. The calibration process is taken into account the performance of the economy in Turkey between the years of 2006–2017. Thus, the model parameters based on the calculation of values for Turkey Economy 2006: 1–2017: 3 period was calibrated by reference. Other parameters in the model have been calibrated using previous studies. Calibrated values are shown in Tab. 7.1.

In the literature, the Calvo parameter 0.50 is used for stickiness of domestic price, because the average duration of price contracts is considered as six months. The parameter value of the inverse elasticity of substitution in consumption is used as 3 in Çebi (2012). This means that the elasticity of substitution in consumption is 0.33 (1/3).

The degree of openness (α) is determined as 0.27 by taking into account the ratio of average imports to GDP, as in Çebi (2012), between 2006 and 2017. On the other hand, with a similar calculation, the steady-state debt / GDP ratio ($\bar{B}$), 0.21 and steady-state consumption / GDP ratio ($\bar{C}$), 0.62, are determined between the same periods. The fixed income tax rate is determined by taking into account the tariff taken as a basis in article 103 of the Income Tax Law. This tariff does not vary by year, but only by income categories. In the study, the fixed income tax of 0.2425 is used as the average of these income categories.

The discount factor (β) is determined as 0.99 because the annual steady-state real interest rate is accepted as 4 %. Based on the study of Lubik and Schorfheide (2007), the elasticity of substitution between domestic and foreign goods (η) and the elasticity of substitution between goods produced in different countries (γ) is determined as 1. Then, ω and λ the coefficients are obtained and $\sigma_a = 1$ is determined as in Çebi (2012).

Tab. 7.1: The Calibration of Parameters, Source: Authors' own calculations

Parameter	Definition	Value
θ	Degree of price stickness	0.5
σ	Inverse elasticity of substitution in consumption	3
α	Degree of openness of the economy	0.27
φ	Inverse elasticity of labour supply	2
β	Discount factor	0.99
σ_α	St. dev. of technology innovation	1
ρ_a	AR coefficient of technology	0.8
ρ_{c^*}	AR coefficient of domestic output	0.8
γ_π	Parameter of the deviation of inflation from its target level according to the equilibrium condition of the economy (in monetary loss functions)	1
ρ_π	Parameter of deviation of inflation from its target level according to the equilibrium condition of the economy (in the financial loss function(	0.5
γ_y	Parameter of the deviation of the output from its potential level according to the equilibrium condition of the economy (in the monetary loss function)	0.4
ρ_y	Parameter of the deviation of the output from its potential level according to the equilibrium condition of the economy (in the financial loss function)	1
γ_r	Parameter of deviation from the equilibrium interest rate according to the equilibrium condition (in the monetary loss function)	0.5
ρ_g	Parameter of deviation from the balanced government expenditure (or financial deficit) according to the equilibrium condition of the economy (in the financial loss function)	0.2

In the monetary and financial loss functions, the parameters of inflation, output, optimal interest and deviation from government spending according to the equilibrium condition of the economy are determined according to the studies of Fragetta and Kirsanova (2010), Çebi (2012), Flotho (2012) and Saulo et al. (2013). In the monetary loss function, the parameter of the deviation of inflation from the target is 1, the parameter of deviation of output from the potential level of is 0.4, and the parameter of the deviation from the equilibrium interest rate is 0.5, according to the equilibrium condition of the economy. In the financial loss function, the parameter of the deviation of inflation from the target is 0.5, the parameter of the deviation of the output from the potential level is 1, and the parameter of deviation from balanced government expenditure parameter is 0.2, according to the equilibrium condition of the economy.

4.1. Endogenous and Exogenous Variables

The endogenous variables in the general equilibrium model are defined as the variables obtained based on the data. Exogenous variables, namely shock variables, are the variables that state shocks that do not arise from the endogenous dynamics of the economy.

In this framework, the variables in the general equilibrium model are summarized in Tab. 7.2.

The endogenous variables used in the model are output gap, domestic inflation rate, debt stock, nominal interest rate, and government expenditure, respectively. The endogenous variables are the natural level of interest rate, technological innovation, foreign consumption, domestic price, interest rate, and government spending shocks. Domestic price, interest, and expenditure shocks reveal real changes for the relevant period after the shocks given to data-based variables. However, the natural level of interest rate, technological innovation, and foreign consumption represent shocks that do not arise from the economy's endogenous dynamics.

4.2. Dynamic General Equilibrium Model within the Framework of Non-cooperative Nash Game

The endogenous processes in the general equilibrium model, which deals with the interaction between policies within the framework of the non-cooperative

Tab. 7.2: Definitions of Variables, Source: Authors' own construction

Endogenous variables	Output gap	$\tilde{y}_t$
	Domestic inflation	$\pi_{H,t}$
	Debt stock	$\tilde{b}_t$
	Nominal interest rate	r_t
	Government expenditure (Fiscal deficit)	$\tilde{g}_t$
Exogenous variables	Natural level of interest rate	r_t^N
	Technology innovation	a_t
	Foreign consumption	c_t^*
	Domestic price shock	ε_t^π
	Interest rate shock	ε_t^r
	Expenditure shock	ε_t^g

Nash game, form the dynamic IS equation, the New Keynesian Phillips curve, the equation for government debt payment constraint, the non-cooperative Nash interest and government spending policy rules, respectively. In order to derive the shocks for domestic inflation, interest, and expenditure, exogenous shocks variables were added exogenously to the New Keynesian Phillips curve, the non-cooperative Nash interest, and expenditure policy rules.

In exogenous processes, firstly, the natural interest rate is derived within the model by using other variables defined in an outward-oriented economy model. Technology and foreign world consumption (production) are included in the model as a shock. These are defined as the AR (1) process, just like domestic inflation, interest, and government spending shock. Tab. 7.3 presents the general equilibrium of the economy, the equations representing the open economy model, and policy rules obtained game theoretically for this scenario.

4.2. Dynamic General Equilibrium Model within the Framework of Cooperative Nash Game

Endogenous and exogenous processes in the general equilibrium model, which deals with the interaction between policies within the framework of cooperative play, are similar to other models. However, interest and government spending rules consist of equations obtained as a result of the scenario where there is cooperation between the monetary and fiscal policymakers. Tab. 7.4 presents the general equilibrium of the economy, the equations representing the open economy model, and the game theoretically obtained policy rules for this scenario.

4.3. Findings for Numerical Analysis

In this part of the study, the stochastic simulation results of the developed game theoretical models are discussed by using counterfactual experiments. As mentioned earlier, the model consists of equations for the dynamic IS, the New Keynesian Phillips curve, and the government debt payment constraint and the interest and government spending policy rules derived for each scenario. In this study, the DYNARE toolbox that works on MATLAB program and developed for the estimation of Dynamic Stochastic General Equilibrium Models is used for the steps in the process of each scenario.

New Keynesian macroeconomic models tend to deal with the disruptive effects of exogenous shocks in an economy and their responses to shocks (Snowdon and Vane, 2005). With the stochastic simulation, the reactions of output, inflation, debt stock, and interest rates are shown for each scenario

Tab. 7.3: First Scenario: Dynamic General Equilibrium Model within the Framework of Non-cooperative Nash Game, Source: Author's own construction

Endogenous Process	Exogenous Process
$\tilde{y}_t = E_t\left\{\tilde{y}_{t+1}\right\} - \frac{1}{\sigma_a}\left(r_t - E_t\left\{\pi_{H,t+1}\right\} - r_t^N\right) - E_t\left\{\Delta\tilde{g}_{t+1}\right\}$	$r_t^N = \frac{\sigma_\alpha(1+\varphi)(\rho_a-1)}{(\sigma_\alpha+\varphi)} a_t + \frac{\varphi\alpha(\omega-1)}{(\sigma_\alpha+\varphi)}(\rho_{c^*} - 1)c_t^*$
$\pi_{H,t} = \beta E_t\left\{\pi_{H,t+1}\right\} + \kappa\tilde{y}_t - \sigma_\alpha\tilde{g}_t + \varepsilon_t^\pi$	$a_t = \zeta_a a_{t-1} + e_t^a$
$\tilde{b}_{t+1} = (r_t - r_t^N) + \frac{1}{\beta}(\tilde{b}_t - \pi_{H,t} + \frac{\bar{C}}{\bar{B}}\tilde{g}_t + \frac{1-\bar{C}-\tau}{\bar{B}}\tilde{y}_t)$	$c_t^* = \zeta_{c^*} c_{t-1}^* + e_t^{c^*}$
$r_t = \Theta_{r,1} r_{t-1} - \Theta_{r,2} r_{t-2} + \Theta_{\pi,0}\pi_{H,t} + \Theta_{y,0}\tilde{y}_t - \Theta_{y,1}\tilde{y}_{t-1} - \Theta_{r^*} r^* + \varepsilon_t^r$	$\varepsilon_t^\pi = \zeta_{\varepsilon^\pi}\varepsilon_{t-1}^\pi + e_t^\pi$
$\tilde{g}_t = -cons + \Psi_{g,+1}E_t\left\{\tilde{g}_{t+1}\right\} + \Psi_{g,1}\tilde{g}_{t-1} + \Psi_{y,+1}E_t\left\{\tilde{y}_{t+1}\right\} - \Psi_{y,0}\tilde{y}_t + \Psi_{y,1}\tilde{y}_{t-1}$ $-\Psi_{\pi,+1}E_t\left\{\pi_{H,t+1}\right\} + \Psi_{\pi,0}\pi_H + \varepsilon_t^g$	$\varepsilon_t^r = \zeta_r\varepsilon_{t-1}^r + e_t^r$ $\varepsilon_t^g = \zeta_g\varepsilon_{t-1}^g + e_t^g$

Tab. 7.4: Second Scenario: Dynamic General Equilibrium Model within the Framework of Cooperative Nash Game, Source: Authors' own construction

Endogenous Process	Exogenous Process
$\tilde{y}_t = E_t\left\{\tilde{y}_{t+1}\right\} - \frac{1}{\sigma_a}\left(r_t - E_t\left\{\pi_{H,t+1}\right\} - r_t^N\right) - E_t\left\{\Delta\tilde{g}_{t+1}\right\}$	$r_t^N = \frac{\sigma_\alpha(1+\varphi)(\rho_a-1)}{(\sigma_\alpha+\varphi)} a_t + \frac{\varphi\alpha(\omega-1)}{(\sigma_\alpha+\varphi)}(\rho_{c^*}-1)c_t^*$
$\pi_{H,t} = \beta E_t\left\{\pi_{H,t+1}\right\} + \kappa\tilde{y}_t - \sigma_\alpha\tilde{g}_t + \varepsilon_t^\pi$	$a_t = \zeta_a a_{t-1} + e_t^a$
$\tilde{b}_{t+1} = (r_t - r_t^N) + \frac{1}{\beta}(\tilde{b}_t - \pi_{H,t} + \frac{\bar{C}}{\bar{B}}\tilde{g}_t + \frac{1-\bar{C}-\tau}{\bar{B}}\tilde{y}_t)$	$c_t^* = \zeta_{c^*} c_{t-1}^* + e_t^{c^*}$
$r_t = \Phi_{r,1}r_{t-1} - \Phi_{r,2}r_{t-2} - \Phi_{g,0}\tilde{g}_t + \Phi_{g,1}\tilde{g}_{t-1} - \Phi_{g,2}\tilde{g}_{t-2} - \Phi_{y,0}\tilde{y}_t + \Phi_{y,1}\tilde{y}_{t-1}$ $-\Phi_{y,2}\tilde{y}_{t-2} + \Phi_{\pi,0}\pi_{H,t} - \Phi_{\pi,1}\pi_{H,t-1} - \Phi_{r^*}r^* + \varepsilon_t^r$	$\varepsilon_t^\pi = \zeta_{\varepsilon^\pi}\varepsilon_{t-1}^\pi + e_t^\pi$ $\varepsilon_t^r = \zeta_r\varepsilon_{t-1}^r + e_t^r$
$\tilde{g}_t = \Omega_{r,0}(r_t - r^*) + \Omega_{r,1}(r_{t-1} - r^*) - \Omega_{r,2}(r_{t-2} - r^*) + \Omega_{g,1}\tilde{g}_{t-1} - \Omega_{g,2}\tilde{g}_{t-2}$ $-\Omega_{y,0}\tilde{y}_t + \Omega_{y,1}\tilde{y}_{t-1} - \Omega_{y,2}\tilde{y}_{t-2} + \Omega_{\pi,0}\pi_{H,0} - \Omega_{\pi,1}\pi_{H,t-1}$	$\varepsilon_t^g = \zeta_g\varepsilon_{t-1}^g + e_t^g$

based on the interaction between policymakers, as a result of a shock in the economy assumed to be in balance. The impulse-response functions here are obtained based on the calibration values of the parameters. Thus, it shows us when the impact of the shocks in the economy on the variables thought to be social welfare indicators started and how long it lasted. In this way, we compare the responses of the endogenous variables to the shocks that will occur in the economy, which is assumed to be in balance for each scenario. Then, we obtain which scenario is more effective, and the balance dynamics of the models analyzed. Also, variants of optimal paths of variables are obtained with stochastic simulation. Thus, the expected value of the social loss function of the economy in equilibrium is calculated for each scenario. In this way, it is examined which scenario minimizes the social loss function. The findings obtained from this point draw a direction other than the impulse-response analysis on the optimal policy interaction.

4.3.1. Analysis of Structural Shocks: Impulse-Response Analysis

Studies on the New Keynesian DSGE models in the literature are generally based on the business cycle fluctuations and the dynamic structure of these fluctuations, and the DSGE models developed by the researchers. In order to explain the sources of business cycles in the economy, the transmission of various structural shocks to the economy is examined. These are done by impulse-response analysis. Structural shocks defined in this study arise from a supply (cost-push shocks), technology, foreign demand, and policy.

During a negative supply shock, coordination between policymakers becomes essential. If there is no coordination between policymakers, then they may follow conflicting policies. For example, a fiscal policymaker may prefer an expansionary policy to reduce the negative output gap. The monetary policymaker, on the other hand, may implement a narrowing policy to restrain the high price increase caused by the negative supply shock. A positive or negative demand shock based on exogenous factors can cause inflation or deflation. Here, again, the coordination of monetary and fiscal policies becomes essential. Policymakers can follow expansionary policies in the event of a negative demand shock while following contractionary policies during a positive demand shock to reduce aggregate demand and control inflation.

In this part of the study, we investigate how structural shocks affect the economy according to the nature of the interaction between policymakers and which scenario among policymakers manages this shock better.

Positive Supply Shock: Technology Shock

Fluctuations in business cycles and instability caused by these fluctuations are caused by shocks in aggregate supply or aggregate demand. Aggregate supply shocks are considered as significant changes in productivity. If the factors that cause productivity changes are positive, then aggregate production will also be affected positively. Factors that positively affect productivity can be defined as positive changes in the quality of production inputs, and these developments will increase aggregate production. In macroeconomic literature, such shocks are called technology or productivity shocks. The real business cycle theory assumes that this technology shock is entirely random. Fig. 7.1 shows how a technological shock affects the economy according to the structure of the interaction between policymakers using impulse response analysis.

In theory, a positive productivity shock positively affects marginal costs. Inflation also decreases as marginal costs fall. However, the decrease in the natural interest rate will stimulate the economy.

In the first column of Fig. 7.1, the response of the variables to such a technology shock is seen in a non-cooperative Nash game between monetary and fiscal policymakers. A positive efficiency shock affects marginal costs positively, reducing inflation. However, this positive effect lasts for a period (quarter). At the same time, the decrease in the natural interest rate positively affects the output even if it is delayed for a while. This delayed effect can be explained by wage/price rigidity in the economy. This increase in output lasts five terms. It is seen that both policymakers react with an expansionary policy to this shock. Gali and Monacelli (2008) emphasize that the optimal policy mix to be applied in the face of a productivity shock is aimed at providing the desired output increase by smoothing the price adjustment over time. Therefore, it is stated that the fiscal deficit should be widened (increasing public expenditures) in order to increase demand. However, such a policy mix causes inflation in the economy and an increase in the debt stock. It can be said that this is caused by both policymakers implementing expansionary policies. Indeed, in this scenario, these reactions of policymakers cause an inflationary effect at the end of the first period. This inflationary effect disappears at the end of the tenth period.

In Fig. 7.1, in the second column, when there is a cooperation between monetary and fiscal policymakers, the responses of variables to technology shock are seen. In this scenario, a positive productivity shock reduces inflation, and this effect lasts for three periods. The decrease in the natural interest rate affects the output positively and the debt stock negatively. In the case of a positive supply

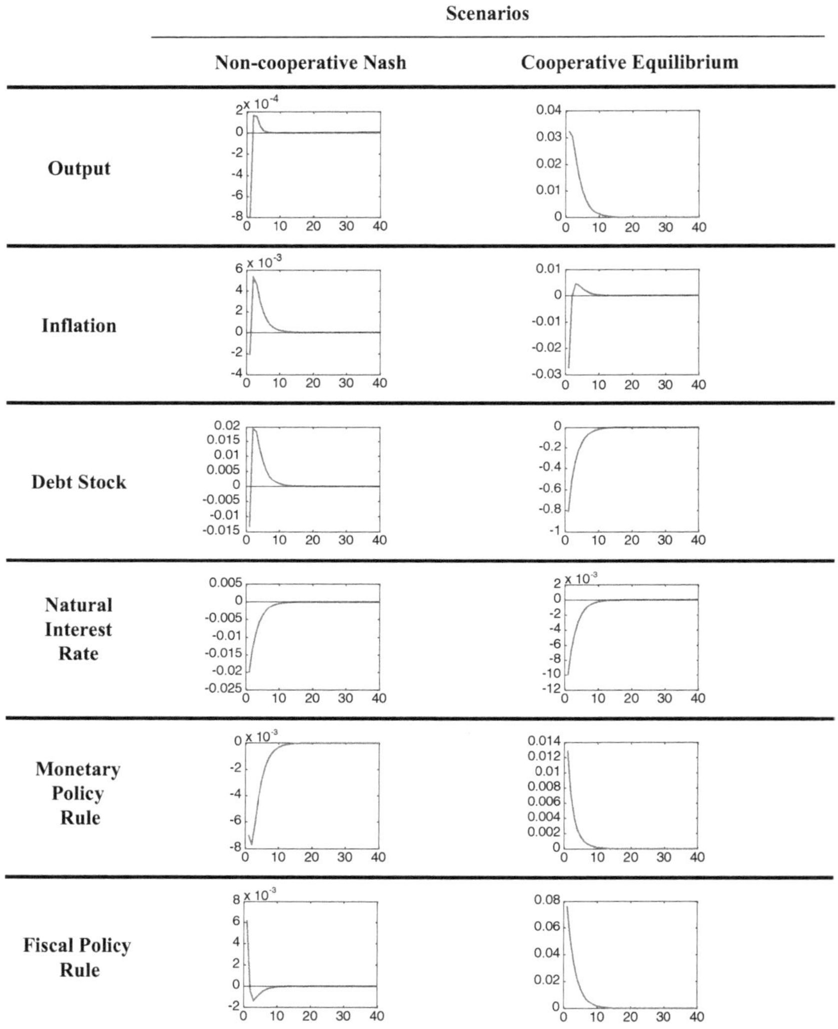

Fig. 7.1: Impulse-Response Results for Productivity Shock, Authors' own calculations

shock, the monetary policymaker reacts with a contractionary policy, while the fiscal policymaker appears to respond with an expansionary policy. This situation is a policy interaction that smooths the price adjustment over time, as stated in Gali and Monacelli (2008), providing the desired output increase.

We result that such policy coordination ensures a better way of stability in the economy, and this situation reveals the importance of cooperation between policymakers. We may say that such a policy mix creates a seven-period inflationary effect in the case of a positive supply shock while maintaining its effect for twelve periods.

Negative Supply Shock: Cost-Push Shocks

It has already been mentioned that aggregate supply shocks are significant changes in productivity. If the factor causing the productivity change is negative, this will affect the aggregate production negatively. For example, factors such as an increase in energy prices, political turmoil, workers' actions, government regulations that will damage incentives, drought, earthquake, or wars will also negatively affect productivity, reducing aggregate supply. In theory, cost-push shocks shift the short-run supply curve (AS) to the left, raising marginal costs. In this case, while the output decreases, inflation increases.

The responses of the variables also depend on the response of monetary and fiscal policymakers. In the case of negative supply shocks, generally, the objectives of monetary and fiscal policymakers tend to conflict. While the monetary policymaker tends to implement a contractionary policy concerning price stability, the fiscal policymaker can take an expansionary policy by considering output stability. Tetik and Ceylan (2016) examine the interaction between fiscal and monetary policies in Turkey. They find that in the case of negative supply shocks, the central bank implement tightening monetary policy, while fiscal authorities conduct expansionary fiscal policy. Therefore, they stated that a negative supply shock could lead to a policy conflict in Turkey.

Fig. 7.2 also shows how a negative supply shock affects the economy according to the structure of the interaction between policymakers and the results of the impulse response analysis.

Fig. 7.2 shows the responses of variables to a negative supply shock in the first column, where there is a non-cooperative Nash game between money and fiscal policymakers. In this scenario, a negative supply shock has increased inflation in the economy. However, this inflationary effect lasts for a while. The monetary policymaker who wants to stabilize inflation implements a strong contractionary monetary policy. The contractionary monetary policy's increase in interest rates and decreases the output. It creates a deflationary effect between the second and fifth periods. The fiscal policymaker who wants to stabilize the output applies an expansionary fiscal policy. Therefore, in a non-cooperative Nash scenario, a negative shock situation can be interpreted as leading to a policy conflict. Afterward,

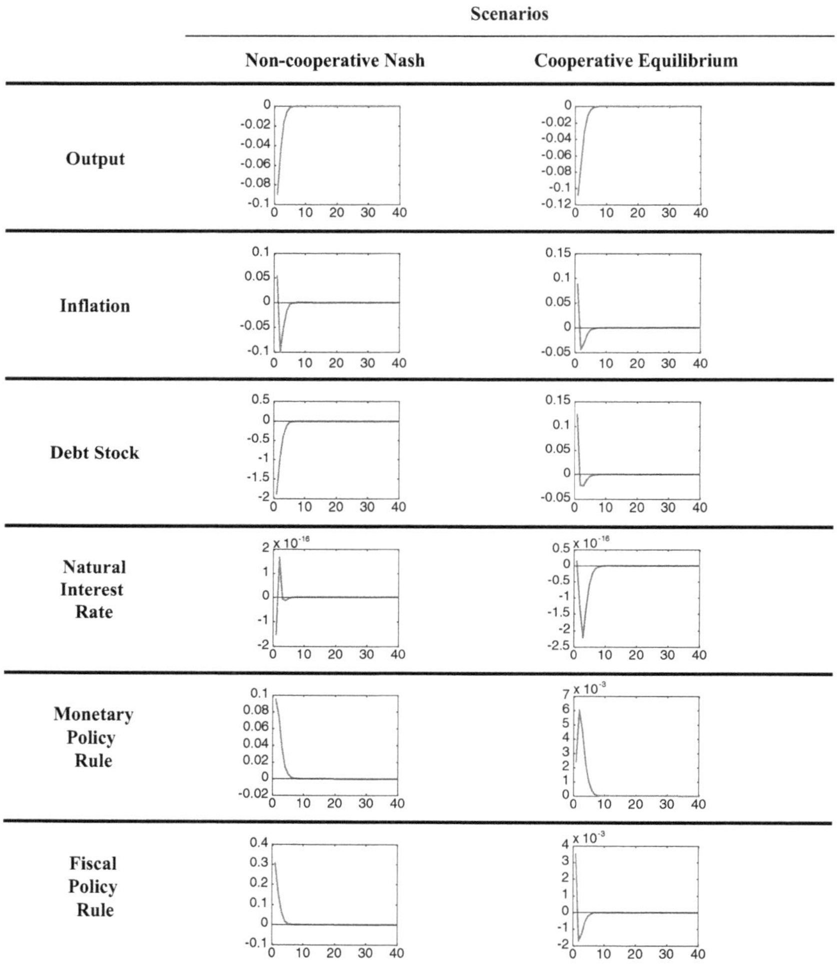

Fig. 7.2: Impulse-Response Results for Domestic Price Shock, Source: Authors' own calculations

the decrease in the debt stock caused by inflation returns to its initial position at the end of the fifth period with the increase in government expenditures.

In the case of cooperation between monetary and fiscal policymakers, the responses of the variables to a negative supply shock are seen in the second column of Fig. 7.2. In this scenario, a negative supply shock increased inflation in the economy, and this effect lasts for two terms. The monetary policymaker, who wants to stabilize inflation, implements a modest contractionary monetary policy. As it is seen from the figure, it is thought that the fiscal policymaker has a contractionary policy option. In this way, the situation of policy conflict disappears. The responses of this policy mix are similar to those in Çebi (2012) and Fragetta and Kirsanova (2010), who investigated optimal interaction. It can be said that both policymakers adopting a contractionary policy reduces the output and creates a deflationary effect between the second and fifth periods as in the non-cooperative scenario. However, the deflationary effect here is not as high as in the non-cooperative scenario. In this scenario, the decrease in the interest rate caused by the policy mix stimulates the output, and it is seen that it returned to its initial position at the end of the fifth period.

Monetary and Fiscal Policy Shocks

The alignment between monetary and fiscal policy objectives and instruments is important for policy coordination. So basically, the effectiveness of economic policy is based on the harmonious operation of objectives and instruments. Effective coordination among policymakers requires information sharing among all players involved in the policy decision-making process. A poorly executed monetary policy may obstruct the implementation of a successful and effective fiscal policy or a poorly executed fiscal policy can prevent successful and effective monetary policy implementation.

For instance, an over restricted monetary policy could cause interest rates to increase fast, thereby increasing government debt payment costs and threatening financial stability (IMF and World Bank, 2003). In monetary policy, price stability is the primary target. If price stability is not directly threatened, policymakers are not recommended to take very restrictive measures.

An excessively expansionary fiscal policy application may also be the main cause of many economic and social problems such as high inflation, budget deficit, and low economic growth. Countries need appropriate financial arrangements to solve these problems. The fiscal policymaker, who carries out such a policy, may push the monetary policymaker to exhibit a wrong policy attitude with excessive borrowing. Failure to take appropriate monetary policy measures as a result of being non-coordinated can damage the private sector by removing it from the credit market and implementation of a bad fiscal policy may slow down economic growth (Raspudic, 2012). Figs. 7.3 and 7.4 show how a positive nominal interest rate shock (a contractionary monetary policy shock) and a positive government spending shock (expansionary fiscal policy

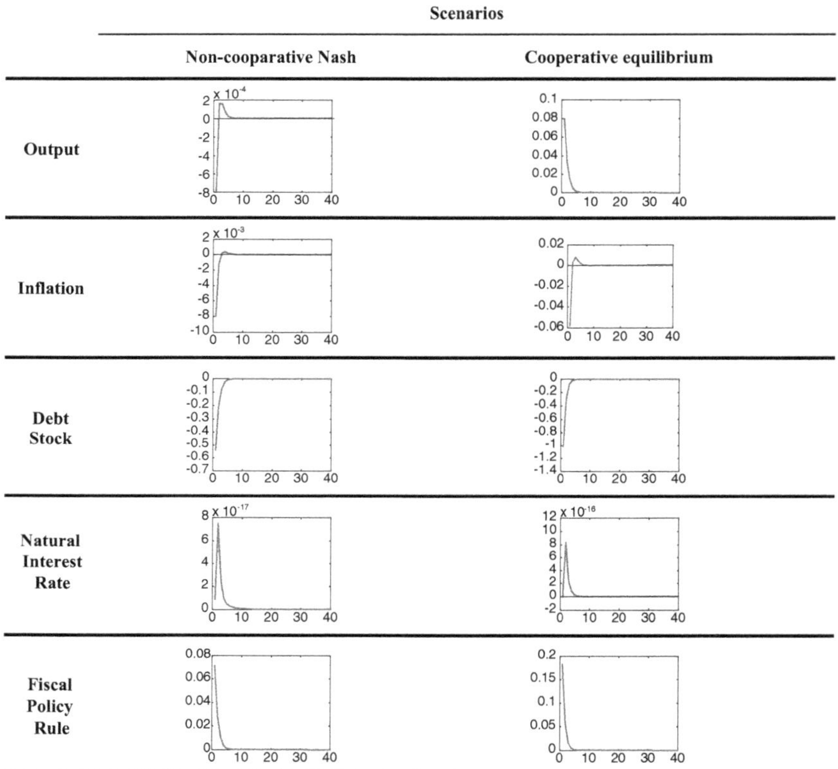

Fig. 7.3: Impulse-Response Results of Interest Rate Shock According to the Scenarios, Source: Authors' own construction

shock) affect the economy according to the nature of the interaction between policymakers and impulse-response analysis results.

Fig. 7.3 shows the responses of variables to the contractionary monetary policy shock in the first column where there is a non-cooperative Nash game between monetary and fiscal policymakers. In this scenario, with the increase in interest rates, inflation and output decrease in the economy and this effect lasts for two periods. As a result of this contractionary policy, natural interest rates in the economy increase and debt stock decreases. The fiscal policymaker, who wants to stabilize the output, reacts an expansionary fiscal policy to this contractionary policy. With the effects of the expansionary fiscal policy, the output increases after the second period and the debt returns to the starting level. It is observed that this fiscal policy preference had an inflationary effect after the fifth period. Later, natural interest rates, which increased further as a result of this policy mix, brought output and inflation to the starting position at the end of the sixth period.

In the case of cooperation between monetary and fiscal policymakers, the responses of the variables to the contractionary monetary policy shock are seen in the second column of Fig. 7.3. In this scenario, with the increase in interest rates, inflation in the economy decreases and this effect lasts for two periods. As a result of the cooperation between policymakers, the output does not decrease as a result of the implementation of the expansionary fiscal policy. On the contrary, it seems that a positive response has been given. The increase in the output along with the effects of the expansionary fiscal policy brings the debt level to its starting position, and it appears to have caused an inflationary effect at the end of the second period. Then increasing natural interest rates put the output and inflation at the beginning of the fifth period.

Fig. 7.4 shows how a positive government spending shock (expansionary fiscal policy shock) affects the economy according to the structure of the interaction between policymakers, and impulse-response analysis results.

Fig. 7.4 shows the responses of variables to the expansionary fiscal policy shock in the first column where there is a non-cooperative Nash game between monetary and fiscal policymakers. From the perspective of the monetary policymaker, the monetary policymaker, whose political priority is considered to be price stability, appears to have a contractionary reaction to the expansionary policy move of the fiscal policymaker. Therefore, in this scenario, it can be said that the monetary policymaker is using the inflationary pressure caused by the widening effect of the policy choice. The positive shock in government spending increases the output. However, inflation reacts negatively due to the contractionary move of the monetary policymaker and the nature of the negative relationship between government spending and marginal costs[9]. Therefore, the inflationary effect of government expenditures appears after the fifth period. Along with the increase in natural interest rates in the economy, the output and inflation return to its starting position at the end of the sixth period.

---

9 Gali and Monacelli (2008) explained the source of the negative relationship between marginal cost and government spending. At a data output level, the increase in government spending increases domestic consumption or creates real appreciation. These two situations tend to negatively affect real marginal cost with negative effects on product wage (expected labor cost).

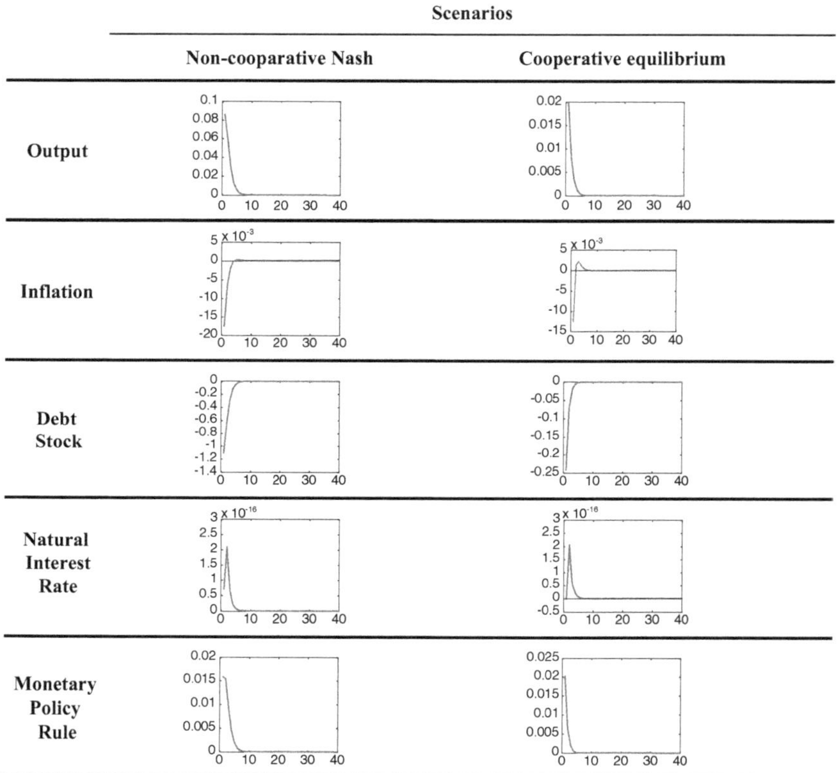

Fig. 7.4: Impulse-Response Results of Government Spending Shock According to the Scenarios, Source: Authors' own construction

The second column of Fig. 7.4 shows the responses of the variables to the expansionary fiscal policy shock when there is a cooperation between monetary and fiscal policymakers. The responses of the variables can be interpreted in the same way as they are similar to the non-cooperative Nash game. However, the return of debt stock and interest rate is faster than the non-cooperative Nash game.

Along with the impulse-response analysis, the effects of efficiency, negative supply, and policy shocks in the economy were examined separately for each scenario. We can say which is the best policy coordination by looking at the effects and aspects of exogenous shocks on variables such as output, inflation, debt stock, and interest, which represent social welfare. We can say that the cooperative solution that we obtained by modeling policy interaction game theoretically for a small-scale open economy, where there is a cooperative situation among policymakers, is the most effective policy coordination for Turkey's economy. The main rationale for this interpretation is that it is the only scenario in which the output reacts positively to the technology shock. The second reason is that, in the cooperative scenario, there are policy preferences to eliminate the policy conflict that may arise against the negative supply shock. Finally, it is observed that the output did not decrease as a result of the government spending shock. Thus, depending on the impulse response analysis, the most effective policy coordination for Turkey's economy to the conclusion that the cooperative solution.

A similar study to this study as its theoretical background is Saulo et al. (2013)'s work. However, However, this study developed for a closed economy, and it evaluated for the Brazilian economy. Saulo et al. (2013), reveal that effective policy coordination for the Brazilian economy is the situation where the monetary policymaker is the leader. There are some difficulties in comparing the findings obtained from this study with other studies. Because the theoretical analysis of the game between the monetary and fiscal policies we have developed for a small-scale open economy makes a new contribution to the literature. Moreover, in the framework of policy analysis before counterfactual experiments in this direction, it has made for Turkey's economy. However, this finding, which we obtained with impulse response analysis, emphasizes cooperation between policymakers, Nordhaus (1994), Henry et al. (1999), Dixit and Lambertini (2003), and Benigno and Woodford (2003).

4.4.2. Social Loss Analysis for Alternative Scenarios

In a small-scale-open economy, along with obtaining the derived policy rules for the alternative scenario, the performance of derived these policy rules, it evaluated using a calibrated model with data on the Turkey economy. From this point of view, firstly, the behavior of each scenario(and the policy rules of these scenarios) against structural shocks analyzed through the impulse-response analysis.

Social Loss Analysis Findings

Social loss calculated using unconditional variance as in Woodford (2003) and Saulo et al. (2013). To calculate the expected loss of the objective (loss) function of the monetary and fiscal policymaker, these loss functions defined by a process similar to the following figure;

Tab. 7.5: Social Loss Values of Alternative Scenarios, Source: Authors' own calculations

$L_t^M = \pi_t^2 + 0.4\tilde{y}_t^2 + 0.5(r_t - r^*)^2$

$L_t^F = 0.5\pi_t^2 + \tilde{y}_t^2 + 0.2\tilde{g}_t^2$

$L_t^S = L_t^M + L_t^F$

	Variance Values							
Scenarios	$\pi_{H,t}$	$\tilde{y}_t$	$\tilde{b}_t$	r_t	$\tilde{g}_t$	L_t^M	L_t^F	L_t^S
Non-cooperative Nash	0.0341	0.0216	6.8467	0.0175	0.1650	0.0515	0.0716	0.1231
Cooperative Equilibrium	0.0154	0.0306	4.0274	0.0083	0.0546	0.0318	0.0493	0.0811

$$L_t^M = \gamma_\pi \pi_t^2 + \gamma_y \tilde{y}_t^2 + \gamma_r (r_t - r^*)^2 \rightarrow L_t^M$$
$$= \gamma_\pi^2 \operatorname{var}(\pi_t) + \gamma_y^2 \operatorname{var}(\tilde{y}_t^2) + \gamma_r^2 \operatorname{var}(r_t - r^*)$$

$$L_t^F = \rho_\pi \pi_t^2 + \rho_y \tilde{y}_t^2 + \rho_g \tilde{g}_t^2 \rightarrow L_t^F = \rho_\pi^2 \operatorname{var}(\pi_t) + \rho_y^2 \operatorname{var}(\tilde{y}_t) + \rho_g^2 \operatorname{var}(\tilde{g}_t)$$

In the light of the calibrated parameters in Tab. 6.2, each policy social loss values shown in Tab. 6.5.

Tab. 7.5 shows the social loss function values obtained as a result of the alternative scenarios of the interaction between the policymakers who considered theoretically in the game. Among the models calibrated with Turkey data, it shows to be more successful coordination between the scenarios with the $L_t^S = 0.0811$ value of cooperative equilibrium solution with minimizing the social loss value.

5. Conclusion

This study examines the interaction between monetary and fiscal policies within the framework of game theory, based on the New Keynesian macroeconomic model. The study derives optimal monetary and fiscal policy rules for an open economy by modeling the interaction between policymakers as a game-theoretical framework.

Policymakers in Turkey, in their report published in ensuring macroeconomic stability, often stress that the work in the importance of coordination and cooperation. However, the problem here is what kind of policy mix will achieve between policymakers against economic shocks and in practice. In this study, it is proposing policy practices aimed at ensuring the coordination between monetary and fiscal policymakers for Turkey's economy. This policy proposal based on the nature of the strategic interaction between policymakers.

An effective policy mix for Turkey's economy seems to be a cooperative scenario. Cooperative interaction between policymakers ensures social welfare in a better way. These results, in practice and the face of economic shocks, to policymakers in Turkey are important to presenting the policy proposal on maintaining macroeconomic stability. The significance of this result is further increased, given the inability to implement economic policy analysis in an experimental framework and the difficulty of game theoretical evaluation of macroeconomic models. So, this study with game theory to handle the interactions between monetary and fiscal policies, and analyze the strategic interaction offers a new contribution to the Turkish economy literature. Moreover, the derived policy rules within this framework thought to assist researchers and policy practitioners in interpreting optimal choices based on the changing conditions of the economy.

In further studies, the game-theoretical optimal fiscal and monetary policies and scenarios based small open economy DSGE models can estimate for Turkey or other countries.

References

Barro, R. J., & Gordon, D. B. (1983a). Rules, discretion and reputation in a model of monetary policy. *Journal of Monetary Economics, 12*(1), 101–121.

Barro, R. J., & Gordon, D. B. (1983b). A positive theory of monetary policy in a natural rate model. *Journal of Political Economy, 91*(4), 589–610.

Benigno, P., & Woodford, M. (2003). Optimal monetary and fiscal policy: A linear-quadratic approach. *NBER Macroeconomics Annual, 18*, 271–333.

Blinder, A. S. (1983). Issues in the coordination of monetary and fiscal policy. NBER Working Paper (982), Retrieved from https://www.nber.org/system/files/working_papers/w0982/w0982.pdf (15.11.2020).

Çebi, C. (2012). The interaction between monetary and fiscal policies in Turkey: An estimated New Keynesian DSGE model. *Economic Modelling, 29*(4), 1258–1267.

Clarida, R., Gali, J., & Gertler, M. (1999). *The science of monetary policy: A new Keynesian perspective* (No. w7147). National Bureau of Economic Research.

Dixit, A., & Lambertini, L. (2003). Interactions of commitment and discretion in monetary and fiscal policies. *The American Economic Review, 93*(5), 1522–1542.

Flotho, S. (2012). *Monetary and fiscal policy in monetary union under the zero lower bound constraint* (No. 20). Discussion Paper Series, University of Freiburg, Department of International Economic Policy.

Fragetta, M., & Kirsanova, T. (2010). Strategic monetary and fiscal policy interactions: An empirical investigation. *European Economic Review, 54*(7), 855–879.

Gali, J., & Monacelli, T. (2004). Optimal fiscal policy in a monetary union. *Manuscript, Universitat Pompeu Fabra.*

Gali, J., & Monacelli, T. (2005). *Optimal monetary and fiscal policy in a currency union* (No. w11815). National Bureau of Economic Research.

Gali, J., & Monacelli, T. (2008). Optimal monetary and fiscal policy in a currency union. *Journal of International Economics, 76*(1), 116–132.

Giannoni, M. P., & Woodford, M. (2002a). *NBER working paper series: Vol. 9419. Optimal interest-rate rules: I. General theory.*

Giannoni, M. P., & Woodford, M. (2002b). *NBER working paper series: Vol. 9420. Optimal interest-rate rules: II. Applications.*

Goodfriend, M., & King, R. G. (1997). The new neoclassical synthesis and the role of monetary policy. *NBER Macroeconomics Annual, 12*, 231–283.

Henry, B., Nixon, J., & Hall, S. (1999). Central bank independence and co-ordinating monetary and fiscal policy. *Economic Outlook, 23*(2), 7–13.

IMF and World Bank. (2003). *Guidelines for public debt management.* Washington, D.C.: IMF.

Kydland, F. E., & Prescott, E. C. (1977). Rules rather than discretion: The inconsistency of optimal plans. *The Journal of Political Economy*, 85(3), 473–491.

Lubik, T. A., & Schorfheide, F. (2007). Do central banks respond to exchange rate movements? A structural investigation. *Journal of Monetary Economics, 54*(4), 1069–1087.

Nordhaus, W. D. (1994). Policy games: Co-ordination and independence in monetary and fiscal policies. *Brookings Papers on Economic Activity*, 2, 139–216.

Raspudić, G. Z. (2012). Coordination between the monetary and public debt management policies in Croatia. *Financial Theory and Practice, 36*(2), 109–138.

Sargent, T. J., & Wallace, N. (1984). Some unpleasant monetarist arithmetic. In *Monetarism in the United Kingdom* (pp. 15–41). UK: Palgrave Macmillan.

Saulo, H., Rêgo, L. C., & Divino, J. A. (2013). Fiscal and monetary policy interactions: A game theory approach. *Annals of Operations Research, 206*(1), 341–366.

Snowdon, B., & Vane, H. R. (2005). *Modern macroeconomics: Its origins, development and current state*. Edward Elgar Publishing, Cheltenham, UK.

Tetik, M., & Ceylan, R. (2016). Investigation of interaction between monetary and fiscal policy in Turkey: SVAR approach. *Journal of Multidisciplinary Developments*, *1*(1), 113–121.

Woodford, M. (2003). *Interest and prices: Foundations of a theory of monetary policy*. Princeton: Princeton University Press.

Suna Korkmaz

Chapter 8 Unemployment and Economic Growth: The Casuality Relationship between Unemployment and Economic Growth in the OECD Countries

Abstract: The governments of the countries implement some policies to solve the economic problems they consider important by examining their own economic conditions. The unemployment problem is seen as an important issue for many countries since it has a social dimension as well as its economic implications. Many countries aim to reduce unemployment by ensuring the economic growth. National governments target to employ more people by following the policies that expand the aggregate demand and increase the amount of goods and services produced in the economy. Therefore, in this study, whether there is a relationship between unemployment and economic growth or not for 8 randomly selected OECD countries (France, Germany, Greece, Italy, Belgium, Poland, Spain, Ireland), is investigated by running the panel causality test. The data set covers the quarterly period between 2016:01 and 2019:02. According to the results of the analysis, unidirectional causality relationship from unemployment to economic growth has been determined.

Keywords: Unemployment, Economic Growth, Panel Causality Test

1. Introduction

National governments aim to control some economic problems and go for a solution according to their own country conditions. For some countries, the inflation problem is a priority, whereas for others, achieving economic growth or reducing unemployment becomes the primary goal. When supply-side macroeconomic policies are adapted to ensure economic growth, demand-side macroeconomic policy is implemented to control unemployment and inflation. During the time supply-side macro economic policy is followed, monetary and fiscal policies are carried out. While demand-side macroeconomic policies are pursued, interventions are also applied on wage limits, interest rates and exchange rates, as well as monetary and fiscal policies.

Unemployment is seen as a serious macroeconomic problem for many countries since it has a social dimension as well as its economic issues. The economic dimension of unemployment is the emergence of a loss in production that will occur in the economy. If the unemployed labor had been employed in the production process, a production would have occurred, meaning it would create a monetary value. Actual production is below potential production since labor is not fully employed in the production process. This causes a production deficit in the economy. It is an undeniable reality where unemployment has a social dimension. People might lose their self-confidence when they are unemployed for a long time and they could give up looking for jobs because of getting offended. It might cause the person to move away from the society. In addition, unemployment might increase the tendency to crime in the society and cause damages both socially and economically. For these reasons, it becomes significant to take measures to reduce unemployment.

2. The Definition and Types of Unemployment

Non-institutional civilian population is the portion of a country's total population over the age of 15, except residents in places such as barracks, prisons and hospitals. Non-institutional civilian population consists of three groups: employed, not working and on an active job search (unemployed), not working and not on an active job search. The part of the non-institutional civilian population consisting of the sum of employed and unemployed persons is called labor force. Therefore, not working and not on an active job search group of the (non-institutional) civilian population represents the persons outside the labor force in the civilian population. This group of the civilian population is called not in labor force (Ünsal, 2017: 115).

Unemployment is the presence of a labor force with a capability and desire, and has willingness to work at the current wage level, but cannot find a job. First of all, in order for a person to be considered as unemployed, that person must have a capacity and desire to work. Secondly, he/she should display a willingness to work at the current wage in the market, and be ready to work as soon as finding a job at this wage level. The unemployment that arises under these conditions is an involuntary situation. Unemployment, which indicates the absence of a part of the laborforce, is measured by the unemployment rate. It is obtained by dividing the number of unemployed persons by the civilian labor force and multiplying that by 100 (Yıldırım et al., 2011: 28).

$$\text{Unemployment Rate} = (\text{Number of persons unemployed}/\text{Civilian Labor Force}) * 100 \qquad (1)$$

For instance, in a representative economy, let the persons employed in the population aged 15 and over be 25 million. In this case if the unemployed is 5 million, the unemployment rate is found to be 16 % as it is shown as follows:

$$\text{UnemploymentRate} = (5/30) * 100 = 0.16 * 100 = 16\%.$$

2.1. Types of Unemployment

Unemployment is categorized in different ways. Unemployment indicators are explained according to age, gender and educational status. However, unemployment is generally categorized under four headings: frictional unemployment, structural unemployment, natural unemployment and cyclical unemployment.

2.1.1. Frictional (Temporary) Unemployment

Frictional unemployment occurs due to the ordinary transitions in the labor market. It is not possible to eliminate such unemployment even when the economy is in full employment. Some people are involved in the labor force for the first time and seek for jobs, while others quit on their jobs to find another because they are not satisfied. These people prefer to be unemployed until they have jobs that satisfy them. From this point of view, a certain amount of frictional unemployment is inevitable or even desired (Yıldırım et al., 2016: 364). If a person finds a job according to his/her abilities and works there, his/her contribution would be higher as a result of the productivity. In addition, the employer would have found the best employee suitable for the company. As the information network between jobseekers and vacant jobs in an economy is developed, the time spent on finding a job is reduced and the temporary unemployment rate gets lower.

2.1.2. Structural Unemployment

In an economy, technology has been constantly changing. There has been a continuous change in products and technologies through the research and development (R&D) activities. The type of unemployment that occurs as a result of changes in labor demand due to structural changes in the economy, where some skills are abandoned or technology advances and there are changes in international competition, is called structural unemployment (Yıldırım et al., 2011: 31). Since technological change has been constantly changing, structural unemployment, just like frictional unemployment, is also a type of unemployment that cannot be eliminated. This type of unemployment lasts longer than frictional unemployment. Individuals who are unemployed due to technological changes have to acquire new skills or have to go elsewhere.

2.1.3. Natural Unemployment

The sum of frictional unemployment and structural unemployment in an economy is defined as natural unemployment.

$$\text{Natural Unemployment} = \text{Frictional Unemployment} + \text{StructuralUnemployment}$$

In an economy, when the current unemployment rate is equal to the natural unemployment rate ($u = u_N$), the wage rate and price level do not change. In other words, inflation does not tend to increase. For this reason, the natural unemployment rate is considered as the unemployment rate that does not accelerate inflation (Bocutoğlu, 2011: 71). If an economy has an unemployment rate of 3 % or 5 %, this unemployment rate is considered natural and is called natural unemployment.

2.1.4. Cyclical Unemployment

It is a type of unemployment that results from economic fluctuations. It emerges in certain periods in the economy. Cyclical unemployment is a short-term unemployment like frictional unemployment, there are two types of cyclical unemployment: seasonal and cyclical unemployment (Ünsal, 2017: 121). Seasonal unemployment occurs when economic activities lose their intensity at certain times of the year (Yıldırım et al., 2011: 31). Workers in the tourism and construction industry are generally unemployed when the workload in the winter season decreases. This situation is also experienced in the agricultural sector.

Cyclical unemployment is a type of unemployment that occurs due to the decrease in aggregate demand during the contraction and recession periods of economic fluctuations (Yıldırım et al., 2016: 365). In the cyclical unemployment, the actual product created in the economy is manufactured below the potential (natural) product.

3. Economic Growth

Economic growth is a concept related to the value of real Gross Domestic Product (GDP) from year to year. Economic growth is the real increase of GDP. If real GDP in an economy is increasing compared to the previous year, it means that the economy is growing. The measure of the economic growth is a concept related to the growth rate. It is the annual rate of increase in real GDP (Bocutoğlu, 2011: 59).

Annual growth rate in an economy is calculated as follows: $g = \frac{Y_t - Y_{t-1}}{Y_{t-1}} * 100$, where g indicates growth rate, Y_t real GDP of the current year, and Y_{t-1} real GDP of the previous year.

The growth rate in Turkey for 2018 according to expenditure approach (chain linked volume index 2009 = 100) is calculated as 2.8 %.

$$g_{2018} = \frac{Y_{2018} - Y_{2017}}{Y_{2017}} * 100 = \frac{1742022926 - 1694133563}{1694133563} * 100$$
$$= \frac{47889363}{1694133563} * 100 = 2,8\%$$

4. Literature Review

Zagler (2003), in his study conducted for the countries with four major European economies (France, Germany, Italy and England), found out that unemployment rate is positively correlated with economic growth in the long run, whereas the increase in unemployment rate decreases economic growth in the short run. Kim (2005) obtained a unidirectional causal relationship between unemployment and economic growth as a result of the Granger Causality Test for Korea with data covering the 1970–2002 period. Kreishan (2011) investigated the relationship between unemployment and economic growth in Jordan for the years between 1970 and 2008 within the context of Okun law. Empirical results show that Okun's law is not valid for Jordan. Kreishan emphasized that structural changes and reforms in the labor market should be implemented to reduce unemployment in Jordan. Mosikari (2013) could not find any causality relationship between unemployment rate and economic growth as a result of the Granger causality test conducted for South Africa with annual data covering the period 1980–2011. Shahid (2014) demonstrated that there was a relationship between unemployment and economic growth in Pakistan in the long run according to Autoregressive Distributed Lag (ARDL) method for the period between 1980 and 2010. Abdul-Khaliq et al. (2014) showed that economic growth had a negative and significant effect on unemployment rate as a result of the pooled EGLS (Cross-section SUR) method for 9 Arab countries with annual data covering the period 1994–2010. Alhdiy et al. (2015) found a Granger causality between unemployment rate and economic growth in Egypt in the short term for the quarterly data between 2006Q1 and 2013Q2. However, no causality relationship was obtained in the long term. Göçer and Erdal (2015) tested the relationship between youth unemployment rate and economic growth using panel data analysis method with the data period 2006–2012 for 18 Central and Eastern European countries, which are above the EU-28 average. The results of the analysis pointed out that only economic growth would not be sufficient alone for reducing youth unemployment in these countries, where the youth unemployment is high. Mohseni and Jouzaryan (2016) revealed that unemployment negatively affects economic growth in the long-term and reduces economic growth as a result of the ARDL method they conducted with data covering the period 1996–2012 for Iran. Dritsakis and Stamatiou (2016) analyzed the relationship between unemployment rate and economic growth in Greece by employing the ARDL method for the annual data covering the period 1995–2015. The findings showed that there was a unidirectional causality relationship from unemployment to economic growth in both the short and long term. Misini and Badivuku-Pantina (2017) revealed a significant and negative relationship between unemployment and economic growth in their study for Kosovo, with annual data covering the period 2004–2014. Accordingly, if the nominal GDP increases by 1 %, unemployment is negatively affected and decreases by an average of 0.43 %. Seth et al. (2018) demonstrated that there was no long-term relationship between unemployment rate and economic growth in Nigeria as a result of the ARDL method they conducted using annual secondary data for the period 1986–2015. Soylu et al. (2018) investigated the relationship between unemployment and economic growth for Eastern European countries by using the panel data method with data covering the period of 1992–2014. Test results have shown that unemployment is positively affected by economic growth. In other words, 1 % increase in GDP in Eastern European countries decreased unemployment rate by 0.08 %. Ellen and Wilson (2019) found a negative relationship between unemployment and economic growth, both in the short and long term, as a result of the ARDL method they employed with the annual data covering the period 1991–2018 for China.

5. Data Set and Methodology

In this study, whether there is a relationship between harmonized unemployment rate (HUR) and economic growth (GDP) in 8 randomly selected OECD countries (France, Germany, Greece, Italy, Belgium, Poland, Spain, Ireland) or not is investigated. In this context, persons not working and on an active job search were selected as unemployment data. The logarithm of this variable is taken and seasonally adjusted. Unemployment data is taken from the electronic data delivery system of OECD. On the other hand, economic growth data in terms of national accounts and at fixed prices is obtained from electronic data delivery system of IMF. The logarithm of the economic growth variable is also taken and seasonally adjusted. The data set covers the period between 2016:01 and 2019:02 on the quarterly basis.

5.1. Panel Unit Root Tests

Performing a unit root test in time series studies is becoming widespread among researchers and it becomes important for the series to be stationary in order to make the results significant in the econometric analysis. In the literature, various panel unit root tests were developed mainly by Levin et al. (2002), Quah (1994), Maddala and Wu (1999), Choi (2001), Kao (1999), Harris and Tzavalis (1999), Hadri (1999), Breitung (2000) and Harris and Sollis (2003) and so on (Baltagi and Kao, 2000; 2).

Apart from that, Bhargava, Franzini and Narendranathan (1982), Boumahdi and Thomas (1991), Breitung and Meyer (1994) proposed a new test in the Fixed Effective Dynamic Model. They intended Durbin Watson (DW) statistics as a new modified form of test statistics based on fixed effect residues and differentiated Ordinary Least Squared (OLS) residues. In micro panels, they suggested their own DW statistics as N approaches infinity. In addition to this, Quah (1994) suggested a unit root test in the panel data model where the N/T ratio is constant, N and T values approach to infinity and have no constant effects.

Levin et al. (2002) have developed this model to allow fixed effects, individual determining trends, and heterogeneous serial correlated errors. Levin et al. (2002) admit that the values of N and T approach to infinity. However, as the N/T ratio approaches to zero, T approaches to infinity at a higher rate than N (Maddala and Wu, 1999: 633). Im et al. (2003) determined that T value approaches to infinity while N value tends to infinity. When the N/T ratio is equal to k, under the assumption of a finite and non-negative k constant, the T and N values approach to infinity as a result of the cross convergence.

Tab. 8.1. Panel Unit Root Tests, Source: Author's own calculations

		I(0) Constant		I(1) Constant	
Variables	**Method**	**Statistic**	**Prob***	**Statistic**	**Prob***
LGDP	Levin Lin & Chu t*	-2.986	0.001*	-6.366	0.000*
	Im Pesaran and Shin W-stat	0.658	0.745	-5.515	0.000*
	ADF-Fisher Chi-square	14.014	0.597	58.180	0.000*
	PP-Fisher Chi-square	15.629	0.479	89.781	0.000*
LHUR	Levin Lin & Chu t*	-0.978	0.164	-9.978	0.000*
	Im Pesaran and Shin W-stat	2.989	0.998	-7.023	0.000*
	ADF-Fisher Chi-square	4.804	0.997	72.959	0.000*
	PP-Fisher Chi-square	7.701	0.957	91.707	0.000*

*Im, Pesaran and Shin; ADF-Fisher and PP-Fisher-Null Hypothesis: Unit root (Individual unit root process), Levin, Lin and Chu Test-Null Hypothesis: Unit root (Common unit root process). Automatic lag lenght selection based on Modified Schwarz Criteria and Bartlett Kernel.

In this study, stationarity of the variables is determined by running Levin et al., Im, Pesaran and Shin (IPS), Augmented Dickey Fuller (ADF), and Phillips-Perron (PP) stationarity tests. From these tests, which are among the first generation stationarity tests, it is seen that GDP and HUR series have only a constant and no trend as a result of all the tests. Accordingly, GDP and HUR series are stationary in the first difference at 5 % significance level according to the LLC, IPS, ADF-Fisher, ADF, and PP-Fisher tests. These results are given in Tab. 8.1.

5.2. Granger Causality Test

The series compared in the application have deterministic elements and are far from being covariance-stationary. For this reason, the deterministic elements such as trend, seasonal mobility are removed from the series and the causality relationship of the series, which became stationary by taking their logarithms and first-order differences, was examined to ensure the covariance-stationary. It is formulated as follows (Şen et al., 2018: 135):

$$\Delta LGDP_{1t} = \alpha_{11} + \sum_{l=1}^{P_1} \beta_{11l}\Delta LGDP_{1t-l} + \sum_{l=1}^{P_1} \delta_{11l}\Delta LHUR_{1t-l} + \varepsilon_{11t} \quad (2)$$

$$\Delta LGDP_{Nt} = \alpha_{1N} + \sum_{l=1}^{P_1} \beta_{1Nl}\Delta LGDP_{Nt-l} + \sum_{l=1}^{P_1} \delta_{1Nl}\Delta LHUR_{Nt-l} + \varepsilon_{1Nt}$$

Tab. 8.2. Granger Causality Test, Source: Author's own calculations

Null Hypothesis:	Obs	F-Statistic	Prob.
ΔLGDP does not Granger cause ΔLHUR	88	2.509	0.087
ΔLHUR does not Granger cause ΔLGDP		3.462	0.036*

H_0 = HUR does not cause GDP
H_1 = HUR cause GDP.
In the first hypothesis, H_0 hypothesis is rejected because the probability value is less than 5 %. So, there is a unidirectional causality relationship from HUR to GDP.
H0 = GDP does not cause HUR
H1 = GDP cause HUR.

$$\Delta LHUR_{1t} = \alpha_{21} + \sum_{l=1}^{P_2} \beta_{21l} \Delta LGDP_{1t-l} + \sum_{l=1}^{P_2} \delta_{21l} \Delta LHUR_{1t-l} + \varepsilon_{21t} \quad (3)$$

$$\Delta LHUR_{Nt} = \alpha_{2N} + \sum_{l=1}^{P_2} \beta_{2Nl} \Delta LGDP_{Nt-l} + \sum_{l=1}^{P_2} \delta_{2Nl} \Delta LHUR_{Nt-l} + \varepsilon_{2Nt}$$

In the equations above, N refers to the number of countries in the panel (i = 1,2, 3, . . .,N), t time period (t = 1,2,3,. . ., T) and "l" lag length. The error terms ε_{1Nt}, ε_{2Nt}, ε_{3Nt} are assumed to be white noise (they have zero mean and constant variance).
In another hypothesis specified in Tab. 8.2, the H_0 hypothesis is accepted because the probability value is greater than 5 %. Therefore, no causality relationship from GDP to HUR was found. According to the results of the analysis, there is a relationship between unemployment and economic growth.

The Panel Granger causality test indicates to a unidirectional causality relationship from unemployment to economic growth. In this study, similar results are obtained with the studies of Kim (2005), Shahid (2014), Alhdiy et al. (2015), Dritsakis and Stamatiou (2016) and Soylu (2018).

Unemployment has a social dimension as well as its economic dimension. When there is unemployment in an economy, it causes goods and services not to be produced and thus product loss. This situation is called as gross domestic product deficit in the economy. For this reason, governments aim to realize the economic growth to reduce the unemployment. Governments implement monetary and fiscal policies that support economic growth. Expansionary monetary and fiscal policies are among the most frequently used policies to support economic growth. As a monetary policy, it can make purchases of open market operations, reduce the rediscount rates, decrease the reserve requirement rate and lower the interest rates. As an expansionary fiscal policy, it can increase the government spending and the transfer payments whereas lower the tax rates. As a result of implementing these policies, the aggregate demand for goods and services will increase. Correspondingly, as the aggregate demand for goods and services increases, production will expand and the income level created in the economy will go up. With the output growth, more people will be employed and therefore unemployment will decrease.

6. Conclusion

In this study, since the unemployment is a major problem for many countries, whether there is a relationship between unemployment (HUR) and economic growth (GDP) or not, is investigated by running a Panel Causality Test for randomly selected 8 OECD countries (France, Germany, Greece, Italy, Belgium, Poland, Spain, Ireland). The data set covers the period between 2016:01 and 2019:02 on the quarterly basis. According to the results of the Panel Granger causality test, unidirectional causality relationship is found from unemployment to economic growth. In a sense, this means that unemployment requires economic growth to occur.

Since the unemployment has become a social problem in the economy in a sense, the governments of the countries aim to realize economic growth. As the economy grows, the number of people employed in the economy will increase, thus unemployment will decrease. To achieve the economic growth, governments implement expansionary monetary and fiscal policies. By expanding the amount of money in the market, they increase the aggregate demand for goods and services. As one of the monetary policy tool, by keeping interest rates low, an increase in investments in the economy can be achieved. The rise in investments in the economy will ensure many people to be employed, thus it will reduce unemployment in the economy. It will also enhance the aggregate demand for goods and services in the economy. On the other hand, national governments can implement some fiscal policies targeting economic growth. Governments can increase their purchase of goods and services by expanding the government spendings in the economy. By lowering the tax rates, they can also boost the demand for the goods and services in the economy, increasing the income that individuals and corporations can spend. In the countries with a social state understanding, governments can increase aggregate demand in the economy by increasing transfer payments.

References

Abdul-Khaliq, S., Soufan, T. and Shihab, R. A. (2014). The Relationship between Unemployment and Economic Growth Rate in Arab Country. *Developing Country Studies*, 4 (7), 62–66.

Alhdiy, F. M., Johari, F., Daud, S. N. M. and Rahman, A. A. (2015). Short and Long Term Relationship between Economic Growth and Unemployment in Egypt: An Empirical Analysis. *Mediterranean Journal of Social Sciences*, 6 (4) S3, 454–462.

Baltagi, B. H. and Kao, C. (2000). Nonstationary Panels, Cointegration in Panels and Dynamic Panels: A Survey, *Center for Policy Research Working Papers*, 16.

Bhargava, A., Franzini, L. and Narendranathan, W. (1982). Serial Correlation and Fixed Effects Model, *The Review of Economic Studies*, 49 (4), 533–549.

Bocutoğlu, E. (2011). *Makro İktisat Teoriler ve Politikalar*, 8. Baskı, Trabzon: Murathan Yayınevi.

Boumahdi, R. and Thomas, A. (1991). Testing for Unit Roots Using Panel Data: Application to the French Stock Market Efficiency. *Economic Letters*, 37 (1), 77–79.

Breitung, J. (2000). The Local Power of Some Unit Root Tests for Panel Data. *Advances in Econometrics*, 15, 161–177.

Breitung, J. and Meyer, W. (1994). Testing for Unit Roots in Panel Data: Are Wages on Different Bargaining Levels Cointegrated. *Applied Economics*, 26 (4), 353–361.

Choi, I. (2001). Unit Root Tests for Panel Data. *Journal of International Money and Finance*, 20, 249–272.

Dritsakis, N. and Stamatiou, P. (2016). The Effects of Unemployment on Economic Growth in Greece. An ARDL Bound Test Approach. *Romanian Economic Journal*, 19 (62), 53–72.

Ellen, K.-A. and Wilson, A. (2019). The Impact of Unemployment on Economic Growth in China. MPRA Paper, No. 96100, mpra.ub.uni-muenchen.de/96100/1/MPRA_paper_96100.pdf

Göçer, İ. and Erdal, L. (2015). The Relationship between Youth Unemployment and Economic Growth in Central and Eastern European Countries: An Empirical Analysis. *Çankırı Karatekin Üniversitesi İktisadi ve İdari Bilimler Fakültesi Dergisi*, 5 (1), 173–188.

Harris and Sollis (2003). *Applied Time Series Modelling and Forecasting*. West Sussex: John Wiley.

Im, K. S., Pesaran, M. H. and Shin, Y. (2003). Testing for Unit Roots in Heterogeneous Panels. *Journal of Econometrics,* 115 (1), 53–74.

Kao, C. (1999). Spurious Regression and Residual-based Tests for Cointegration in Panel Data. *Journal of Econometrics*, 90 (1), 1–44.

Kim, D.-K. (2005). Unionization, Unemployment, and Growth in Korea: A Cointegration Approach. *Atlantic Economic Journal*, 33 (2), 225–233.

Kreishan, F. M. (2011). Economic Growth and Unemployment: An Empirical Analysis. *Journal of Social Sciences,* 7 (2), 228–231.

Levin, A., Lin, C.-F., and Chu, C.-S. (2002). Unit Root Tests in Panel Data: Asymptotic and Finite-Sample Properties. *Journal of Econometrics*, 108, 1–24.

Maddala, G. S. and Wu, S. (1999). A Comparative Study of Unit Root Tests with Panel Data and a New Simple Test. *Oxford Bulletin of Economics and Statistics*, 61 (1), 631–652.

Misini, S. and Badivuku-Pantina, M. (2017). The Effect of Economic Growth in Relation to Unemployment. *Journal of Economics and Economic Education Research*, 18 (2), 1–9.

Mohseni, M. and Jouzaryan, F. (2016). Examining the Effects of Inflation and Unemployment on Economic Growth in Iran (1996–2012). *Procedia Economics and Finance*, 36, 381–389.

Mosikari, T. J. (2013). The Effect of Unemployment Rate on Gross Domestic Product: Case of South Africa. *Mediterranean Journal of Social Sciences*, 4 (6), 429–434.

Quah, D. (1994). Exploiting Cross Section Variation for Unit Root Inference in Dynamic Data. *Economics Letters*, 44 (1–2), 9–19.

Şen, H., Kaya, A. and Alpaslan, B. (2018). Education, Health, and Economic Growth Nexus: A Bootstrap Panel Granger Causality Analysis for Developing Countries. *Sosyoekonomi*, 26 (36), 125–144.

Seth, A., John, M. A. and Dalhatu, A. Y. (2018). The Impact of Unemployment on Economic Growth in Nigeria: An Application of Autoregressive Distributed Lag (ARDL) Bound Testing. *Sumerianz Journal of Business Management and Marketing*, 1 (2), 37–46.

Shahid, M. (2014). Effect of Inflation and Unemployment on Economic Growth in Pakistan. *Journal of Economics and Sustainable Development*, 5 (15), 103–106.

Soylu, Ö. B., Çakmak, İ. and Okur, F. (2018). Economic Growth and Unemployment Issue: Panel Data Analysis in Eastern European Countries. *Journal of International Studies*, 11 (1), 93–107.

Ünsal, E. M. (2017). *Makro İktisat,* 11. Baskı, Ankara: Murat Yayınları.

Yıldırım, K., Bakırtaş, İ., Yılmaz, R. and Esen, E. (2011). *Makro İktisada Giriş*, 6. Baskı, Ankara: Pelikan Kitabevi.

Yıldırım, K., Karaman, D. and Taşdemir, M. (2016). *Makroekonomi*, 13. Baskı, Ankara: Seçkin Yayınevi.

Zagler, M. (2003). A Vector Error Correction Model of Economic Growth and Unemployment in Major European Countries and an Analysis of Okun's Law. *Applied Econometrics and International Development*, 3 (3), 93–118.

Özlem Ayvaz Kızılgöl and Özlem Kuvat

Chapter 9 Analysis of the OECD Countries' Better Living Index with the Entropy Based GRA and WASPAS Methods

Abstract: Increasing interest in welfare assessment in recent years has enabled the use of a wide variety of statistical and decision-making techniques to measure well being at regional and national levels. One of the most important studies conducted to determine the welfare level of countries is the Better Life Index, which was created by the Organisation for Economic Co-operation and Development (OECD). OECD collects data from countries and compiles the Better Life Index, which gives more details about people's daily life. With this contribution, people can compare countries' living standards under different indicators. In this study, better life evaluation is made by using the multi-criteria decision making methods, Gray Relational Analysis (GRA) and the Weighted Aggregates Sum Product Assessment (WASPAS). Criterion weights in the study were determined by the entropy method. The methods were applied to 15 alternative countries and 24 indicators in the OECD Better Life Index data. Looking at the results of the analysis, United Kingdom ranked first and Latvia ranked last, according to the GRA method. According to the WASPAS method, United States ranked first, while Latvia ranked last. According to the findings, it was seen that the ranking results were close to each other. In the analysis, the biggest order difference was realized for Spain, United States and Austria.

Keywords: Better Life Index, Entropy, Gray Relational Analysis, WASPAS

1. Introduction

Recent economic events and developments related to welfare have attracted great attention in the literature. Welfare has a great importance not only for developing countries but also for all the world economies, because the measurement of welfare indicates to what extent social progress is achieved in the countries. Therefore, welfare is an important factor for societies and individuals. As the welfare of societies and individuals increases, the economies of the countries develop and economic development takes place (Eren Şenaras and Çetin, 2016: 35).

The well-being of people is the main objective of development economics. Welfare began to be measured with the human development approach in the

1990s. In the 2000s, universal rights and freedoms came to the fore (Eren Şenaras and Çetin, 2016: 35). With the globalization, technological developments and the diversification of communication tools that started in the 1990s, the changing living conditions have modified the well-being measurement criterions (Koçhisarlı and Özarı, 2019: 471; Akar, 2014: 2). While the models in which only income is frequently used lose their importance, other variables have begun to be included in the models as an indicator of welfare (Başol, 2018: 75). There was a need for more comprehensive indices similar to GDP but including global threats such as climate change, environment, income, education, health and quality of life of societies (Kulesza and Ucieklak-Jez, 2012: 184). In this process, the necessity of developing new approaches in defining and measuring welfare has emerged. According to Stiglitz, Sen and Fitoussi (2009), multiple criteria are required to define and measure well-being, not just a single criterion like GDP. Accordingly, the criteria used to measure the quality of life and well-being are the required living standards, such as income and consumption; personal activities including health, education and work; political participation, social connections and relationships, climate, economic and physical safety environment (Koçhisarlı and Özarı, 2019: 471; Gündoğan Aşık and Altın Yavuz, 2018: 2549; Başol, 2018: 75; Eren Şenaras and Çetin, 2016: 36; Stiglitz et al., 2009: 14).

In light of these developments, the OECD has developed a new index that defines and measures well-being more broadly. The organization named this index, which it put into practice in 2011, as the "Better Life Index" (Başol, 2018: 75). The index currently has 24 criteria (see Tab. 9.1). For each criterion, countries are evaluated on a scale from 0 to 10. A country's score is obtained by the weighted average of the criteria. In this index, all indicators defining well-being are listed side by side instead of hierarchical order (Kerényi, 2011: 518). The index aims to measure the welfare level and its changes in the countries. It also provides the opportunity to make evaluations between countries with multiple criteria determined in economic and social fields. In addition to determine the global wealth of countries, it also addresses different welfare indicators in various fields (Koçhisarlı and Özarı, 2019: 472; Kasparian and Rolland, 2012: 2223). The index allows countries to be ranked and compared in a better, faster and easier way. By measuring the welfare and better quality of life of countries in various fields, presenting their performances comparatively, it enables countries to produce more qualified solutions in the issues they are weak (Kulesza and Ucieklak-Jez, 2012: 188). Thus, countries can develop policies on the criteria they fall behind and implement them to maximize the welfare of individuals.

The OECD offers the rankings of countries based on each indicator used in the better life index. Therefore, it does not make a general ranking by using all indicators. The aim of this study is to rank for OECD countries with GRA and WASPAS, which are Multi Criteria Decision Making (MCDM) methods, as an alternative approach in measuring life standards and quality and well-being by using better life index data. Entropy method was used for weighting in the evaluation of the indicators, thus facilitating the application without binary comparison in the study. It is thought that this study, which has been empirically analyzed with current data of the better life index and MCDM techniques, which are rarely used, will contribute to the literature.

The other parts of the study are discussed as follows: Empirical studies in the literature will be examined in the second section, and entropy in the third one. After the introducing GRA and WASPAS methods in the fourth and fifth sections respectively, the variables used in the analysis will be explained and the findings will be interpreted in the sixth section. Finaly the results and the assessment will be given in the conclusion section.

2. Literature

Determining the quality of life, which has been the focus of attention of researchers in recent years, has become a frequently studied topic in the literature. MCDM is one of the methods generally used in the studies. Various researches that make empirical analysis using these methods are mentioned below.

Akdamar (2019) examined 35 OECD countries using 4 labor market indicators. Labor market indicators are 4 sub-indicators (labor market insecurity, employment rate, long-term unemployment rate and personal earnings) under the heading "Labor Force" among 11 performance indicators in OECD's "Better Life Index". Hierarchical clustering analysis and multidimensional scaling analysis were used in the study. OECD countries are divided into 4 clusters as a result of hierarchical clustering analysis. According to the multidimensional scaling analysis, a low stress value was obtained and the positions of OECD countries were shown in a two-dimensional space with a good to excellent fit. The analysis results pointed out that the most important indicator in the clustering of countries is labor market insecurity. Ela and Soysal Kurt (2019) aimed to compare the macroeconomic performances of 8 Sub-Saharan African countries in 2016 with the TOPSIS method. For this, they used 4 macroeconomic indicators consisting of GDP growth rate, inflation rate, unemployment rate and current account balance (as percentage of GDP) variables. According to the analysis results, Ivory Coast and Tanzania showed the best macroeconomic performance, while South Sudan displayed the worst macroeconomic performance. Koçhisarlı and Özarı (2019) aimed to rank the Scandinavian countries with TOPSIS method, one of the MCDM methods, using the OECD's better life index indicators. Thus, they determined which of the four countries had better standards when considering the better life index criteria. As a result of the analysis, it was found that the country in the first place, that is the country with the best performance, is Denmark. Türe (2019) used a methodological approach that drives the GRA with the Entropy base in order to rank the welfare levels of 34 OECD countries. Welfare measurement was examined for the 15-year period (2000–2014), taking into account the two-dimensional framework of the OECD. In the study, it was found that Iceland, Australia, Norway and Switzerland reached the highest welfare level. Hungary, Greece, Turkey and Mexico were observed to have a relatively low level of prosperity. Yıldız et al. (2019) analyzed 31 European Union member countries by examining the criteria set by the European Union to evaluate the life quality of the countries. Criterion weights were acquired by using the binary comparison matrix, which was obtained by employing the Pythagorean Fuzzy Analytic Hierarchy Process (AHP) method and Modified Delphi Method. The TOPSIS method was used to rank 31 countries according to the quality of life. The top 5 countries with high quality of life were found to be Norway, Denmark, Switzerland, Finland and Sweden. Kılıç Depren and Bağdatlı Kalkan (2018) have ranked the countries using the 2017 better life index data created by the OECD. They determined the criterion weights with Entropy and obtained the order with the Multimoora method. They stated that the rankings obtained by the entropy-based Multimoora method gave accurate and reliable results both statistically and socio-economically. Gündoğan Aşık and Altın Yavuz (2018) aimed to classify OECD countries with multivariate statistical techniques according to the better life index for 2016. With the help of this classification, they investigated whether the effects of variables affecting life satisfaction were statistically significant or not. They used 6 different classification techniques in their studies. These are discriminant analysis, robust discriminant analysis, logistic regression analysis, robust logistic regression analysis, logistic ridge regression analysis and robust logistic ridge regression analysis. According to authors, the results from the statistical models depend on assumptions. Başol (2018) aimed to determine the dynamics affecting life satisfaction in 35 OECD member countries, using the better life index data for 2016. For this purpose, he has used structural equation modeling and model development strategy. Analysis results showed that health and positive job quality positively affect life satisfaction, while income and negative job quality negatively affect life satisfaction. Monica (2018) focuses on potential weighting schemes and their effects on the final value of variables along with the order they produce. After describing the basic features and elements of well-being criteria and collection procedures in general, she presented the results of an empirical study based on the Better Life Index. The main findings of this research are the results showing the effect of different weight combinations. Descriptive statistics and correlation analysis were applied to show the findings of varying weight simulations. This article concludes with additional questions that outline further research directions. Peiro′-Palomino and Picazo-Tadeo (2018) proposed a composite welfare indicator for 35 OECD countries, as well as South Africa, Russia and Brazil during the 2013–2016 period. In the first stage of the study, countries were ranked by using data envelopment analysis with the benefit-of-the-doubt principle and MCDM techniques on the basis of welfare indicators, and in the second stage, groups related to the wealth level were determined using hierarchical clustering analysis. Sevgin and Kundakçı (2017) sorted European Union countries and Turkey for the year 2013 according to development levels by using six economic indicators with the MOORA and TOPSIS methods. At the end of the study, it was determined that Croatia, Bulgaria, Slovenia, Greece and Turkey were ranked last while Luxemburg, Switzerland and Denmark were ranked near to the top. Ömürbek, Eren, and Dağ (2017) have demonstrated the life quality of European Union member countries with ARAS and MOORA methods. They formed the weights of the indicators used with entropy. As a result of the study, Finland ranked first in both methods. Genç, Avcı and Sevgin (2017) aimed to analyze the efficiency of the Organization of the Black Sea Economic Cooperation member countries by using macroeconomic variables such as imports, unemployment and inflation as input, and macroeconomic variables such as employment, export and per capita GDP as output. For efficiency analysis, ARAS, TOPSIS, and MOORA methods are used. AHP method is employed to find the weighting scores. According to the analysis, it was seen that the MOORA and TOPSIS methods gave results closer to each other. In the rankings made by three different methods, the Russian Federation, Azerbaijan and Romania took the first places, whereas Serbia, Armenia and Albania took the last places. Orakçı and Özdemir (2017) determined the human development indexes of European Union member countries and Turkey by using the variables elected from Human Development Index and European Life Quality Survey. In the study, MOORA and Gray Relational Analysis methods were used to determine the human development levels of the countries. The effect levels of variables were evaluated with CRITIC and Entropy weighting methods. As a result of the study, the top three countries having the highest human development levels were the United Kingdom, Holland and Denmark based on MOORA-Reference point while the top three countries having the highest human development level were Luxemburg, Finland and Austria based on MOORA-Ratio and Gray Relational Analysis method. Önay (2016) evaluated the OECD's Better Life Index with TOPSIS, MOORA Ratio System and MOORA Reference Point Approach methods. The ranking of the countries was obtained by applying the methods to 24 criteria and 36 countries that generate the index. There are some differences between the rankings of countries according to the methods. Despite of the changes in the ranking, some countries are at the top it. The USA and Switzerland dominate the first two rows of the ranking list for each of the three methods. The United States, Switzerland, and Canada dominate the top three rankings for the TOPSIS and MOORA-Ratio System methods. Eren Şenaras and Çetin (2016) evaluated OECD countries in terms of a better life index by using the multidimensional scaling method. According to the findings, it is established that in the primary dimension America, Australia, Denmark, Sweden, Switzerland, Canada, Norway and New Zealand were perceived similarly, whereas Mexico, Chile and Turkey were perceived as the most different countries. The first studies on the Quality of Life Index were made by Kasparian and Rolland (2012). In their work, they have created a Better Quality of Life Index on the basis of various data obtained from OECD countries. Based on the 2011 dataset, they systematically tested all integer weight sets from zero to five for each country and each dimension (for 34 countries). They conclude that the innovative framework of Better Life Index as a better life model defines the quasi-hierarchy among the evaluated countries; because binary comparisons depend very little on the weight selection set. They also released the constraint of integer weights of dimensions. Moreover they stated that "the Better Life Index defines a hierarchy of the countries, which is only marginally affected by the choice of the weights". Özden (2012) measured the economic performance of the European Union member countries and Turkey for the year 2010 by using eight economic variables. He then ranked the countries according to these indicators. As a result of the study, it was determined that Luxembourg has the highest economic performance, while Greece has the lowest economic performance. At the end of the study Turkey took the 24th place of 28 countries. Kaya et al. (2011) made the life quality ranking of European Union and candidate countries by using VIKOR method. The ranking has been taken separately for the years 2003, 2005 and 2007. In addition, 12 main criteria and related sub-criteria given in the European quality of life questionnaire were used. As a result of the research, it was determined that Sweden and Denmark had the best quality of life in 2005, and Spain had the best quality of life in 2003 and 2007. It was concluded that Turkey approached to the last place in every three years.

3. Entropy

Entropy method is one of the widely used methods to determine the criterion weights in MCDM problems. It is an effective method in terms of probability theory for a formulated measure of uncertain information. It is widely used to determine the relative importance of criteria based on the evaluation information made by decision makers. In this method, the relative importance of each criterion is reflected with the intrinsic decision information and objective weights are calculated according to the entropy value. Objective weights based on entropy value are determined according to the following steps (Zhou, Lin, Wang, Zhou and He, 2016: 9):
Step 1: While the number of evaluation criteria C_1 , C_2 , .., C_n is n and the alternative number A_1 , A_2 , .., A_m is m, x_{ij} indicated the performance of the ith alternative and jth criterion. Accordingly the decision matrix is given in the Equation 1 below.

$$X = \begin{bmatrix} x_{11} & x_{12} & \dots & x_{1n} \\ x_{21} & x_{22} & \dots & x_{2n} \\ \vdots & \vdots & \vdots & \vdots \\ \vdots & \vdots & \vdots & \vdots \\ x_{m1} & x_{m2} & \dots & x_{mn} \end{bmatrix} \tag{1}$$

For the normalization of the X decision matrix, P_{ij} values are determined as given in the Equation 2 below (Zhou et al., 2016: 9):

$$P_{ij} = x_{ij} / \sum_{i=1}^{m} x_{ij} \tag{2}$$

Step 2: Using the P_{ij} values, e_{ij} entropy information is calculated for each criterion. ($e_0 = 1/lnm$) is the entropy constant. Its formula is given in the Equation 3 (Ghorbani, Bahrami and Arabzad, 2012: 523):

$$e_j = -e_0 \sum_{i=1}^{m} p_{ij} \ln p_{ij} = -(1/\ln m).\sum_{i=1}^{m} p_{ij} \ln p_{ij} \quad j = 1, 2, \dots n \tag{3}$$

Step 3: The weight for each criterion is determined. d_j is the degree of diversification and is formulized as $d_j = 1 - e_j$. The calculation for the weight is given in the Equation 4 (Ghorbani et al., 2012: 523):

$$w_j = d_j / \sum_{j=1}^{n} d_j \tag{4}$$

4. Gray Relational Analysis-GRA

The principle of GRA used in MCDM problems is to analyze the similarity relationship between reference sequence and alternative sequence. The selected alternative sequence, which has the closest similarity to the reference sequence, gives the best scheme of the decision problem (Wu, 2017: 7915). The stages are given as follows:

Step 1: The m criteria sequence that will be subject to comparison regarding the decision problem are determined. The representation $x_i = (x_i(j), \ldots x_i(n))$, $i = 1, 2, \ldots, m; j = 1, 2, \ldots n$ can be used while specifying the sequences. In MCDM problems, the alternatives are x_i and the values taken by the alternatives for each criterion are displayed with $x_i(j)$ (Yıldırım, 2014: 232):

After the sequences are created, the decision matrix expressed with the X matrix is obtained as it is given in Equation 5 (Ecer and Boyukaslan, 2014: 65):

$$X = \begin{bmatrix} x_1(1) & x_1(2) & \ldots & x_1(n) \\ x_2(1) & x_2(2) & \ldots & x_2(n) \\ \vdots & \vdots & \vdots & \vdots \\ \vdots & \vdots & \vdots & \vdots \\ x_m(1) & x_m(2) & \ldots & x_m(n) \end{bmatrix} \tag{5}$$

Step 2: After the decision matrix is created, the reference sequence and comparison matrix are generated. The reference sequence to be determined to compare the factors in the decision problem is shown as $x_0 = (x_0(j))$ $j = 1, 2, \ldots, n$. Here $x_0(j)$, indicates the highest value among the normalized values of jth criterion. The reference sequence is added to the first row of the decision matrix created in the previous step and transformed into a comparison matrix (Yıldırım, 2014: 232).

Step 3. Normalization process and creation of normalization matrix vary depending on the purpose. The calculations made according to the purposes are given in Equation 6, 7 and 8. $x_{ob}(j)$ in the Equation 8 is determined as the optimal value and it is the target value of criterion j and satisfies the condition $\max_j x_i(j) > x_{ob}(j) > \min_j x_i(j)$ (Yıldırım, 2014: 232):

$$x_i^* = \frac{x_i(j) - \min_j x_i(j)}{\max_j x_i(j) - \min_j x_i(j)} \text{ Larger the better (beneficial) condition} \quad (6)$$

$$x_i^* = \frac{\max_j x_i(j) - x_i(j)}{\max_j x_i(j) - \min_j x_i(j)} \text{ Smaller the better (cost) condition} \quad (7)$$

$$x_i^* = \frac{|x_i(j) - x_{ob}(j)|}{\max_j x_i(j) - x_{ob}(j)} \text{ Closest to the desired value (Optimal) condition} \quad (8)$$

Following the normalization steps, the decision matrix is transformed into a normalization matrix and denoted by X^*. The representation of the matrix is given in the Equation 9 (Ecer and Boyukaslan, 2014: 65):

$$X^* = \begin{bmatrix} x_1^*(1) & x_1^*(2) & \dots & x_1^*(n) \\ x_2^*(1) & x_2^*(2) & \dots & x_2^*(n) \\ \vdots & \vdots & \vdots & \vdots \\ \vdots & \vdots & \vdots & \vdots \\ x_m^*(1) & x_m^*(2) & \dots & x_m^*(n) \end{bmatrix} \quad (9)$$

Step 4: To create the absolute value table, the value $\Delta_{0i}(j)$ of the absolute difference between x_0^* and x_i^* is calculated as in the Equation 10 given below (Wu, 2017: 7915):

$$\Delta_{0i} = |x_0^*(j) - x_i^*(j)| \quad i = 1, 2, \dots, m; j = 1, 2, \dots n$$

$$\Delta_{0i} = \begin{bmatrix} \Delta_{01}(1) & \Delta_{01}(2) & \dots & \Delta_{01}(n)) \\ \Delta_{02}(1) & \Delta_{02}(2) & \dots & \Delta_{02}(n) \\ \vdots & \vdots & \vdots & \vdots \\ \vdots & \vdots & \vdots & \vdots \\ \Delta_{0m}(1) & \Delta_{0m}(2) & \dots & \Delta_{0m}(n) \end{bmatrix} \quad (10)$$

Step 5: The elements of the gray relational coefficient matrix for the criteria are calculated using the Equation 11 given below. The parameter Δ in the equation is the Distinguishing Coefficient and takes values between 0 and 1 interval. It is seen in the literature that 0.5 is generally used to minimize the error (Huang, Jane and Chang, 2010: 1015):

$$\gamma_{0i}(j) = \frac{\Delta_{\min} + \varsigma\Delta_{\max}}{\Delta_{0i}(j) + \varsigma\Delta_{\max}}$$

$$\Delta_{max} = \max_{\forall i} \max_{\forall j} \Delta_{0i}(j)$$

$$\Delta_{min} = \min_{\forall i} \min_{\forall j} \Delta_{0i}(j) \tag{11}$$

Step 6: Gray relational grades are calculated. The gray relational grade Γ_{0i} refers to the correlation level between x_i^* sequence and x_0^* reference sequence. It indicates the degree of similarity between the comparability sequence and the reference sequence. w_j is the weight of criterion j and generally depends on decision makers' decision or the nature of the proposed problem. It also satisfies the $\sum_{j=1}^{n} w_j$ condition (Kuo, Yang and Huang, 2008: 83).

Considering the criterion weights, the relational grade of the sequences can be calculated as given in the Equation 12. For decision making processes, if any alternative has the highest value of Γ_{0i}, it indicates that it is the most important alternative (Ecer and Boyukaslan, 2014: 65).

$$\Gamma_{0i} = \sum_{j=1}^{n} [w_i(j) . \gamma_{0i}(j)] \quad i = 1, 2, \ldots, m \tag{12}$$

5. WASPAS

In the WASPAS method, while m is the number of alternatives and n is the number of evaluation criteria, x_{ij} indicates ith alternative and jth criterion. And the decision matrix taken into account is given in the Equation 13 below:

$$X = \begin{bmatrix} x_{11} & x_{12} & \ldots & x_{1n} \\ x_{21} & x_{22} & \ldots & x_{2n} \\ \vdots & \vdots & \vdots & \vdots \\ \vdots & \vdots & \vdots & \vdots \\ x_{m1} & x_{m2} & \ldots & x_{mn} \end{bmatrix} \tag{13}$$

While applying the WASPAS method, the combination of two well-known MCDM (multi-criteria decision making) approaches, namely the weighted sum model (WSM) and the weighted product model (WPM), is used (Chakraborty and Zavadskas, 2014: 2).

Step 1: In the first stage, linear normalization of decision matrix elements is provided by using the equations given in the Equation 14 below (Chakraborty, Bhattacharyya, Zavadskas, and Antucheviciene, 2015: 78):

$$\text{For beneficial criteria,} \quad \bar{x}_{ij} = x_{ij} / \max_i x_{ij}$$

$$\text{For non-beneficial criteria,} \quad \bar{x}_{ij} = \min_i x_{ij} / x_{ij} \tag{14}$$

Step 2: The relative importance values for each alternative are calculated according to the WSM and WPM methods as given in the Equation 15. Here w_j is the criterion weights (Stanujkić and Karabašević, 2018: 33):

$$Q_i^{WSM} = \sum_{j=1}^{n} w_j.(\bar{x}_{ij})$$

$$Q_i^{WPM} = \prod_{j=1}^{n} (\bar{x}_{ij})^{w_j} \tag{15}$$

Step 3: In cases where two models have equal power, joint optimality value is calculated according to the Equation 16 given below (Chakraborty and Zavadskas, 2014: 3):

$$Q_i = 0,5Q_i^{WSM} + 0,5Q_i^{WPM} = 0,5\sum_{j=1}^{n} w_j.(\bar{x}_{ij}) + 0,5\prod_{j=1}^{n} (\bar{x}_{ij})^{w_j} \tag{16}$$

6. Empirical Analysis

In this study, 15 countries, which take place in Better Life Index with complete data based on their ranking under 11 main criteria and 24 sub-criteria, are included. These main criteria are Housing, Income, Jobs, Community, Education, Environment, Civic engagement, Health, Life Satisfaction, Safety, Work-Life Balance. The analyzed countries in alphabetical order are: Austria,

Tab. 9.1: Better Life Index Indicators, Source: OECD

	Main Criteria		Indicator/ Sub Criteria	Unit
1	Housing	HO1	Dwellings without basic facilities	Percentage
2		HO2	Housing expenditure	Percentage
3		HO3	Rooms per person	Ratio
4	Income	I1	Household net adjusted disposable income	US Dollar
5		I2	Household net wealth	US Dollar
6	Jobs	J1	Labour market insecurity	Percentage
7		J2	Employment rate	Percentage
8		J3	Long-term unemployment rate	Percentage
9		J4	Personal earnings	US Dollar
10	Community	CO1	Quality of support network	Percentage
11	Education	ED1	Educational attainment	Percentage
12		ED2	Student skills	Average score
13		ED3	Years in education	Years
14	Environment	EN1	Air pollution	Micrograms per cubic metre
15		EN2	Water quality	Percentage
16	Civic engagement	CI1	Stakeholder engagement for developing regulations	Average score
17		CI2	Voter turnout	Percentage
18	Health	HE1	Life expectancy	Years
19		HE2	Self-reported health	Percentage
20	Life Satisfaction	L1	Life satisfaction	Average score
21	Safety	S1	Feeling safe walking alone at night	Percentage
22		S2	Homicide rate	Ratio
23	Work-Life	W1	Employees working very long hours	Percentage
24	Balance	W2	Time devoted to leisure and personal care	Hours

Belgium, Canada, Denmark, Estonia, Finland, France, Germany, Italy, Latvia, Poland, Slovenia, Spain, United Kingdom and United States (OECD, 2020).

The indicators considered and their codes and units are given in the Tab. 9.1.

During the performance of the analysis, the ones with benefit and cost characteristics regarding to indicators were separated, and maximization and minimization were positioned. Considering the average and range values given in the Tab. 9.2, it is seen that countries can take different values for the indicators and that indicators have different units. Thanks to the normalization process on the decision matrix in ENTROPI, GRA and WASPAS methods, this problem has been solved and the value ranges of the criteria have been shortened. Criterion weights are calculated by employing the equations of the entropy method given in the second part of the study. These weights are used in the GRA and WASPAS stage.

According to the results obtained, the indicator with the highest value is the "Dwellings without basic facilities" sub criterion. The following criteria are "Homicide rate", "Long-term unemployment rate", "Labor market insecurity". Subsequent criteria take rapidly declining low values. The change of the criteria weights is given in the Fig. 9.1. The course of the curve indicating the cumulative values shows that the weight sum of the high-weighted criteria has a value close to a 100 %.

Tab. 9.2: Descriptive Statistics and Entropy Weights for Better Life Index Indicators, Source: Authors' own calculations

No	Code	Max/ min	Average	Min	Max	Range	Standard deviation	Entropy	Entropy rank
1	H1	min	2.0	0.1	13.9	13.8	3.6	0.4196	1
2	H2	min	21.3	17.0	26.0	9.0	2.2	0.0022	16
3	H3	max	1.8	1.1	2.6	1.5	0.4	0.0104	10
4	I1	max	28073.2	16275	45284	29009.0	7040.2	0.0130	9
5	I2	max	297030.7	70160	632100	561940.0	149472.3	0.0522	6
6	J1	min	6.9	2.7	23.1	20.4	5.0	0.0823	4
7	J2	max	69.1	58.0	75.0	17.0	5.0	0.0011	19
8	J3	min	2.7	0.7	7.7	7.0	2.0	0.0968	3
9	J4	max	41524.6	23683	60558	36875.0	10298.4	0.0135	8
10	CO1	max	91.5	86	95	9.0	2.6	0.0002	22
11	ED1	max	82.4	59	92	33.0	9.9	0.0032	14
12	ED2	max	502.5	485	524	39.0	12.7	0.0001	24
13	ED3	max	17.9	16.5	19.8	3.3	1.0	0.0006	20
14	EN1	min	12.5	6.0	22.0	16.0	4.3	0.0241	7
15	EN2	max	84.9	71.0	95.0	24.0	7.2	0.0015	18
16	CI1	max	2.3	1.3	3.1	1.8	0.5	0.0098	11
17	CI2	max	69.9	53	89	36.0	10.0	0.0043	13
18	H1	max	80.6	74.7	83.4	8.7	2.3	0.0002	23
19	H2	max	68.4	47	88	41.0	10.6	0.0050	12
20	L1	max	6.6	5.7	7.6	1.9	0.6	0.0018	17
21	S1	max	74.8	58.4	86.1	27.7	8.2	0.0026	15
22	S2	min	1.5	0.2	5.5	5.3	1.6	0.1935	2
23	W1	min	5.2	1.3	12.2	10.9	3.0	0.0615	5
24	W2	max	15.2	13.8	16.5	2.6	0.8	0.0005	21

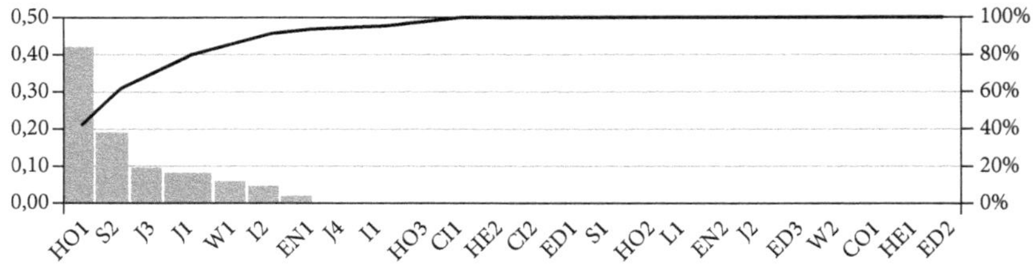

Fig. 9.1. Entropy Weights, Source: Authors' own calculations

Then, in the study, it is tried to determine the optimum values for each country by using Entropy based GRA and WASPAS MCDM methods. The gray relational grade Γ_{0i} for the GRA method and the joint optimality value Q_i for the WASPAS method were determined with the help of the equations given in the Sections 3 and 4. Rankings were made for countries according to these values. The Tab. 9.3 shows the values and the performance ranking of the countries.

Tab. 9.3. Sort for Entropy_GRA and Entropy_WASPAS, Source: Authors' own calculations

	Entropy_GRA		**Entropy_WASPAS**	
	Γ_{0i}	**rank**	Q_i	**rank**
Austria	0.033	5	0.013	10
Belgium	0.030	12	0.011	12
Canada	0.035	3	0.021	5
Denmark	0.035	4	0.015	6
Estonia	0.024	14	0.009	14
Finland	0.033	6	0.013	8
France	0.032	9	0.013	9
Germany	0.036	2	0.021	4
Italy	0.031	11	0.010	11
Latvia	0.018	15	0.007	15
Poland	0.029	13	0.010	13
Slovenia	0.033	7	0.013	7
Spain	0.032	10	0.026	2
United Kingdom	0.036	1	0.023	3
United States	0.033	8	0.029	1

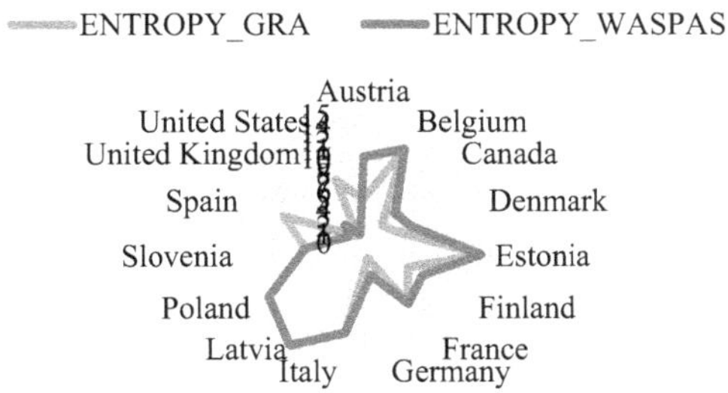

Fig. 9.2. Radar Chart, Source: Authors' own calculations

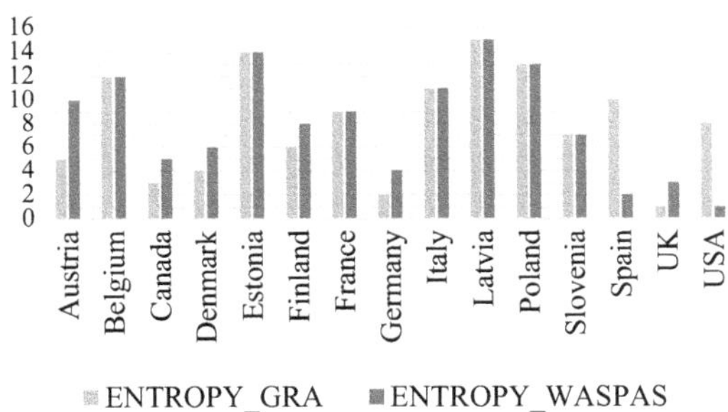

Fig. 9.3. Histogram, Source: Authors' own calculations

As a result of ranking the countries using the entropy-based GRA method, United Kingdom ranked first, followed by Germany, Canada, Denmark, Austria. According to the entropy-based WASPAS method, United States ranks first whereas Spain, United Kingdom, Germany, Canada formed the following ranking. The last ranked countries are in the same order by both methods. Sorting from the 11th row, these countries are Italy, Belgium, Poland, Estonia and Latvia.

The comparison of the ranking of the countries according to two methods is shown in the Figs. 9.2 and 9.3. Differentiation between countries can be monitored according to Γ_{0i}ENTROPY_GRA value for entropy based GRA and Q_i ENTROPY_GRA optimality values for entropy based WASPAS.

According to the radar chart, it is seen that the ranking results are close to each other and the rankings generally overlap with each other. However, the biggest ranking difference occurred for Spain, United States and Austria.

According to the histogram, the ranking depends on the methods and the similarities of these rankings are seen.

7. Conclusion

In this study, 15 OECD countries were listed based on the indicators in the Better Life Index, using the GRA and WASPAS methods, which do not require dual comparison and are easy to apply. 24 sub-criteria under the 11 main criteria, namely "Housing", "Income", "Jobs", "Community", "Education", "Environment", "Civic engagement", "Health", "Life Satisfaction", "Safety", "Work-Life Balance", are examined.

First of all, weights regarding to sub-criteria that represent the indicators were determined using the entropy method. According to the findings, the indicator that gets the highest value and takes the first place is the "Dwellings without basic facilities" sub criterion. The following criteria are listed as "Homicide rate", "Long-term unemployment rate", "Labor market insecurity", "Employees working very long hours" and "Household net wealth". Following these 6 indicators, the criterion weights of the rest get considerably low values.

After determining the weights with entropy, country comparisons are made. Considering the differentiations in the calculated Entropy-based GRA $\Gamma_{0i}$and Entropy-based WASPAS $Q_i$values, it is seen that there are differences between countries according to the indicators in the life index. According to this, in the countries with high values, the resources allocated for indicators are presumably elevated and the individuals living in these countries are likely to be conscious.

As a result of ranking the countries using the entropy-based GRA method, United Kingdom ranks first, while Latvia ranks last. According to the entropy-based WASPAS method, United States ranks first, while Latvia ranks last. According to the findings, it is observed that the ranking results are close to each other and the rankings mostly overlap with each other. The analysis outcome shows that the biggest order difference occur for Spain, United States and Austria. When the last ranking countries are considered, it becomes evident that the policymakers should make an effort to develop services with a more positive impact in order to experience developments in favor of these countries. In order to eliminate inequalities between countries, a way to improve the life-related variables of countries that are behind in terms of indicators should be sought. The programs, prepared more efficiently and productively, might carry these countries to higher rankings as a result of the better life index assessment. Such studies, which will be carried out regularly due to changing economic conditions, can guide the decision-makers to take the necessary precautions by giving an idea about the positions of their countries.

For Better Life Index, USA ranked first in the study conducted by Kılıç Depren and Bağdatlı Kalkan (2018) using the MULTIMOORA method and

Önay (2016) using the TOPSIS and MOORA-Ratio System method. This result is the same with the first rank of the WASPAS method conducted in the recent study even though the years and the data are different. According to Önay (2016)'s MOORA-Reference Point Approach method, Switzerland ranked first, while USA ranked second. When the rankings in the studies are evaluated, it is seen that the results obtained are similar.

The findings show that MCDM methods can give appropriate results for countries to take into account the model countries and their practices in order to determine the policies that would increase the welfare and improve the life quality. In the following studies, comparative analyzes can be presented by obtaining rankings between countries with different MCDM methods. Thanks to these methods, information about the general situation of the countries in terms of different indicators can be obtained and studies can be carried out to improve the situation of the countries in lower ranking position. The ability to obtain the values in countries with incomplete data will enable the analysis to be made for a wider area, as well as allowing the time series analysis of the data collected for different years will let various methods to be used.

References

Akar, S. (2014). Türkiye'de Daha İyi Yaşam Endeksi: OECD Ülkeleri ile Karşılaştırma. *Journal of Life Economics*, 1(1), 1–12.

Akdamar, E. (2019). OECD Ülkelerinin Bazı İşgücü Piyasası Göstergeleri Kullanılarak Kümeleme Analizi ve Çok Boyutlu Ölçekleme Analizi İle İrdelenmesi. *Akademik Araştırmalar ve Çalışmalar Dergisi*, 11(20), 50–65.

Başol, O. (2018). OECD Ülkelerinde Yaşam Tatmini Üzerine Bir Değerlendirme. *İş, Güç, Endüstri İlişkileri ve İnsan Kaynakları Dergisi*, 20(3), 67–86.

Chakraborty, S., and Zavadskas, E. K. (2014). Applications of WASPAS Method in Manufacturing Decision Making. *Informatica*, *25*(1), 1–20.

Chakraborty, S., Bhattacharyya, O., Zavadskas, E. K., and Antucheviciene, J. (2015). Application of WASPAS Method as an Optimization Tool in Non-traditional Machining Processes. *Information Technology and Control*, *44*(1), 77–88.

Ecer, F., and Boyukaslan, A. (2014). Measuring Performances of Football Clubs Using Financial Ratios: The Gray Relational Analysis Approach. *American Journal of Economics*, 4(1), 62–71.

Ela, M., and Soysal Kurt, H. (2019). Comparison of Macroeconomic Performances of Sub-Saharan African Countries with TOPSIS Method. *Gümüşhane Üniversitesi Sosyal Bilimler Enstitüsü Elektronik Dergisi*, 10(3), 547–555.

Eren Şenaras, A., and Çetin, I. (2016). OECD Ülkelerinde Refahın Daha İyi Yaşam Endeksi İle Analizi. *PARADOKS Ekonomi, Sosyoloji ve Politika Dergisi*, 12(2), 31–51.

Genç, A., Avcı, T., and Sevgin, H. (2017). Karadeniz Ekonomik İşbirliği Üye Ülkelerine İlişkin Etkinlik Analizi: TOPSİS, ARAS ve MOORA Yöntemleriyle Bir Uygulama. *Pamukkale Journal of Eurasian Socioeconomic Studies*, 4(2), 15–40.

Ghorbani, M., Bahrami, M., and Arabzad, S. M. (2012). An Integrated Model for Supplier Selection and Order Allocation; Using Shannon Entropy, SWOT and Linear Programming. *Procedia-Social and Behavioral Sciences*, *41*, 521–527.

Gündoğan Aşık, E., and Altın Yavuz, A. (2018). Investigation of Life Satisfaction in OECD Countries with Multivariate Analysis Methods. *Journal of Social and Hımanities Sciences Research*, 5(26), 2547–2561.

Huang, K. Y., Jane, C. J., and Chang, T. C. (2010, December). A Hybrid Model for Portfolio Selection Based on Grey Relational Analysis and RS Theories. In *2010 International Computer Symposium (ICS2010)* (pp. 1014–1019). IEEE.

Kasparian, J., and Rolland, A. (2012). OECD's "Better Life Index": Can Any Country Be Well Ranked?. *Journal of Applied Statistics*, 39(10), 2223–2230.

Kaya, P., İpekçi Çetin, E., and Kuruüzüm, A. (2011). Çok Kriterli Karar Verme ile Avrupa Birliği ve Aday Ülkelerinin Yaşam Kalitesinin Analizi. *İktisat Fakültesi Ekonometri ve İstatistik Dergisi*, 80–94.

Kerényi, Á. (2011). "The Better Life Index of the Organisation for Economic Co-operation and Development". *Public Finance Quarterly*, 56(4), 518–538

Kılıç Depren, S., and Bağdatlı Kalkan, S. (2018). Ülkelerin Konumlarının Daha İyi Yaşam Endeksine Göre Belirlenmesi: Entropi Tabanlı Multimoora Yaklaşımı. *Trakya Üniversitesi Sosyal Bilimler Dergisi,* 20(2), 353–366.

Koçhisarlı, S., and Özarı, Ç. (2019). İyi Yaşam Endeksi Göstergeleri Dikkate Alınarak İskandinav Ülkelerinin TOPSİS Yöntemi İle Değerlendirilmesi. *Akademik Sosyal Araştırmalar Dergisi,* 7(94), 466–480.

Kulesza, M., and Ucieklak-Jez, P. (2012). "Poland and Selected Countries in the Light of OECD's Better Life Index". *Prace Naukowe Akademi im. Jana Daugosza w Częstochowie, Pragmatates Oikonomias*, 6, 183–191,

Kuo, Y., Yang, T., and Huang, G. W. (2008). The Use of Grey Relational Analysis in Solving Multiple Attribute Decision-Making Problems. *Computers and Industrial Engineering*, *55*(1), 80–93.

Monica, G. T. (2018). The Weight of Weighting-An Empirical Study Based on the OECD Better Life Index. *The Businessand Management Review*, 9(3), 443–450.

OECD Better Life Index, Retrieved from http://www.oecdbetterlifeindex.org/#/11111111111 (15.04.2020).

Ömürbek, N., Eren, H., and Dağ, O. (2017). Entropi-ARAS ve Entropi-MOOSRA Yöntemleri İle Yaşam Kalitesi Açısından AB Ülkelerinin Değerlendirilmesi. *Ömer Halis Demir Üniversitesi İktisadi ve İdari Bilimler Fakültesi Dergisi*, 10(2), 29–48.

Önay, O. (2016). Multi-criteria Assessment of Better Life via TOPSIS and MOORA Methods. *International Journal of Business and Social Science*, *7*(1), 225–234.

Orakçı, E., and Özdemir, A. (2017). Telafi Edici Çok Kriterli Karar Verme Yöntemleri İle Türkiye ve AB Ülkelerinin İnsani Gelişmişlik Düzeylerinin Belirlenmesi. *Journal of Economics and Administrative Sciences*, XIX(1), 61–74.

Özden, Ü. H. (2012). AB'ye Üye Ülkelerin ve Türkiye'nin Ekonomik Performanslarına Göre VIKOR Yöntemi ile Sıralanması. *İstanbul Ticaret Üniversitesi Sosyal Bilimler Dergisi*, 21(1), 455–468.

Peiro´-Palomino, J., and Picazo-Tadeo, A. J. (2018). OECD: One or Many? Ranking Countries with a Composite Well-Being Indicator. *Social Indicators Research*, 139, 847–869.

Sevgin, H., and Kundakçı, N. (2017). TOPSIS VE MOORA Yöntemleri ile Avrupa Birliği'ne Üye Olan Ülkelerin ve Türkiye'nin Ekonomik Göstergelere Göre Sıralanması. *Anadolu Üniversitesi Sosyal Bilimler Dergisi*, 17(3), 87–107.

Stanujkić, D., and Karabašević, D. (2018). An Extension of the WASPAS Method for Decision-Making Problems with Intuitionistic Fuzzy Numbers: A Case of Website Evaluation. *Operational Research in Engineering Sciences: Theory and Applications*, *1*(1), 29–39.

Stiglitz, J. E., Sen, A., and Fitoussi, J.-P. (2009). Report by the Commission on the Measurement of Economic Performance and Social Progress, Paris. Retrieved from http://www.stiglitz-sen-fitoussi.fr/documents/rapport_anglais.pdf (08.05.2020).

Türe, H. (2019). OECD Ülkeleri için Refah Ölçümü: Gri İlişkisel Analiz Uygulaması. *Ankara Hacı Bayram Veli Üniversitesi İktisadi ve İdari Bilimler Fakültesi Dergisi,* 21(2), 310–327.

Wu, W. (2017). Grey Relational Analysis Method for Group Decision Making in Credit Risk Analysis. *EURASIA Journal of Mathematics, Science and Technology Education*, *13*(12), 7913–7920.

Yıldırım, B. F. (2014). Gri İlişkisel Analiz. In: *Operasyonel, Yönetsel ve Stratejik Problemlerin Çözümünde Çok Kriterli Karar Verme Yöntemleri*, Eds: Yıldırım, B. F., and Önder, E., Bursa, Turkey, Dora Yayıncılık, 227–242.

Yıldız, A., Ayyıldız, E., Taşkın Gümüş, A., and Özkan, C. (2019). Ülkelerin Yaşam Kalitelerine Göre Değerlendirilmesi için Hibrit Pisagor Bulanık Ahp-Topsis Metodolojisi: Avrupa Birliği Örneği. *Avrupa Bilim ve Teknoloji Dergisi*, 17, 1383–1391.

Zhou, F., Lin, Y., Wang, X., Zhou, L., and He, Y. (2016). ELV Recycling Service Provider Selection Using the Hybrid MCDM Method: A Case Application in China. *Sustainability*, *8*(5), 482, 1–22.

Hale Kırer Silva L. and Rüya Eser

Chapter 10 Income Inequality in Turkey: A Fractal Point of View

Abstract: Income inequality is one of the most studied topics since the existence of economics. Its analysis within the economic complexity gained momentum in the 2000s. In this study, the scaling indicator is used as a measure of income inequality in complex systems. In addition, the effects of income inequality on energy consumption have been analyzed considering the complexity of the systems. In this context, fractal dimensions of income distribution are calculated on the basis of the scaling indicator for Turkey and its regions. After that its relationship with energy use, Gross Domestic Product (GDP) and population density are examined.

Keywords: Inequality, Complexity, Fractal Dimension, Scaling (Indicator), Energy Consumption

1. Introduction

The investigation of income inequality in economic systems particularly started with the Pareto golden rule in the literature at the end of the 19th century, and continues to this day. Inequality is defined as any economic or social feature that causes some individuals to be worse off than others. Fair income distribution is a political subjective statement about income distribution rather than a scientific issue. However, the increasing inequality raises the risk of instability and is the biggest social problem of countries on top of corruption and unemployment. The deterioration of income distribution causes the income inequality to be seen as an important economic and social problem. For these reasons, economic growth and sustainable development are the main objectives of economic policies in order to eliminate inequality by accurately measuring the distribution of income.

There are several methods to measure the inequality in income distribution, and most of the studies on income distribution employ indices such as Gini and Lorenz, which are based on the normal distribution assumption. However, knowing that the economic wealth and income of 99 % and 1 % have differentiated even more for the last thirty to forty years, especially the wealth and income of the 1 % and 0.1 % or 0.01 % or 0.001 %, economists called this situation "fractal inequality". The meaning of fractal inequality does not only mean that the rich have moved away from the average citizens in that country, but the richer you are, the farther you are (Lowrey, 2014). Within this framework, studies in the context of complex systems have been increasing.

Scarcely there are some studies conducted regarding the complex systems in Turkey, particularly the number of studies examining them based on the regions is very limited. Thus, this study intends to measure the income distribution inequality in Turkey through a fractal dimension. In addition, the relationship between development indicators such as energy use, GDP and population density, with the income distribution inequality based on the calculated fractal dimension is reviewed from the perspective of complex systems. In this direction, the scaling indicator for measuring income distribution inequality is calculated for regions. It is then examined whether income inequality, measured using these scaling indicators, affects energy consumption, GDP and population density in different regional economies or not.

The study consists of five sections. The second one emphasizes the complex and fractal structure of economics. The third section contains theoretical information and data regarding the method of the study. In the fourth section, the findings obtained as a result of the analysis are presented and the study is completed with the conclusion section where the findings are evaluated.

2. The Fractal Nature of Economics and Income Distribution Dynamics

Studies on income distribution inequality generally use methods based on averages that do not achieve non-linearity in the systems and therefore, they are criticized (Khan and Heinecker, 2018). However, the economy as a complex system is adaptable, that is, it has an evolutionary structure and is affected by social, political and physical processes. In the economy there are a significant number of factors related to the organic structure of the economy as a whole, and the behavior of the system is unpredictable by the understanding of the components in it, and the relationships are not linear. Economies are complex adaptive systems and should also exhibit similar scaling properties like other complex systems. Therefore, it is not appropriate to use orthodox (traditional) statistical methods in complex systems.

One way to examine inequality (disorder) in complex systems is to look at the entropy or scaling within the systems. The two basic concepts for characterizing a data set are entropy and fractal dimension. While the metric entropy measures how much a data set (an object) differs from itself (defined as the number of covering spheres), fractal dimension measures how the number of the required spheres to cover all points in a data set is scaled with the dimensions of these spheres (Yu et al., 2015).

Fractals are structures that repeat themselves at different scales. Many fractal structures consist of self-similarity parts. For this reason, in an object similar to itself, the elements that form the object are similar to the whole object, the patterns are renewed in gradually smaller scales, and when the shape of small objects is enlarged, they look the same and similar parts to the object itself are obtained (Eser, 2016). The fact that an object has the feature of resembling itself means that it includes repetition of itself in different scales. An example is a broccoli pattern zooming in on repetitive patterns. However, fractals can also be amorphous quantities, in this case characterized by the distribution known as the power law (or non-scale-free) distribution. Therefore, a fractal is said to be scale-free due to its scale invariance (Takayasu and Takayasu, 2010). Scale invariance is a property of a variable (an observation) that remains unchanged in different scales (time or space), and it means that the variable (observation) repeats itself at different scales.

Fractal dimension is a statistical index that measures the complexity of a given pattern within given spatial dimensions. There are several methods[1] and algorithms to measure the fractal dimension. Box-counting method is the one used in this study. In this framework, the formulas can be written as follows: where N indicates the number of cells used to cover the object (building/shore), ε scaling factor and D the fractal dimension (Sparavigna, 2016):

$$N \propto \varepsilon^{-D}$$

$$log_{\varepsilon}N = -D = \frac{logN}{log\varepsilon}$$

Probability distribution of the variable representing the fractal is as follows:

$$\mathrm{P}\left(\mathrm{X} \geq \mathrm{x}\right) \propto \mathrm{x}^{-\alpha}$$

Power law distribution;

---

1 Some of the methods developed are: (1) Hausdorff dimension (2) Self-similarity dimension (3) Box-counting dimension (4) Topological dimension (5) Euclidean dimension (6) Kolmogorov dimension (7) Lyapunov dimension (8) Divider or Ruler dimension. These are all interrelated. However, some are significant for certain situations, but not for others (Xiong et al., 2012).

$$p(x) = Cx^{-\alpha}$$

The dimension classes of the given parameter are distributed at various scales so that the number of p elements on each x scale is related according to the equation px^{α}, where α is the power law exponent with values between 0.75 and 2.5, sometimes referred as fractal dimension. Fractals exhibit a power law effect as they get smaller at a fixed rate and are determined by rank / frequency distributions. The power law distribution demonstrates that power and number in a population are inversely correlated. In other words, typically these systems do not have aberrantly sized elements and the number of component elements decreases as the scale to which the element belongs increases in size. Regarding network terms, the system exhibits "scale-free" structuring (Khan and Heinecker, 2018). Such structuring is found in natural systems in the magnitute of earthquakes, lunar craters, solar explosions, lakes, mountains, clouds and seacoasts. They always look like smaller parts of themselves and because of their scaling invariance, for example, the vast majority of lakes are small while some are very large (Pueyo, 2014). It is also encountered in many man-made dynamic systems, especially in cities, companies, sales, wages and organizational structures in terms of network links, manager connections, biotechnology networks (Eser, 2016).

The idea of describing natural phenomena with statistical scaling analysis, self-similarity and self-affine character has a long history and many studies have been conducted on this subject (Xiong et al., 2012) However, although the power law in economics dates back decades to studies of Pareto (1897), Auerbach (1913) and Zipf (1949), it became widespread by Mandelbrot (1963, 1982)'s pioneering studies and has been a milestone in the fractal geometry (Eser, 2016).

In this context, the relationship between entropy-based non-power and power law distributions has begun to play a central role in modeling dynamic systems. The economists' use of entropy ideas in measuring income distribution is based on the generalized entropy-based Theil measure (Theil, 1967) and their search for generalization of various measures used to examine income distributions. However, the Atkinson measure, which can better distinguish skewness of tails, is widely used in income inequality, since the Theil measurement has a more general result (Rosser, 2016).

In addition, according to the studies conducted by Dragulescu and Yakovenko (2001) and Yakovenko and Rosser (2009) wealth distribution in the economy follows the power law distribution, whereas income distribution reflects the combination of the Boltzmann-Gibbs distribution and entropy that explain the poorest 97–98 %, and the Pareto power law distribution that is better for the top income level (the richest 2–3 %) where wealth dynamics can play a more important role (Rosser 2016). In the study conducted for Turkey, Kırer (2011) obtained that the income distribution of the richest 1–3 % segment of the population follows a Pareto distribution, while the income distribution of the rest of the population is compatible with a completely different distribution.

The advantage of fractal theory lies in the irregular and non-smooth relationships that are common in the real world and cannot be solved using traditional models. The fractal theory using the temporal and spatial statistical scaling law and the power law characteristic can reveal that complex dynamic systems are common in the real world (Xiong et al., 2012). It has been shown in studies that living organisms and many other dynamical systems follow a power law in scaling the sizes of their various components. However, part of the problem of discovering the relationship between inequality or disequilibrium in the systems and its effects on energy consumption is the lack of indicator systems that can take into account the complexity underlying such interaction.

3. Methodology and Data

3.1. Methodology

Economies are complex adaptive systems and should demonstrate similar scaling characteristics as other complex systems. In this study, the scaling indicator of income distribution based on the fractal dimension is examined to determine how scaling in economic systems affects the environmental indicators. In this direction, the box-counting method in Khan and Heinecker (2018)'s study is employed as a basis.

The box-counting method used to measure fractal size is generally adopted in quantitative evaluation and classification of images and geographical areas. Accordingly, when the current figure is overlapped with a paper consisting of boxes, it is observed how many boxes can be counted to cover the entire figure. Then the process is repeated by decreasing one side length of the boxes. Since this time, smaller boxes are used, more boxes are counted. In other words, box-counting consists of determining the number of $N(x)$ cells required to cover the structure to be measured, depending on the x size of the cells. For different values of cell size x, the cells covering the shape are counted and then represented in logarithmic coordinates as $logN = f(logx)$. Finally, the slope of a linear regression is an estimate of the fractal dimension. The mathematical expression[2] of this is as follows (Andronache et al., 2016);

$$D = \frac{logN\left(x\right)}{log\left(\frac{1}{x}\right)} \tag{1}$$

where, "x" indicates the side length of the box used and "N (x)" is the number of adjacent and non-overlapping boxes of side "x" required to cover the area of the object. D gives the box-counting[3] fractal dimension of the shape. For this formula to give the correct D value, the "x" value must approach to zero. The smaller the boxes are the better results are obtained.

In the recent study, to derive the fractal exponent, the box-counting dimension formula is used as expressed in the Equation 1. However, since the method is applied to numerical data instead of a specific geographical area, clustering in the form of boxes have been formulated and calculated as an income distribution between 20 sequential percentiles. Since we have a data set on the distribution of income by percentage of the population, rather than "boxes" in a geographic area, the cluster is divided into virtual boxes each covering 20 % of the population. Thus, in the applied method, the "box" of the box-counting method is any 20 % population block.

Accordingly, the variables x, $N\left(x\right)$ and D in the Equation 1 imply, respectively, the certain percentage of the area covered by the population group x (box size, that is the population group of 20 %), the percentage of income per specified 20 % population (that is the number of boxes falling in the x interval), and the box-counting dimension of the income (that is the fractal dimension).

The next step in the box-counting method is to count all the boxes that fall under a certain income group (cluster). The 'box' in the box-counting method is similar to the cumulative 20th percentile of income in the data-based method, and clustering is based on the income distribution rather than the percentage of the box covered by the income held. This is represented by the term $N\left(x\right)$ in the Equation (1). The adaptive box-counting for the methodology is the percentage of income per given population percentage block. Fig. 10.1 illustrates how the box-counting method is applied to income distribution data.

2 Box-counting formula is $N\left(x\right) = c\left(\frac{1}{x}\right)^{D}$ or $N\left(x\right) = cx^{-D}$. This equation can also be expressed as follows: $log\ N\left(x\right) = -D\log\left(x\right) + log\left(c\right)$. In the Equation 1, c is assumed as one (c=1).

3 Box-counting dimension is 1 if it is linear; 2 if it belongs to an area such as a square, and 3 if it is three-dimensional like a cube.

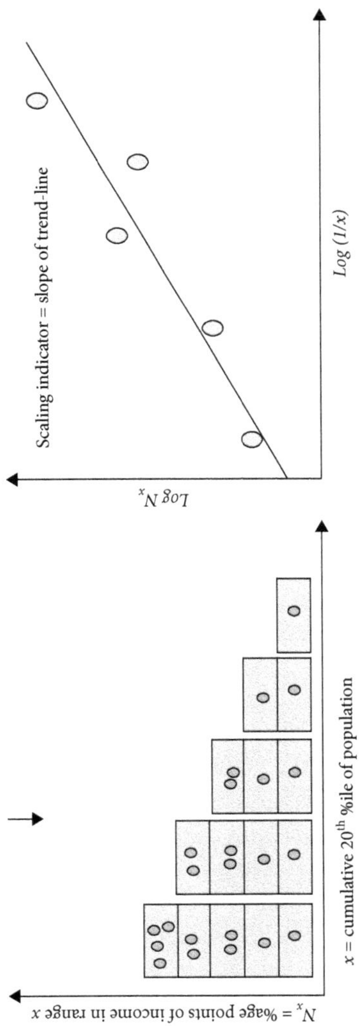

Fig. 10.1. Adaptation of the Box-Counting Method to a Numeric Based Data, Source: Khan and Heinecker, 2018. Note: While the left figure represents the data based scaling indicator, the right one shows the slope of the scaling indicator.

Thus, the cumulative income for jth percentile in the p percentile of the population is formularized as follows;

$$a_j = \sum_{i=1}^{j} a_i$$

where a_i implies the percentage of income held by the population block i and p the percentage of population in each block.

For the scaling exponent, the number of $N(x)$ boxes falling in a given x interval is the percentage of the income share in the j percentile; a_j, $N(x)$ can simply be expressed as:

$$N(x) = a_j = \sum_{i=1}^{j} a_i$$

Similarly, for any percentage j, x is given as the total population falling within the jth percentile. Therefore, x = 1 / (j × p). The scaling indicator, D, can be expressed as;

$$D = \frac{logN(x)}{log\left(\frac{1}{x}\right)} = \frac{log\ a_j}{log\left(\frac{1}{x}\right)}$$

Using the Richardson-Mandelbrot slope, the D value is calculated by plotting a_j and $\frac{1}{x}$ on the log-log scale and estimating the slope of the regression line. As a_j and x are measured in percentage, D is a dimensionless quantity (Khan and Heinecker, 2018).

The fractal indicator is the measure of the difference, that is, inequality within the system. It means that the greater the value of the indicator, the less inequality. When there is high inequality, a much smaller scaling indicator value (the slope of the trend line) is obtained.

The fractal dimension based scaling indicator of the income distribution of the countries is calculated by plotting the cumulative income share according to the cumulative population percentage. When it is plotted in log-log scales, the obtained slope of the line indicates the fractal dimension-based scaling indicator of the income distribution within the country (Khan and Heinecker, 2018).

The indicator calculated based on the fractal dimension does not presuppose that inequality should be measured according to a linear income distribution. It is not necessary to assume the 1:1 equality of the calculated indicator, that is 50 % of the income, which is reduced to a half of the population, is ideal as in

Gini. Instead, it takes the nature of the power-law distribution of income data, and by measuring the power-law exponential, a way to examine how strong the middle segment in the economic distribution (allocation) is offered.

3.2. Data

Turkey has 81 provinces located in 7 geographical areas. In Turkey the income distribution percentiles by provinces are not published. For this reason, income distributions according to 26 regions defined as "Level 2"[4] by the Turkish Statistical Institute (TURKSTAT) were employed in this study. The income distribution and GNP data used in the application are from the Income and Living Conditions Statistics database released by TURKSTAT (TURKSTAT, 2020a, 2020b), and the population density data are obtained from the Address Based Population Registration System (ABPRS) results (TURKSTAT, 2020c) database.

Data on electricity consumption are taken from the Electricity Market Annual Market Development Report (EMRA, 2020a) published by the Republic of Turkey Energy Market Regularity Authority (EMRA). We calculate the per capita electricity consumption by dividing the number of consumers in the province by the amount of electricity consumption on the provincial basis, which is included in the Electricity Market Monthly Sector Report (EMRA, 2020b).

Later, per capita electricity consumption and GDP per capita figures and population density figures were taken as a grouping according to the "Level 2" regions. The World Bank's *World Development Indicators database* (World Bank, 2020) was taken to compare Turkey with other countries in terms of the fractal dimension of the income distribution.

While the fractal dimension analysis of income distribution regarding throughout Turkey covers the period between 2002 and 2019, the analysis in

4 In the statistical region units classification by TURKSTAT, provinces are defined as 'Level 3'; Neighboring provinces, which are economically, socially and geographically similar, are grouped as "Level 1" and "Level 2", taking into account regional development plans and population sizes. Statistical regional units within the scope of "Level 3" are 81 and they are at the provincial level. Each province defines a statistical regional unit. 'Level 2' statistical regional units have been defined as a result of grouping neighboring provinces within the scope of 'Level 3', and there are 26 of them. 'Level 1' statistical regional units are defined as a result of the grouping of 'Level 2' statistical regional units, and there are 12.

terms of regions is made only for 2008, because all the data for electricity consumption, GDP and population density are available for this year.

4. Findings and Assesments

4.1 Income Distribution

4.1.1 Fractal Dimension of Income Distribution for Turkey

Fractal dimension based scaling index values of the calculated income distribution for the years 2002–2019 for Turkey are given in the Tab. 10.1. As it is seen, the R^2 values are greater than 0.98 for the analyzed period in Turkey, indicating a strong power law distribution. When the values obtained are evaluated, income difference, in other words inequality, tends to improve from 2002 to 2019, whereas it worsens from 2008 on (Tab. 10.1).

Then, according to the calculated fractal dimension values to determine the cross-country income distribution differences, the result of Turkey for 2017 is compared to Germany which is one of the advanced countries and similar to Turkey in terms of population size, Russia which has much higher population size, and Brazil which is similar to Turkey in terms of economic structure. For this purpose, the cumulative income share of the countries in the log-log scale is calculated according to the cumulative population percentage and the slope of the regression line (Fig. 10.2). When it is plotted in log-log scales, the slope of the line gives the fractal dimension-based scaling indicator of the income distribution of the country (Khan and Heinecker, 2018).

Fractal dimension based scaling indicator of national income distribution is calculated by plotting cumulative income share against the cumulative

Tab. 10.1. Income Distribution Slope Values for Turkey, Source: Authors' own calculations

Years	Fractal Dimension (D)	R^2	Years	Fractal Dimension (D)	R^2	Years	Fractal Dimension (D)	R^2
2002	0.4677626	0.990278	**2008**	0.5048408	0.989181	**2014**	0.467659	0.990461
2003	0.4589757	0.989786	**2009**	0.4997588	0.989734	**2015**	0.484176	0.991834
2004	0.4793265	0.987414	**2010**	0.5026498	0.990027	**2016**	0.475814	0.992754
2005	0.4611185	0.988619	**2011**	0.484482	0.99027	**2017**	0.472809	0.993499
2006	0.4975572	0.988336	**2012**	0.482836	0.989912	**2018**	0.469225	0.993042
2007	0.5098723	0.988855	**2013**	0.481565	0.990144	**2019**	0.486856	0.992471

population percentage. Once plotted on log-log scales the resulting slope of the line would be the fractal dimension based scaling indicator for the distribution of income within the country.

However, it is crucial to state that, in this plotting, the twenty percentile taken in clustering of the population or binning is constant, only the income distribution changes, and the regression degree of freedom is one. Therefore, high R^2 values are only indicative of a power law distribution, not exactly an accurate prediction (Khan and Heinecker, 2018).

The Fig. 10.2 shows that Turkey has a lower percentage of income share in its population compared to Germany. Thus, the starting point income share of the richest 20 % in Turkey is higher than in Germany and the slope of the trend line is less. The income distribution inequality in Russia is between Turkey and Germany, which means income inequality is worse than in Germany but better than in Turkey. Brazil is the country with the worst income distribution and the country with the lowest scaling indicator value. The slope of the trend line thus catches the inequality between these countries.

To understand why the trend exists, one must consider what 'scaling' means. The higher the slope or scaling indicator, the less the difference in income distribution. In short, if the slope becomes horizontal and the indicator value is high, the low income inequality, the steepness of the slope and the smallness of the indicator value indicate that the income inequality is high. The larger the scaling indicator, the smaller the change in the distribution of incomes among different population groups.

4.1.2. Fractal Dimension of Income Distribution in the Regions of Turkey

Scaling indicators by regions were calculated on the basis of "Level 2". The results are shown in the Tab. 10.2.

When the fractal dimension values of 2018 for all regions are examined, among the 26 regions calculated, TR10 (Istanbul) has the lowest fractal dimension with 0.420357, while TRB1 (Malatya, Elazığ, Bingöl and Tunceli) has the highest value with 0.589916. In other words, the region with the worst income distribution is TR10 (Istanbul), followed by TR21 (Tekirdağ, Edirne, Kırklareli) with 0.475271 and TR62 (Adana, Mersin) with 0.470694. The best income distribution at Level 1 is Central East Anatolia, West and East Black Sea. The regions with the worst income distribution are Istanbul, the Mediterranean and West Marmara.

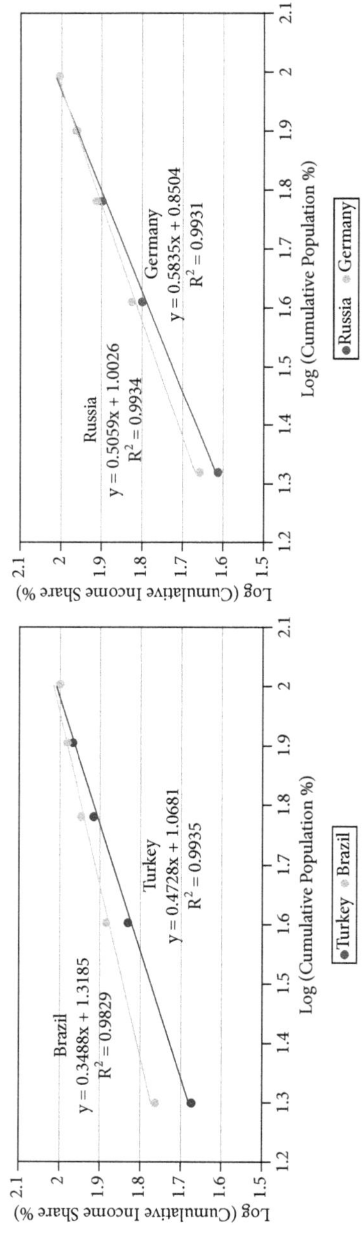

Fig. 10.2. Scaling Indicator as a Measure of Disparity of Income Distribution in Turkey, Brazil, Russia and Germany (2017)

Tab. 10.2. Scaling Indicators Based on Fractal Dimension for Income Distribution in Turkey According to Classification of Statistical Regional Units, Source: Authors' own calculations

Level 1	Level 2	Level 2 Fractal Dimension (D) Values	Level 1 Fractal Dimension (D) Values (Average)
İstanbul	TR10 (İstanbul)	0.420357	0.420357
West Marmara	TR21 (Tekirdağ, Edirne, Kırklareli)	0.475271	0.500446
	TR22 (Balıkesir, Çanakkale)	0.525621	
Aegean	TR31 (İzmir)	0.517540	0.544533
	TR32 (Aydın, Denizli, Muğla)	0.568492	
	TR33 (Manisa, Afyon, Kütahya, Uşak)	0.547566	
East Marmara	TR41 (Bursa, Eskişehir, Bilecik)	0.549656	0.552148
	TR42 (Kocaeli, Sakarya, Düzce, Bolu, Yalova)	0.554641	
West Anatolia	TR51 (Ankara)	0.488461	0.501548
	TR52 (Konya, Karaman)	0.514636	
Mediterranean	TR61 (Antalya, Isparta, Burdur)	0.526093	0.495052
	TR62 (Adana, Mersin)	0.470694	
	TR63 (Hatay, Kahramanmaraş, Osmaniye)	0.488368	
Central West Anatolia	TR71 (Kırıkkale, Aksaray, Niğde, Nevşehir, Kırşehir)	0.559217	0.548974
	TR72 (Kayseri, Sivas, Yozgat)	0.538732	
West Black Sea	TR81 (Zonguldak, Karabük, Bartın)	0.574858	0.551856
	TR82 (Kastamonu, Çankırı, Sinop)	0.547261	
	TR83 (Samsun, Tokat, Çorum, Amasya)	0.533450	
East Black Sea	TR90 (Trabzon, Ordu, Giresun, Rize, Artvin, Gümüşhane)	0.550442	0,550442
North East Anatolia	TRA1 (Erzurum, Erzincan, Bayburt)	0.580959	0.549112
	TRA2 (Ağrı, Kars, Iğdır, Ardahan)	0.517265	
Central East Anatolia	TRB1 (Malatya, Elazığ, Bingöl, Tunceli)	0.589916	0.568761
	TRB2 (Van, Muş, Bitlis, Hakkari)	0.547606	
South East Anatolia	TRC1 (Gaziantep, Adıyaman, Kilis)	0.542825	0.512866
	TRC2 (Şanlıurfa, Diyarbakır)	0.489767	
	TRC3 (Mardin, Batman, Şırnak, Siirt)	0.506007	
	TR Turkey	**0.469547**	

It shows how higher inequality in income intensity distribution leads to a lower scaling indicator value. The scaling indicator for regions is inversely correlated to the inequality, and the higher the scaling indicator is, the lower the inequality. When the findings are evaluated in general, it is seen that the income distribution is worse in developed regions.

The Fractal dimension based scaling indicator for income distribution in sample regions is calculated by plotting on log-log scale the cumulative income distribution and cumulative population percentage and taking the slope of the regression line. The R^2 value is greater than 0.95 for all the linear fits for all regions, indicating a strong power law distribution. The values are shown in the Fig. 10.3.

Log-Log plot in the Fig. 10.3 shows how higher disparity of income density distribution leads to a lower scaling indicator value for the six sample regions. The indicator is also a measure of disparity within the system. Comparing the regions in the Fig. 10.3 for instance: TR10 (Istanbul) has a higher population covered by its lowest density income and lesser population covered by its highest density income compared to TRB1. Thus there is a greater disparity between extremes in Istanbul compared to TRB1 and thus it has a much higher scaling indicator value (slope of the trend-line).

A higher fractal size for regions, less inequality, a lower indicator of scaling (higher inequality) means that a larger percentage of income is concentrated in the richer percentage of the population.

A higher value of the scaling indicator means that the change in the distribution of certain features at different scales are steeper. For example, some regions with a higher income have a greater population density compared to the lower fractal dimension regions. In general, lower scaling indicator values are indicative of a higher inequality in the distribution of elements across the system, meaning that a high percentage of income is obtained by a very few people. Lower scaling indicator values mean that the spread of income density (difference between minimum and maximum) for regions is greater and this indicates inequality for economies.

4.2. The Relationship between Income Distribution Scaling Indicator and the Development Indicators

Determining the relation of income distribution inequality with other indicators of development will also show how reliable the measurement based on fractal dimension is. Income inequality is associated to a number of important sociological issues. In this context, in this study, the relationship between scaling indicator and economic development indicators, namely energy consumption, GDP and population density is investigated. To establish the veracity and utility of the scaling indicator of disparity, its correlation with electricity consumption, GDP and population density are studied.

Particularly, the primary reason for selecting energy consumption efficiency as a dependent variable in the analysis is the significance of electricity consumption towards making human development more sustainable. If disparity in economic systems can be shown to be co-occurring with energy consumption then it becomes imperative to consider this parameter in development policies and planning.

The most appropriate curves that give the relationship of the income distribution scaling indicator in the regions with the electricity consumption per capita and GDP are obtained by using the Least Squares Regression. As expected, electricity used is quite strong linearly correlated with fractal dimensions shown in Fig. 10.4. In the regression analysis between the income inequality indicator and electricity consumption, the R^2 value is found 16.66 %, and the P value of the x values calculated as the scaling indicator as a result of the regression is less than 0.05 ($p < 0.05$), indicating that it is statistically significant (Tab. 10.3).

The correlation between the fractal dimension based scaling indicator of national income distribution and GDP per capita in the regions is studied using linear and non-linear regression. The R^2 value for the GNP in the power law distribution is higher as 10.36 % and it is 19.44 % in the lognormal distribution. This situation reveals that there is a relationship between the income inequality indicator and GNP. Fractal dimension and GDP per capita are dependent each other as shown in Fig. 10.4. This means the overall scaling indicator that is fractal dimension is being affected by a "long tail" or the profile of one extreme. However, the P value of the calculated x values is 0.1087, and since $p > 0.05$, it is not statistically significant (Tab. 10.3).

The relationship between the scaling indicator and population density is the highest with the R^2 value of 29.85 %, compared to the other two variables examined. The P value of the calculated x value is also found to be significant.

As shown in the Fig. 10.4, the response of electricity consumption indicators to scaling based disparity indicators is non-linear. Regionally, energy use declines with the increasing inequality in income distribution. In other words, energy consumption rises with a more fair distribution of income. Similarly, with the fair income distribution in the regions, GDP also grows.

Population density and fractal dimention are correlated. It is observed that fractal dimention is power law dependent on population density as shown in

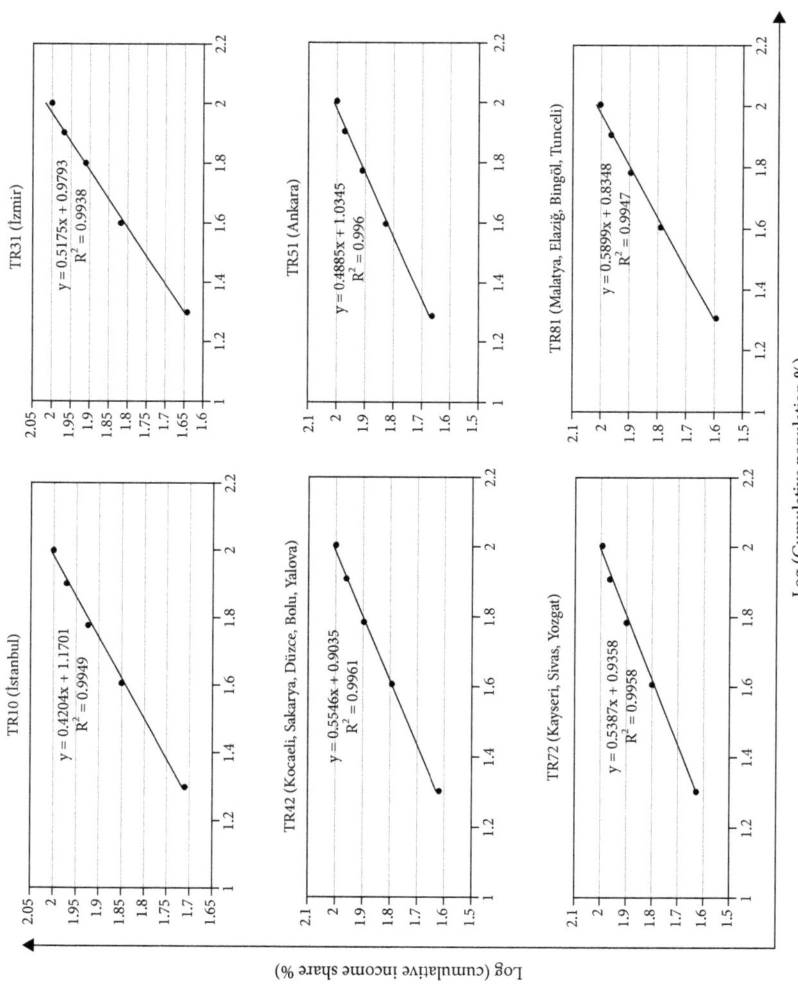

Fig. 10.3. Calculation of Scaling Indicator for 6 Sample Regions (Provinces), Source: Authors' own calculations

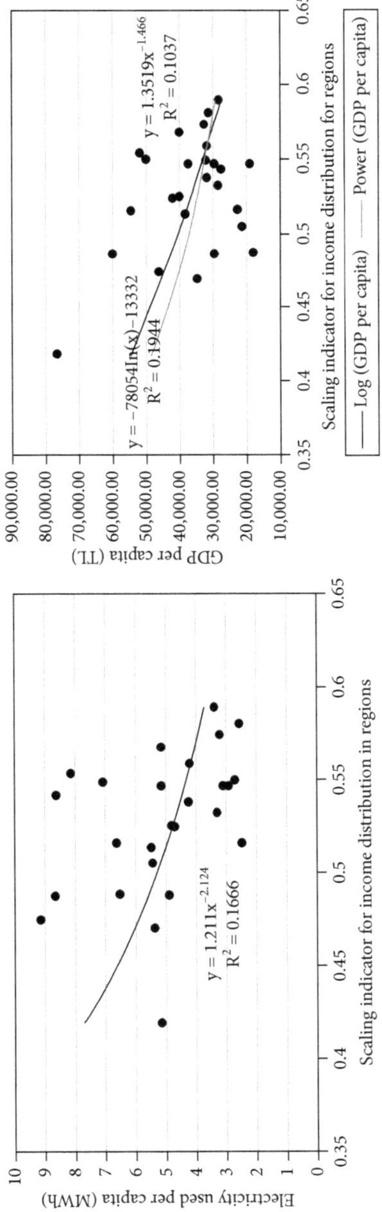

Fig. 10.4. Relationship of Income Distribution Inequality with Electricity Consumption and GNP

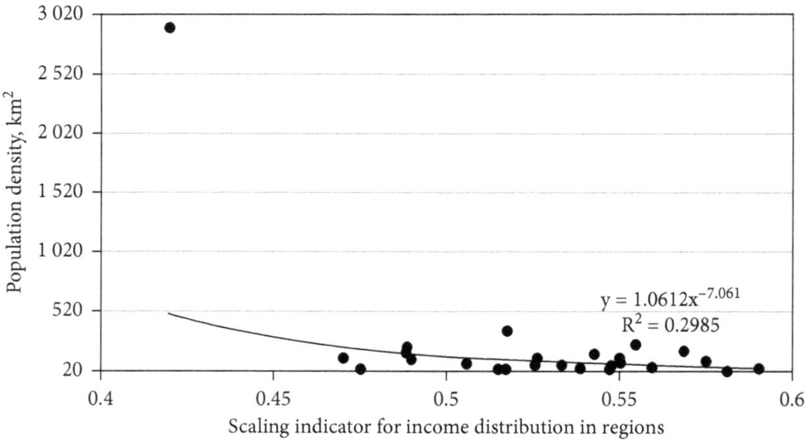

Fig. 10.5. The Relationship between Income Distribution Inequality and Population Density

the Fig. 10.5. It is seen that the population density is less in regions with better income distribution.

To understand why the relationship between energy consumption and scaling indicator exists, it is necessary to examine what scaling shows. Lower scaling indicator values imply the inequality for regions. For these reasons, energy consumption decreases as the inequality increases. Also, a lower scaling indicator might correspond to a higher energy consumption because the richest 20 % might be consuming a disproportionately large percentage of energy per capita. The increase in energy consumption with lower inequality might be partially due to the excessive increase in energy consumption of the high-income segments of the economy.

Given why inequality affects energy use, from a system point of view, when scaling the dimension (size) distribution within a system becomes different, that is, when economies have high income inequality, this disequilibrium would have two effects. First, the share of the energy consumption by highest 20 percentile would disproportionately increase. Second, it would complicate the task of regulation for providing energy efficiently to all their citizens in different ways (Khan and Paul Heinecker, 2018).

Another finding is that GNP and population density in complex systems are related to scaling according to a power law. Furthermore, power law correlations are weak with R^2 values less than 0.5 and the only interpretation that can be

Tab. 10.3. Regression Results of Scaling Indicator with Development Indicators

	R^2	X value	Pvalue
Energy Consumption (Per capita, MWh)	0.16663	-2.12366	0.03842
GDP (Per capita, TRY)	0.10366	-1.46599	0.10871
Population density per km^2	0.29854	-7.06062	0.00388

made with any certainty about this result is that the changing scaling indicator value is related to the trend of the change in energy consumption, GDP and population density (Khan and Heinecker, 2018).

Results beyond this may be indicative. However, they may not be fully supported by the data and require further work with different data. For this reason, it would be more appropriate to work with all the data that gives the distribution among individuals instead of a single data such as calculating indicators according to the population density of countries or regions, energy use per capita and GNP per capita.

5. Conclusion

This study uses the fractal dimension-based scaling indicator for income inequality in national economies, which is a measure of system complexity and does not ideally assume any distribution. The scaling indicator is calculated for the income distribution in the sequential 20 percentiles in Turkey. It is also shown that income distribution densities are distributed in the form of power law, and the exponent of the power law, which means that the fractal dimension of the scaling indicator has an effect on energy consumption, GDP and population density in the regions. It is concluded that the increasing inequality decreases the energy use and GNP in the economies of the region and increases the population density.

One of the issues of the traditional inequality indicators is that such indicators do not capture the rapidly accumulating wealth at the top of the distribution. The indicator computed based on the fractal dimension has the possibility to capture this increasing inequality. However, to show the income accumulation in a smaller population group instead of five 20 percentiles would yield better results. In contrast, data from all over the world are not available to document the share of income holding by the richest 0.1 % or 0.01 % of the population. There are also technical clustering problems, especially due to the nature of the data in economics. With the development of clustering methods, it would be possible to reach more detailed results for studies related to income distribution in the economies.

The relationships between income inequality and other indicators across the economic system appear to be largely non-linear responses. Although it is interesting that the concept of power law and fractal dimension used in natural sciences can provide a measure of inequality for economies, the findings based on these concepts imported from physical sciences into economics or built according to scaling dimension sizes by analogy are still considered limited by mainstream economists.

References

Andronache, I. C., D.Peptenatu, Ana-MariaCiobotaru, A. K.Gruia, N.M. Gropoşilă. (2016). Using fractal analysis in modeling trends in the national economy, Procedia Environmental Sciences 32, 344–351.

Auerbach, F. (1913). Das Gesetz der Bevolkerungskoncentration. Petermanns Geographische Mitteilungen, 59, 74–76.

Dragulescu, A. A., V. M. Yakovenko. (2001). Exponential and power-law probability distributions of wealth and income in the United Kingdom and the United States, *Physica A* 299, 213–221.

EMRA. (2020a). Elektrik Piyasası Yıllık Sektör Raporları, Retrieved from https://www.epdk.gov.tr/Detay/Icerik/3-0-24-3/elektrikyillik-sektor-raporu (02.08.2020)

EMRA. (2020b). Elektrik Piyasası Aylık Sektör Raporu, Retrieved from https://www.epdk.gov.tr/Detay/Icerik/3-0-23/elektrikaylik-sektor-raporlar (02.08.2020).

Eser, R.. (2016). "Kompleksite İktisadı, Kendi Kendine Organize Olan Kritiklik ve Firma Dinamikleri", Yıldız Teknik Üniversitesi Sosyal Bilimler Enstitüsü Doktora Tezi.

Khan, F. &, P.Heinecker. (2018). Inequality and energy: Revisiting the relationship between disparity of income distribution and energy use from a complex systems perspective, Energy Research & Social Science, 42, 184–192.

Kırer, H. (2011). Türkiye ve Almanya'nın kişisel gelir dağılımına ekonofizik yaklaşım, Yıldız Teknik Üniversitesi, Sosyal Bilimler Enstitüsü, Doktora Tezi, Tez No: 289428.

Lowrey, A. (2014). "Even Among the Richest of the Rich, Fortunes Diverge", The New York Times, Feb 10, 2014.

Mandelbrot, B. (1963). New Methods in Statistical Economics. Journal of Political Economics, 71(5), 421-440.

Mandelbrot, B. (1982). The Fractal Geometry of Nature. New York. Freeman.

Pareto, V. (1897). Cours d'Economie Politique. Paris. Rouge & Cie.

Pueyo, S. (2014). Ecological Econophysics for Degrowht, Sustainability, 6, 3431–3483; doi:10.3390/su6063431.

Rosser, J. B. (2016). Entropy and Econophysics, Retrieved from http://cob.jmu.edu/rosserjb/ENTROPY%20AND%20ECONOPHYSICS.pdf (12.05.2020)

Sparavigna, A. C. (2016). "Entropies and fractal dimensions", Philica, Philica, 2016. Retrieved from https://hal.archives-ouvertes.fr/hal-01377975 (15.07.2020).

Takayasu, M. & H. Takayasu. (2010). Fractals and Economics. Chapter 10. In *Complex Systems in Finance and Econometrics, Selected Entries from the Encyclopedia of Complexity and Systems Science. 2-vol. set,* edited by Meyers, R.A. New York: Springer-Verlag. pp. 444–463.

Theil, H. (1967). Economics and Information Theory. Amsterdam: North Holland.

TURKSTAT. (2020a). Gelir Dağılımı ve Yaşam Koşulları İstatistikleri, Retrieved from http://www.tuik.gov.tr/PreTablo.do?alt_id=1011, (02.09.2020).

TURKSTAT. (2020b). Ulusal Hesaplar, Bölgesel Hesaplar, İl Bazında Gayrisafi Yurt İçi Hasıla, Kişi Başına Gayrisafi Yurtiçi Hasıla, İstatistiki Bölge Birimleri Sınıflaması, Retrieved from http://www.tuik.gov.tr/PreHaberBultenleri.do?id=30889 (02.09.2020).

TURKSTAT. (2020c). Adrese Dayalı Nüfüs Kayıt Sistemi Sonuçları, "İl ve cinsiyete göre il/ilçe merkezi, belde/köy nüfusu ve nüfus yoğunluğu", Retrieved from http://www.tuik.gov.tr/PreHaberBultenleri.do?id=33705 (02.09.2020).

World Bank. (2020). World Development Indicators, http://datatopics.worldbank.org/world-development-indicators/, erişim 20.07.2020.

Xiong, Gang, ShuningZhang, XiaoniuYang. (2012). "The fractal energy measurement and the singularity energy spectrum analysis", Physica A 391, 6347–6361.

Yakovenko, V.M. & J.B. Rosser, Jr. (2009), Colloquium: Statistical mechanics of money, wealth, and income, *Reviews of Modern Physics* 81, 1704–1725.

Yu, William, N.M. Daniels, D. C. Danko & B.Berger. (2015). Entropy-scaling search of massive biological data https://www.ncbi.nlm.nih.gov/pmc/articles/PMC4591002/

Zipf, G. K. (1949). Human Behavior and the Principle of Least Effort, Reading, MA, Addison-Waley.

Erdal Alancıoğlu

Chapter 11 Analysis of Environmental Kuznets Curve Hypothesis with SD Model: The Case of the G8

Abstract: In this paper, the relationship between economic development and environmental degradation is analyzed based on ecological footprint data and SD (Society-Economy-Energy) environment model. This relationship was examined using ecological footprint, economic growth, technological development, energy density, urbanization, population variables. For this purpose, we investigated the period of 1990 – 2016 using panel ARDL analysis. Unlike other studies, the SD environmental model was based on. The findings provide strong evidence that the Environmental Kuznets curve hypothesis is valid in G8 economies. Furthermore, long-term statistically significant relationships between other variables and environmental degradation were determined.

Keywords: Ecological Macroeconomics, Environmental Kuznets Curve, Ecological Footprint, Panel ARDL, SD Model, G8 Countries

1. Introduction

The Environmental Kuznets Curve (EKC) hypothesis, which models the relationship between economic development and environment and claims that there is an inverted-U shaped relationship between economic development and environmental degradation, is the model with the widest area of application in the literature (Bozkurt & Okumuş, 2017: 58).

According to the EKC hypothesis, environmental pressure tends to increase faster than income growth in the early stages of economic development. Then it slows down, reaches a turning point and decreases with increasing income (Rothman & De Bruyn, 1998; Kang et al., 2016).

Economies demonstrate a concave relationship with environmental degradation. In other words, the closer they are to the turning point in which economic development causes environmental recovery, the economic growth is less disruptive to the environment (Pontarollo & Muñoz, 2020: 1).

Empirical analyses of the Environmental Kuznets Curve (EKC) were first initiated by Grossman and Krueger (1991), Shafik and Bandyopadhyay (1992), Panayotou (1993), Selden and Song (1994). In the literature, different cases were examined for different indicators of pollution. There are also studies, which aim to verify EKC by using various research methods.

The EKC hypothesis proposed by Grossman and Krueger (1996) assumed an inverted U-shaped relationship between different environmental pollutants and income per capita. As income increases, environmental pressure increases to a certain level; then it starts decreasing. Some studies have proven that the EKC is inverted U-shape (Ozturk & Acaravci, 2013; Ahmed & Long, 2012). Özkoç et al. (2017) analyzed the relationship between economic development and environment using the data of 91 countries for the period between 1964 and 2009 by panel data method. According to the findings of the analysis, there were both short and long-term correlations among the variables. It also proved that there was an inverted U-shaped relationship in low-income countries. Unlike the previous studies focusing on traditional prediction techniques, Kang et al. (2016) investigated the CO2- EKC hypothesis of China for the period of 1997–2012 using a spatial panel data model. The findings showed that the relationship between economic growth and CO2 emissions was shaped as inverted U. It was verified that the effects of spatial spreading affected the shape of the EKC.

Bozkurt and Okumuş (2017) tested the relationship between economic growth, energy consumption, commercial liberalization, urbanization and CO2 emissions for 33 developed countries using the data of 1980–2013 with panel data analysis. According to the findings of the study, the EKC hypothesis was not valid for the country group included in the analysis. The effect of energy consumption on CO2 emissions was positive. In developed countries, the effect of commercial liberalization on CO2 emissions was found to be statistically insignificant.

Alam et al. (2016) examined the effects of income, energy consumption and population growth on CO2 emissions for the economies of India, Indonesia, China and Brazil with the ARDL bounds testing approach. He found that the increase in income and energy consumption also increased CO2 emissions. Although the relationship between CO2 emissions and population growth was statistically significant for India and Brazil, it was insignificant or China and Indonesia for both short term and long term.

Asongu et al. (2016) analyzed the relationship between energy consumption, CO2 emissions and economic growth for 24 African countries for the period of 1982–2011 using the panel ARDL method. A long-run relationship was detected between the variables. Furthermore, it was found that a one-way causality was running from economic growth to energy consumption and CO2 emissions. Despite all these studies, the EKC hypothesis was not empirically supported by the studies conducted by Farhani and Ozturk (2015), Ozturk and

Al-Mulali (2015), Begum et al. (2015), Dogan and Turkekul (2016), Özokçu and Özdemir, (2017).

This study aims to determine the validity of the Environmental Kuznets curve hypothesis in G8 countries (USA, Russia, England, France, Germany, Italy, Japan, Canada) based on the SD model. Since other environmental models cannot accurately predict environmental degradations, we preferred the SD model to solve complex problems that change over time. Although there are many studies in the literature investigating the EKC hypothesis for G8 countries, there are no studies testing the hypothesis using this model. Therefore, we hope that our study will contribute to the literature in this particular aspect.

The study has been structured as follows; Section 2 explains the properties of the theoretical model and data. Section 3 explains the methods used in empirical studies, including econometric approaches. Section 4 discusses the empirical findings. The study is finalized with the conclusion part, which includes a general evaluation and policy recommendations.

2. Model and Data

In this study, we preferred to use the SD (Society-Economy-Energy) model as the environmental model. SD model was first created by Forrester in 1956. It is a method for solving complex and dynamic system issues. Accordingly, the SD model has superior position in the field of environmental policy. It is widely used in experiments to make medium and long-term system decisions in areas such as society, economy and environment.

The SD model has three systems such as society, economy and energy consumption. The community subsystem covers the population and urbanization variables. The economy subsystem includes primary, secondary industry GDP variables, and technology input. The energy consumption subsystem consists of the energy consumption of industry, transportation, living and commercial service variables (Fu et al. 2015: 78).

Tab. 11.1 presents information on the variables selected to be used in the analysis according to the SD model. The data sample was converted to the panel data format. We used the data of 27 years (1990 – 2016) for 8 developed countries. The reason for choosing this country group is that, besides being industrialized and high income, they also demonstrate an intense level of urbanization. We thought that the energy consumption was high in these countries, which also increased the negative impact on the environment.

In the study, we used the ecological footprint indicator, which is believed to detect the environmental degradation level more accurately compared to CO2

Tab. 11.1 A selection of the SD model parameters, Source: Author's own construction

Parameter	**Symbol**	**Definition**	**Unit**
Ecological Footprint	EF	Environmental degradation indicator	In per capita form
GDP per capita	GDP	GDP per capita	Dollars
Secondary industry proportion	GDP2	The proportion of the value of the secondary industry to the GDP	%
Energy consumption intensity	EI	Industry energy consumption per unit of GDP	%
Technological development index	TD	Technological development indicator	%
Urbanization level	POP	Urban population proportion of the total population	%
Population	URB	Growth in the population	%

emissions. The reason for this is that the "ecological footprint" indicator developed by Wackernagel and Rees (1996) does not only take into consideration the carbon footprint but it also includes indicators such as crop-land, grazing land, forest, built-up land and fishing ground (Destek, 2018: 269).

The ecological footprint (EF) variable was obtained from the Global Footprint Network database in per capita terms. The economic growth (GDP) variable is in per capita terms and based on 2010 dollar exchange rate. Energy intensity (EI) is an indicator of how much energy is used to produce one unit of economic output. The energy intensity level of primary energy is the ratio between energy supply and gross domestic product measured in purchasing power parity. The variable of urbanization level (URB) is the ratio of urban population to the total population. The variable of population (POP) refers to the growth in population. Like other variables, the technological development index was also obtained from the World Bank Development Indicators Database (WDI).

Tab. 11.2 shows the descriptive statistics of the variables. As mentioned earlier in the data source, all variables are converted to natural logarithm, except for the POP variable. The statistics in Tab. 11.2 show that economic growth, for the G8 countries, is an average of 10,150 and quite high with a standard deviation of 0.743 compared to the ecological footprint (1.204).

The empirical model formed by using the ecological footprint as an indicator of environmental degradation is as follows:

Tab. 11.2: Common sample descriptive statistics (data in logarithms), Source: Author's own calculations

Variables	EF	GDP	GDP2	EI	TD	URB	POP
Mean	1.204	10.150	103.575	1.732	10.262	4.341	0.440
Median	1.104	10.358	107.295	1.654	9.911	4.348	0.383
Maximum	1.764	10.966	120,265	2.666	12.858	4.515	1.507
Minimum	0.830	7.1935	51.746	1.091	7.687	4.200	-1.853
Std. Dev.	0.242	0.7434	13.931	0.396	1.424	0.067	0.469
Skewness	0.983	-2.1402	-1.930	0.515	0.438	-0.020	-0.382
Kurtosis	2.521	7.3455	6.509	2.365	2.147	3.606	4.352
Jarque-Bera (JB)	36.91	334.85	244.959	13.200	13.442	3.328	21.746
Probability of JB	0.000	0.0000	0.000	0.001	0.001	0.189	0.000

$$\begin{aligned} \ln EF_t &= \alpha_0 + \alpha_1 \ln GDP_t + \alpha_2 \ln GDP_t^2 + \alpha_3 \ln EI_t + \alpha_4 \ln TD_t \\ &\quad + \alpha_5 \ln URB_t + \alpha_6 \ln POP_t + \mu_t \end{aligned} \tag{1}$$

Among the variables in the model, lnEF is the natural logarithm of the ecological footprint in per capita terms representing environmental degradation; lnGDP is the natural logarithm of real GDP in per capita terms used to represent economic development (economic growth); lnGDP2 represents the square of the natural logarithm of real GDP in per capita terms; lnEI is the natural logarithm of the energy intensity variable used to represent technological development, lnTD represents the natural logarithm of the technological development index, lnURB is the natural logarithm of the ratio of the population living in the cities used to the total population representing the level of urbanization, and lnPOP represents the natural logarithm of population growth rate.

3. Econometric Estimation Approach

To test the unit roots (or stationarity), we used various tests for panel datasets, taking into account the sample sizes and the asymptotic properties of the tests. These tests were developed by Levin et al. (2002) [hereafter LLC], Im et al. (2003) [hereafter IPS], Fisher ADF and Fisher PP. All these tests are considered to be the first-generation panel unit root tests because they assume independence between cross-section units. LLC and IPS tests include individual and specific trends. The purpose of the IPS test is to rectify the restrictive LLC hypothesis, namely the homogeneous nature of the autoregressive root under the alternative hypothesis. The null hypotheses of all tests indicate the presence of a unit root (Da Silva et al., 2018: 49).

Pesaran et al. (1999) proposed the Pooled Mean Group estimator (PMG) within the ARDL framework. Pesaran et al. (1999) stated that the homogeneity in the long-run relationship could be attributed to several factors. And these factors are arbitration condition, common technologies, or the institutional development, which was covered by all groups.

According to the methodology of Pesaran et al. (1999), the ARDL model, which includes the long-run relationship between variables, may be as follows:

$$EF_{it} = \sum_{j=1}^{p} \alpha_{ij} EF_{i,t-j} + \sum_{j=0}^{q} \delta\prime_{ij} x_{i,t-j} + \mu_i + \varepsilon_{it} \quad (2)$$

where X is the vector of the explanatory variables.

The Equation 2 model allows parameters to change between units. Pesaran and Smith (1995) and Pesaran et al. (1999) showed that the MG estimator would produce consistent estimates of the average of the parameters for each country and group. Nevertheless, on condition that the long-term coefficients are homogeneous between the groups, a more efficient estimator can be used. In order for the model to be read as an error correction mechanism, the variables have to be co-integrated. Therefore, in the next section, we will first present the stationarity tests of the variables and finally, the panel estimator (Da Silva et al., 2018: 49).

4. Empirical Results

The results of the panel unit root tests are presented in Tab. 11.3 and Tab. 11.4. According to results of the fixed and fixed trendy LLC and IPS panel unit root tests, all variables, except for POP, were found to have unit root at level.

According to the unit root test statistics calculated when the difference of the variables was taken, the null hypothesis was rejected. It was concluded that the variables were stationary at I (1). Drawing on Tabs. 11.3 and 11.4, it could be concluded that EF and GDP are integrated variables; thus, the panel ARDL model could be used. This finding was drawn from the results of most of the panel unit root tests.

Tab. 11.5 presents strong evidence that the EF variable has long-term effects on GDP and other variables. We would like to point out that reciprocal paths of

Tab. 11.3 Panel unit root results: series in level

Variable	LLC		IPS		Fisher-ADF		Fisher-PP	
	İntercept	**Trend**	**İntercept**	**Trend**	**İntercept**	**Trend**	**İntercept**	**Trend**
EF	-0,868	0,011	-1,351	-0,988	23,860	-15,733	27,326	15,668
	[0.192]	[0.495]	[0.088]	[0.838]	[0.092]	[0.471]	[0.038]	[0.476]
GDP	-2.208	-0,971	-0,038	-0,231	14,083	-12,873	12,529	5,933
	[0.013]	[0.834]	[0.484]	[0.591]	[0.592]	[0.682]	[0.706]	[0.988]
GDP2	-2.041	1,010	0,039	0,215	13,575	12,877	11,898	6,118
	[0.020]	[0.843]	[0.515]	[0.585]	[0.630]	[0.681]	[0.751]	[0.986]
EI	1.279	-0,859	4,942	-1.406	1,047	26,725	1,274	54,741
	[0.899]	[0.195]	[1,000]	[0.079]	[1,000]	[0.044]	[1,000]	[0.000]
TD	-1,559	-0,494	0,183	0.795	15,398	11,332	19,025	15,807
	[0.059]	[0.310]	[0.572]	[0.786]	[0.495]	[0.788]	[0.267]	[0.466]
URB	-0,325	-1,051	2,688	2,424	15,196	14,089	28,896	6,223
	[0.372]	[0.146]	[0.996]	[0.992]	[0.510]	[0.592]	[0.024]	[0.985]
POP	-1,483	-1,247	-1,551	-2,374	25,621	-34,197	27,439	26,181
	[0.069]	[0.106]	[0.060]	[0.008]	[0.059]	[0.005]	[0.036]	[0.051]

Tab. 11.4 Panel unit root results: series in first difference, Source: Author's own calculations

Variable	LLC		IPS		Fisher-ADF		Fisher-PP	
	İntercept	**Trend**	**İntercept**	**Trend**	**İntercept**	**Trend**	**İntercept**	**Trend**
EF	-5,886	-5,134	-6,996	-6,471	78,119	68,236	141,893	143,548
	[0.000]	[0.000]	[0.000]	[0.000]	[0.000]	[0.000]	[0.000]	[0.000]
GDP	-5,730	-4,311	-5,571	-3,764	60,737	40,933	67,882	47,372
	[0.000]	[0.000]	[0.000]	[0.000]	[0.000]	[0.000]	[0.000]	[0.000]
GDP2	-5,721	-4,261	-5,595	-3,742	61,003	40,789	68,796	47,495
	[0.000]	[0.000]	[0.000]	[0.000]	[0.000]	[0.000]	[0.000]	[0.000]
EI	-6,707	-6,567	-8,1562	-7,586	92,155	81,036	171,659	923,89
	[0.000]	[0.000]	[0.000]	[0.000]	[0.000]	[0.000]	[0.000]	[0.000]
TD	-6,577	-6,214	-6,220	-5,247	68,937	55,555	114,189	112,075
	[0.000]	[0.000]	[0.000]	[0.000]	[0.000]	[0.000]	[0.000]	[0.000]
URB	-7,001	-92,178	-4,527	-67,446	270,060	59,615	8,400	9,231
	[0.000]	[0.000]	[0.000]	[0.000]	[0.000]	[0.000]	[0.000]	[0.000]
POP	-6,565	-5,019	-8,805	-7,341	98,280	78,306	120,908	128,397
	[0.000]	[0.000]	[0.000]	[0.000]	[0.000]	[0.000]	[0.000]	[0.000]

Tab. 11.5 Panel ARDL PMG long-run estimates (LNEF is the dependent variable)

Variables	Estimate	t-Statistic	Probability
LNGDP	15.36647	2.063248	0.0426**
LNGDP2	-1.668175	-2.282019	0.0254**
LNEI	0.259978	6.193731	0.0000*
LNTD	-0.095220	-7.588171	0.0000*
LNURB	0.244025	1.904521	0.0608***
POP	0.018764	3.848722	0.0003*

*, ** and *** indicate significance levels 1, 5 and 10 %, respectively.

these long-term effects have been observed with a lot of evidence. However, the long-term effects of EF on GDP (and vice versa) are only significant at 5 % level.

We determined that all variables, except for GDP2 and TD, had a positive and significant effect on the ecological footprint. According to the findings; GDP creates a 1 % increase in energy consumption intensity, urbanization and population while it increases ecological footprint by 15 %, 0,05 %, 0,25 %, 0,24 % and 0,02 % respectively. In contrast, GDP2 and the technological development variable reduce the ecological footprint by 1,66 % and 0,09 %, respectively.

Tab. 11.6 presents the short-term estimates and describes the error correction model corresponding to the established cointegration relationships or long-run equilibriums. While the error correction term (ECT) is zero at equilibrium, a non-zero ECT indicates that pairs of linkages deviate from the long-term equilibrium. Therefore, ECT helps adjust and partially restore the cointegration relationship. The underlying restoration of the equilibrium requires ECT (i) to have an expected sign and (ii) be in the right interval. Basically, a negative ECT between 0 and 1 is essential for a stable error correction mechanism. A positive ECT coefficient indicates deviation from balance. It is concluded that a negative ECT sign is required for the restoration of equilibrium after an exogenous shock (Asongu et al., 2016: 6569).

Our findings show that the ECT coefficient is negative (-0.635) within an interval of 0 and 1 as expected. The error correction coefficient of the model has also been found to be significant. Accordingly, a stable error correction mechanism works in our analysis. According to the results in Tab. 10.6, it can be stated that any shock or unexpected effect that will occur in the short term will be corrected by 0.63 % every year in the long term. In the short term; while the effect of the GDP variable on the ecological footprint is negative (-217,798), the coefficient of the GDP2 variable is positive (20,933) and significant. The coefficients of other variables are not statistically significant.

Tab. 11.6: PMG short-run estimate, LNEF is the dependent variable, Source: Author's own calculations

	Estimate	t-Statistic	Probability
ECT	-0.635435	-2.211610	0.0301**
D(LNEF(-1))	0.042570	0.381640	0.7038
D(LNGDP)	187.9272	0.864123	0.3904
D(LNGDP(-1))	-217.7980	-2.320846	0.0231**
D(LNGDP2)	-17.47390	-0.844535	0.4011
D(LNGDP2(-1))	20.93360	2.302957	0.0241**
D(LNEI)	-0.039773	-0.397545	0.6921
D(LNEI(-1))	-0.470553	-4.799895	0.0000*
D(LNTD)	0.304971	1.185316	0.2397
D(LNTD(-1))	0.090892	0.692025	0.4911
D(LNURB)	-10.27660	-0.643784	0.5217
D(LNURB(-1))	26.07118	1.612557	0.1112
D(POP)	-0.010803	-0.195653	0.8454
D(POP(-1))	-0.009246	-0.222436	0.8246
Constant	-29.38810	-2.213774	0.0300**

*, ** and *** indicate significance levels 1, 5 and 10 %, respectively.

5. Conclusion, Limitations and Suggestions for Future Research

In this study, in order to analyze the relationship between economic development and environmental degradation, we tested the validity of the EKC hypothesis for G8 economies. In the study, the SD environment model was taken as the empirical model, unlike the studies examining the validity of the EKC hypothesis.

According to the findings of panel ARDL analysis; short-term and long-term coefficient estimates of GDP are -217,79 and 15,366, respectively while the short-term and long-term coefficient estimates of GDP square are 20,933 and -1,668. For the EKC hypothesis to be valid, the impact of GDP and GDP2 variables on the ecological footprint is expected to be positive and negative, respectively. Our findings are supportive of the validity of the EKC hypothesis in G8 countries. This finding is consistent with those of Iwata et al. (2010), Cho et al. (2014), Kasman and Duman (2015), Al-Mulali and Ozturk (2016), Li et al. (2016), Destek et al. (2016), Balaguer and Cantavella (2016).

There is an inverted U-shaped relationship between the level of income and ecological footprint. Therefore, an increase in the GDP level causes a certain level of environmental degradation. Then, the increase in income level leads to environmental recovery. Developed economies such as G8 countries have transformed their product mix into the service sector due to having a higher level of GDP. In this way, they can shift their pollution to other countries. Kearsley and Riddell (2010) claim that developed economies specialize in service industries and light manufacturing, not in "dirty" production compared to developing countries. Environmental policies and institutionalization in G8 countries lead to stricter environmental regulations. Having a higher institutional capacity is another factor that explains the EKC model.

Furthermore, we found a positive relationship between ecological footprint and energy consumption, which is one of the variables added based on the SD model. Accordingly, increasing the energy consumption intensity by 1 unit in the long term increases environmental degradation by 0.25 %. Likewise, urbanization level and population growth in G8 countries also cause environmental degradation. One unit increase in both variables increases environmental degradation by 0.24 % and 0.01 %, respectively. On the other hand, increasing technological development reduces environmental degradation in accordance with the theory. According to the coefficient estimate; 1 unit of technological development in the long term causes recovery by 0.09 %. The results are in accordance with the theory.

Based on all these results, the trend towards renewable energy sources can be increased in order to reduce environmental degradation in G8 countries. R&D expenditures can be channeled to environmentally friendly technologies. In addition, alternative energy sources should be sought. Policies should be developed in order to reduce the high amount of carbon that is likely to spread. These types of environmental projects can be funded.

Finally, there are some limitations in our study. One of them is the availability of data. Ecological footprint data is available until 2016. For this reason, the observation range was determined as 1990–2016 in the analyzes. Further research using the GMM approach could also be conducted in order to develop a common policy on climate change and environmental pollution.

References

Ahmed K., & Long W. (2012). Environmental Kuznets curve and Pakistan: An empirical Analysis. *Procedia Economics and Finance*, *1:* 4–13.

Alam M. M., Murad M. W., Noman A. H. M., & Ozturk, I. (2016). Relationships among carbon emissions, economic growth, energy consumption and population growth: Testing Environmental Kuznets Curve Hypothesis for Brazil, China, India and Indonesia. *Ecological Indicators, 70*: 466–479.

Al-Mulali U., & Ozturk I. (2016). The investigation of environmental Kuznets curve hypothesis in the advanced economies: The role of energyprices. *Renewable and Sustainable Energy Reviews, 54*: 622–1631.

Asongu S., El Montasser G., & Toumi H. (2016). Testing the relationships between energy consumption, CO2 emissions, and economic growth in 24 African countries: A panel ARDL approach. *Environmental Science and Pollution Research, 23(7)*: 6563–6573.

Balaguer J., & Cantavella M. (2016). Estimating the environmental Kuznets curve for Spain by considering fuel oil prices (1874–2011). *Ecological Indicators, 60:* 853–859.

Begum, R. A., Sohag K., Abdullah S. M. S., & Jaafar M. (2015). CO2 emissions, energy consumption, economic and population growth in Malaysia. *Renewable and Sustainable Energy Reviews, 41*: 594–601.

Bozkurt C., & Okumuş İ. (2017). Gelişmiş ülkelerde çevresel Kuznets eğrisi hipotezinin test edilmesi: Kyoto protokolünün rolü, *İşletme ve İktisat Çalışmaları Dergisi, 5(4):* 57–67.

Cho C. H., Chu Y. P., & Yang H. Y. (2014). An environment Kuznets curve for GHG emissions: A panel cointegration analysis. *Energy Sources, Part B: Economics, Planning and Policy, 9(2)*:120–129.

Da Silva P. P., Cerqueira P. A., & Ogbe W. (2018). Determinants of renewable energy growth in Sub-Saharan Africa: Evidence from panel ARDL. *Energy, 156*: 45–54.

Destek M. A. (2018). Çevresel Kuznets eğrisi hipotezinin Türkiye için incelenmesi: STIRPAT modelinden bulgular. *Cumhuriyet Üniversitesi İktisadi ve İdari Bilimler Dergisi, 19(2):* 268–283.

Destek M. A., Balli E., & Manga M. (2016). The relationship between CO2 emission, energy consumption, urbanization and trade openness for selected CEECs. *Research in World Economy, 7(1):* 52–58.

Dogan E., & Turkekul B. (2016). CO2 emissions, real output, energy consumption, trade, urbanization and financial development: Testing the EKC hypothesis for the USA. *Environmental Science and Pollution Research, 23(2)*: 1203–1213.

Farhani S., & Ozturk I. (2015). Causal relationship between CO2 emissions, real GDP, energy consumption, financial development, trade openness, and urbanization in Tunisia. *Environmental Science and Pollution Research, 22(20):* 15663–15676.

Forrester J. W. (1956). Dynamic models of economic systems and industrial organizations (2003 republication of a "Note to the Faculty Research Seminar, November 5, 1956" and MIT "D-memo" zero). *System Dynamics Review, 19(4):* 331–345.

Fu B., Wu M., Che Y., Wang M., Huang Y., & Bai Y. (2015). The strategy of a low-carbon economy based on the STIRPAT and SD models. *Acta Ecologica Sinica, 35(4):* 76–82.

Global Footprint Network Database. (2020). [online] Available at: <https://data.footprintnetwork.org/#/exploreData> Accessed 10 February 2020.

Grossman G. M., & Krueger A. B. (1991). Environmental impacts of a North American free trade agreement (No. w3914). *National Bureau of Economic Research.* doi:10.3386/w3914.

Grossman G. M., & Krueger A. B. (1996). The inverted-U: What does it mean?. *Environment and Development Economics, 1(1):* 119–122.

Im K. S., Pesaran M. H., & Shin Y. (2003). Testing for unitroots in heterogeneous panels. *Journal of Econometrics, 115(1):* 53–74.

Iwata H., Okada K., & Samreth S. (2010). Empirical study on the environmental Kuznets curve for CO2 in France: The role of nucleare nergy. *EnergyPolicy, 38(8):* 4057–4063.

Kang Y. Q., Zhao T., & Yang Y. Y. (2016). Environmental Kuznetscurve for CO2 emissions in China: A spatial panel data approach. *Ecological Indicators, 63:* 231–239.

Kasman A., & Duman Y. S. (2015). CO2 emissions, economic growth, energy consumption, trade and urbanization in new EU member and candidate countries: A panel data analysis. *Economic Modelling, 44:* 97–103.

Kearsley A., & Riddel M. A. (2010). A further inquiry into the pollution haven hypothesis and the environmental Kuznets curve. *Ecologial Economics, 69(4):* 905–919.

Levin A., Lin C. F., & Chu C. S. J. (2002). Unit root tests in panel data: Asymptotic and finite-sample properties. *Journal of Econometrics, 108(1)*: 1–24.

Li T., Wang Y., & Zhao D. (2016). Environmental Kuznets curve in China: New evidence from dynamic panel analysis. *Energy Policy, 91:* 138–147.

Özkoç H., Yıldırım A., & Kudubeş E. (2017). Çevresel Kuznets eğrisinin geçerliliğinin düşük ve üst orta gelirli ülkeler için sınanması: 1964–2009 dönemi. *Mehmet Akif Ersoy Üniversitesi Sosyal Bilimler Enstitüsü Dergisi, 9(22):* 327–340.

Özokcu S., & Özdemir Ö. (2017). Economic growth, energy, and environmental Kuznets curve. *Renewable and Sustainable Energy Reviews, 72:* 639–647.

Ozturk I., & Acaravci A. (2013). The long-run and causal analysis of energy growth, openness and financial development on carbon emissions in Turkey. *Energy Economics. 36*: 262–267.

Ozturk I., & Al-Mulali U. (2015). Investigating the validity of the environmental Kuznets curve hypothesis in Cambodia. *Ecological Indicators, 57*: 324–330.

Panayotou T. (1993). Empirical tests and policy analysis of environmental degradation at different stages of economic development. *ILO Working Paper 992927783402676*. International Labour Organization.

Pesaran M. H., & Smith R. P. (1995). Estimating long-run relationships from dynamic heterogeneous panels. *Journal of Econometircs, 68(1)*: 79–113.

Pesaran M. H., Shin Y., & Smith R. P. (1999). Pooled mean group estimation of dynamic heterogeneous panels. *Journal of American Statistical Association, 94 (446):* 621–634.

Pontarollo N., & Muñoz, R. M. (2020). Land consumption and income in Ecuador: A case of an inverted environmental Kuznets curve. *Ecological Indicators, 108,* 105699.

Rothman D. S., & Bruyn S. M. (1998). Probing into the environmental Kuznets curve hypothesis. *Ecological Economics, 25*: 143–145.

Selden T. M., & Song D. (1994). Environmental quality and development: Is there a Kuznets curve for air pollution emissions? *Journal of Environmental Economics and Management, 27(2):* 147–162.

Shafik N., & Bandyopadhyay S. (1992). Economic growth and environmental quality: Imeseries and cross-country evidence. *Policy Research Working Papers no. 904*. World Bank Publications.

Wackernagel M., & Rees W. (1996). *Our ecological foot print: Reducing human impact on the earth* (Vol. 9). New Society Publishers.

World Bank. (2020). World Development Indicators, [online] Available at: <https://databank.worldbank.org/source/world-development-indicators> Accessed 15 February 2020.

Berna Tuncay

Chapter 12 Generic Competition and Price Regulation in Pharmaceuticals: Evidence from the European Union[1]

Abstract: The purpose of this study is to examine the extent of generic competition in European countries, given an understanding of these countries' different pharmaceutical price regulations. In particular, this study investigates the competitive effects of generic entry among the five largest European pharmaceutical markets; the United Kingdom, Germany, France, Italy and Spain, and employs fully interacted model with comprehensive IMS data set for 10 years (1994–2003), in order to estimate the effect of generic entry on drug prices at the product level. Accordingly, this analysis finds that generic entry has a negative effect on prices in countries with free pricing originator market, whereas in countries with strict price and reimbursement regulation, generic competition is ineffective and/or counterproductive. Low regulated prices for originator products do not encourage generic entry following patent expiration. This finding is consistent with less generic firms and less competitive late entrants in regulated environments. Thus, strict price regulation undermines price competition in the off-patent market.

Keywords: Pharmaceuticals, Generic Entry, Price Competition, Market Regulation, Reference Pricing, Fully Interacted Model

1. Introduction

In recent decades, one of the priorities of the European Union (EU) health care system has been controlling pharmaceutical expenditures. In order to more effectively control pharmaceutical expenditures, EU countries have employed regulatory policies designed to generate lower costs while improving efficiency. Pharmaceutical pricing and reimbursement regulatory systems are often very complex, as they are customized to respond to the specific economic and health care needs of a country. Collectively, these systems provide comprehensive and

1 This study is produced from Berna Çolak Tuncay's PhD thesis named "Generic Competition and Price Regulation in the European Union Pharmaceutical Market: The Case of Cardiovascular Medicines" submitted to the University of South Florida in 2014.

up-to-date information, which is useful for monitoring price competition in both on-patent and off-patent pharmaceutical markets.

The pharmaceutical industry is subject to a high degree of effective competition because it includes such a large number of rival producers, and because these rivals then compete among one another by responding to the price-sensitive demand for drugs (Scherer, 2000). Patents and the lack of good substitutes for new drugs provide substantial monopoly power, which encourage national governments in the EU to develop price control policies (Danzon and Chao, 2000). When patents expire, generic substitutes enter the market and introduce price competition to the originator drug market. Ultimately, the extent to which generics capture the market share from branded original drugs depends on the government's regulatory policies. In other words, the characteristics of the off-patent and in-patent pharmaceutical markets create the potential for price competition, which can be encouraged by pricing and reimbursement regulations.

Many irregularities exist within EU pharmaceutical market, some of which are insurance and third party payers, information asymmetry, and agency relationships. Essentially, this means that prices may not respond to the entry of new products as is normally predicted. Additionally, this atypical pattern may also lead to low levels of elasticity of demand (Vandoros and Kanavos, 2013). Because of these irregularities, pricing and reimbursement regulations are used to offset market failures. In the EU, the status of off-patent pharmaceutical markets is determined largely by policy developments and market regulations. National health care systems are extremely influential in affecting the penetration of generic medicines in pharmaceutical markets. The market for generic drugs has received more serious attention in EU countries over the past few years, primarily due to new policies that promote the use of off-patent drugs. Germany is the most highly developed generic market in Europe; it is also the largest pharmaceutical market in Western Europe. In contrast, generic markets in the UK, France, Italy, and Spain are not as developed as Germany. Countries within the EU use formalized pricing regulations to control generic prices, which support generic uptake following the patent's expiration. The most commonly used regulatory policies are reference pricing and price caps (Vandoros and Kanavos, 2013). Reference pricing is the most popular regulatory policy used in off-patent markets within EU countries. Under reference pricing, prices among similar products (or prices for the same product in other EU countries) are compared and grouped together in order to determine a maximum reimbursement price. European countries that use reference pricing in off-patent markets include Germany, France, Italy and Spain. Another policy, used in the UK, is price capping. Under price capping, generic prices are set at a maximum percentage of branded prices (Vandoros and Kanavos, 2013). Moreover, both within and across these countries, different interventions are being applied to in-patent markets. For example, in Germany, markets for on-patent drugs are largely unregulated and prices are set relatively freely. In the UK, originator medicine prices are free from direct regulatory intervention, but are subject to a rate of return regulation, where drug companies are allowed to make a profit of up to 21 % return on capital invested. France, Italy, and Spain, on the other hand, use direct price controls for originator drugs, where fixed maximum pharmaceutical prices are set.

This paper examines the extent of competition between generic products under different regulatory regimes in the EU pharmaceutical industry. In particular, the study investigates the effect of generic competition on drug prices at the product level among the five largest European countries – the UK, Germany, France, Italy and Spain – given an analysis of comprehensive Intercontinental Medical Statistics (IMS) data over the span of 10 years (1994–2003). This analysis finds that generic competition has a significant negative effect on price for Germany, whereas for the countries with stricter price regulation (the United Kingdom, France, Italy, and Spain), the number of generic competitors has either no effect or a positive effect on prices. As Danzon and Chao (2000) point out, this is consistent with evidence that in countries with strict regulation, generic competitors are predominantly either licensed co-marketers or new versions of old molecules that manufacturers introduce in order to obtain a price increase. On the other hand, in countries with relatively free pricing regime, successive generics enter at lower prices, and prices at the product levels are negatively related to the number of generics.

The remainder of the paper is organized as follows: Section 2 summarizes a literature review describing the nature of off-patent market competition. Section 3 outlines the data and empirical strategy implemented in this study. Section 4 presents empirical results. Section 5 provides concluding remarks and suggestions for future research in the field.

2. Literature

Price competition has been an important topic in various empirical studies of the pharmaceutical industry. However, empirical studies in literature does not provide a clear explanation for the nature of generic competition due to heterogeneity in the methodologies used, the range of products considered, the study periods chosen, and the methods of estimation.

Jönsson (1994) and Vandoros and Kanavos (2013) suggest that countries with strict price regulations have lower prices than countries with less strict price regulations. On the other hand, the studies of Grabowski and Vernon (1992), Rizzo and Zeckhauser (2009) and Caves et al. (1991) show that prices do not decrease after generics enter the market; they argue that generic entry only leads to a slower rate at which drug prices increase. Danzon and Chao (2000) identify how, in less regulated markets, competition has kept prices low. Anis et al. (2003) state that in cases where less regulation is imposed, substantially more competition exists. Their study concludes that pricing regulations fail to achieve the goal of lowering prices. Garattini and Tediosi (2000) and Rovira and Darba (2001) find that countries with strict price regulation policies have lower overall prices than countries with less strict regulations. On the other hand, Reekie (1996) claims that competition yields low prices in markets with less strict regulation in Germany. Brekke (2007) finds that reference-pricing policy increases generic competition, resulting in lower brand-name market shares. Puig-Junoy (2010) reports that the reference pricing system causes a reduction in the consumer price of all pharmaceuticals subject to this system, to a varying degree in different countries and different periods of time. Podnar et al. (2007) addresses how the Slovenian pharmaceutical market is influenced by reference pricing and states that the reference pricing system causes an increase in the share of generic drugs. Similarly, Adriaen et al. (2008) examine the pricing strategies of generic medicines following patent expiry in Belgium and conclude that pricing strategies are influenced by regulatory aspects, such as, successive reductions in reference prices. Finally, Augurzky et al. (2009) show that the introduction of a reference pricing policy reduces the market prices of the affected products by approximately 7 %.

Several studies stated above suggest that generic competition has less of an effect on prices in strictly regulated markets. One possible explanation is that, pricing and reimbursement regulations keep the prices of branded drugs lower, and this reduces the motivation for generics to enter the market. Conversely, in less-regulated regimes, innovators of effective drugs can profit from higher prices, which subsequently attract the entry of generics. In countries where the pharmaceutical market is managed by less-regulated regimes, markets generate a sharp distinction between innovators and imitators (Magazzini et al., 2004).

Overall, pharmaceutical markets respond to significant imperfections both from the demand side and supply side, which leads to significant differences among markets. One way to pursue further research in this field is to examine the effect of generic competition among different markets (Kanavos and Srivastava, 2008). Therefore, in order to shed light on this topic, this paper focuses on how drug prices change over time as a consequence of generic competition, taking into consideration different pricing regulatory regimes across the countries examined.

3. Data and Empirical Methodology

This section explains the nature of the IMS data in detail and the empirical strategy, fully interacted model, implemented in the study.

3.1. Data

This study analyzes retail prices of drugs used to treat cardiovascular disease (CVD), the third-leading cause of death in OECD countries. Importantly, the effectiveness of CVD drug therapies is short-term, so patients must continually receive treatment to maintain its health benefits. The study sample consists of drugs from eight CVD therapeutic categories (C1A, C2A, C3A, C4A, C7A, C8A, C9A, C10A), which cover both newer and older innovations that form the core of pharmacotherapy for CVD.

Data used in this study were obtained from IMS Health, an international pharmaceutical consulting company that collects sales and price data from various countries. Data are collected at the level of the pharmaceutical market supply and distribution chain that provides reliable information. The IMS Health measure for all dosage forms and strengths is the IMS standard unit (SU). The SU is a single dose for example, one tablet or capsule, five liquid milliliters (i.e. one teaspoon), or one ampoule or vial of an injected product. Prices are measured at the ex-manufacturer level and converted from local currencies to euros by IMS Health using constant exchange rates. A country's SU price for a molecule is its volume-weighted average price per dose over all presentations, including generic, licensed, OTC, and parallel imported products (Danzon and Furukawa, 2003; Timur, 2006). Products are categorized by the Anatomic Therapeutic Category (ATC) system, which is developed and maintained by European Pharmaceutical Marketing Research Association, EphMrA (EphMrA, 2006). Products are categorized in the sales, medical and promotional audits according to the EphMrA/PBIRG Anatomical Classification System, the main principle of which is that there is only one Anatomical Classification code allocated to a product/pack. This allows each product to be classified consistently in all countries (EphMrA, 2006; Timur, 2006).

The IMS data used here are on all drug sales through retail pharmacies for 10 years between 1994 and 2003. The study restricts the sample to single-molecule "global" products, that is, products that contain a single active ingredient (molecule) and are available in all five countries. A given molecule may have multiple products (defined by molecule, manufacturer, and IMS product name) – for example, originator brand, licensees, parallel imports, and generics – and each product may have multiple packs, defined by strength, presentation forms, and pack sizes. Although the sample of molecules is uniform across countries, the number of products per molecule, manufacturers, and packs differ across countries. The main unit of analysis here is the product, aggregated over packs for each product.

The sample includes the five largest pharmaceutical markets in the European Union: Germany, the United Kingdom (UK), Italy, Spain, and France. These countries are also the leading pharmaceutical markets in the world after the US and Japan. The study sample contains 259 molecules with a total of 3347 products. The study further restricts the sample to molecules that are available in all five countries as described above. Germany is specified as the baseline country because it contains the most products, it is the largest market in the EU, and it is the relatively least regulated market in the EU.

3.2. Variable Definitions

Price. For each pack, IMS reports the price per standard unit. This study defines the average price per standard unit for each product as the volume-weighted average over all forms and packs of the product. For the regression analysis the paper uses the log transformation of price and of all explanatory variables where proportional effects are expected.

Quality Variables. This study controls for several "quality" characteristics that impact the product's efficacy and its price. Molecule Age, measured as (log) months from the last observation month to the launch date of the first product in the molecule in that specific country. Molecule Age is an inverse indicator of therapeutic effectiveness, assuming that more recent compounds are generally more effective. Molecule Age is the same for all products in a molecule but is country specific. Strength is the mean grams of active ingredient per standard unit, averaged over all packs within the product. One can expect a positive relationship between Strength and price. Form Code is the number of different product formulations for each molecule and product, and is intended to reflect choice and convenience available to patients. Forms include different types of tablets, capsules, ampoules, powders, drops, syrups, syringes, and liquids, along with different strengths and pack sizes. The coefficient is expected to be positive, assuming that manufacturers launch new forms only where the expected increase in price is sufficient to cover the fixed costs of developing a new form.

Competition (Market) Variables. Measures of competition distinguish between generic and therapeutic substitutes. Generic Competitors is the number of generically equivalent products in the molecule, including originator, licensed, and parallel imported products, as well as post patent generic imitators. The expected effect of generic imitators on price is negative in markets where manufacturer prices are unregulated. Therapeutic Substitute Molecules is the number of molecules within the same three-digit therapeutic category ATC3. These drugs are competitors that are chemically distinct but used to treat the same indication, thus reflecting increased availability of substitutes and should thereby be negatively related with price. Pack Size is the number of SUs averaged over all packs in a molecule. This market variable is converted to standard units according to IMS (2005) guidelines. Price is expected to be inversely related to Pack Size in countries with competitive retail pharmacy, where manufacturers, particularly generics, compete by offering volume discounts to pharmacists on large packs.

3.3. Descriptive Statistics of IMS Data

Tab. 12.1 shows summary statistics for the product-level variables by country. This analysis categorizes the variables as quality characteristics and competition (market) characteristics. As reported in Tab. 12.1, the mean ***Price*** per product shows some variations across countries. Quality characteristics are summarized in the first section of Tab. 12.1. The mean ***Strength*** per product does not differ significantly across countries. More effective molecules are assumed to have a higher level of strength, implying a positive relationship between strength and price. The overall mean for ***Molecule Age*** is 22 years. The high sample mean age for all countries reflects the influence of a few very old molecules (Danzon and Chao, 2000). As Timur et al. (2011) says "molecule age is expected to be inversely related with price, since newer treatments are typically introduced precisely because they are more effective, and thus have a higher value, than older treatments". ***Form Code*** along with different strengths and pack sizes suggests a positive relationship with price.

Competition (market) characteristics are summarized in the second section of Tab. 12.1. The average SU ***Pack Size*** is significantly lower in France, Italy, and Spain, which require more unit pack dispensing than Germany and the United Kingdom. Economies of scale at the manufacturer level will imply

Tab. 12.1: Overall Mean; (Overall), [Within] Standard Deviation Values; N Unit of Observation: Products, Retail Pharmacy, 1994 – 2003, Source: Author's own calculations

Variable	Germany	France	United Kingdom	Italy	Spain	Overall
SU Price (Local Euro)	0.5208 (1.1888) [0.1871] 5039	0.2116 (0.2051) [0.0135] 1022	0.6290 (3.1275) [0.1456] 945	0.3109 (0.7629) [0.1189] 1822	0.2337 (0.2597) [0.0478] 1298	0.3584 (1.3227) [0.1513] 10126
<u>Quality:</u>						
Strength(g)	0.0529 (0.0884) [0.0089] 5039	0.1276 (0.4011) [0.0046] 1022	0.0523 (0.0831) [0.0101] 945	0.0939 (0.1468) [0.0295] 1822	0.0768 (0.1375) [0.0145] 1298	0.0708 (0.1663) [0.1041] 10126
Molecule Age	24.0784 (13.4493) [2.8724] 8160	21.4869 (11.8051) [2.8732] 1530	24.5141 (14.3001) [2.8733] 1410	21.9339 (10.9312) [2.8937] 2650	16.8350 (11.1338) [2.8730] 1910	22.6181 (12.9345) [3.0572] 15660
Form Code	3.3351 (4.4552) [2.0342] 8240	1.1574 (1.1126) [0.6454] 1550	3.0574 (4.5637) [1.4828] 1410	1.2215 (1.1186) [0.5444] 2650	1.3994 (1.4475) [0.7835] 1910	2.5061 (3.7171) [1.7960] 15760
<u>Competition:</u>						
Pack Size	90.0948 (22.3983) [6.7413] 5039	33.1120 (13.4247) [2.0104] 1012	68.4500 (83.7458) [51.6193] 945	27.8134 (15.7158) [2.7000] 1822	40.9572 (16.9818) [2.6861] 1298	64.8498 (41.7574) [21.1523] 10116
Generic Competition	18.4353 (16.3496) [5.0843] 8240	3.9309 (3.6622) [2.0654] 1550	5.5673 (6.1620) [1.7857] 1410	6.6290 (6.4981) [2.1331] 2650	4.9062 (5.2283) [3.9564] 1910	12.2327 (14.0546) [4.5613] 15760
Therapeutic Substitute Molecule	19.5940 (7.4819) [1.4054] 8240	14.4954 (4.7608) [1.2526] 1550	13.0198 (4.0079) [1.3880] 1410	16.6022 (5.3471) [1.5518] 2650	15.1722 (6.2132) [1.2986] 1910	17.4654 (6.9412) [1.7413] 15760

a negative relationship between price and pack size. ***Generic Competitors*** are manufacturers of products containing the molecule, including originators, licensees, parallel imports and generics. The overall mean is 12, ranging from 4 in France, 5 in Spain, 6 in Italy, and 6 in the United Kingdom to 18 in Germany. Germany has the highest number of generic competitors in the sample consistent with the high mean age of the sample, which also reflects laxer regulations in Germany. This implies that global molecules are the most valuable ones and attract the most products per molecule. Consistent with this, the mean of ***Therapeutic Substitute Molecules*** (molecules in the ATC categories) is higher in Germany than in France, Italy, Spain and the United Kingdom. Therapeutic Substitute Molecules also reflect increased availability of substitutes that range from 13 in the United Kingdom to 19 in Germany, with an overall mean of 17.

3.4. Fully Interacted Model

This study investigates the competitive effect of generic entry on pharmaceutical prices by employing the fully interacted model to address cross-country differences in product specifications. The fully interacted model estimates the effect of quality and competition (market) characteristics on price among the five largest European pharmaceutical markets between 1994 and 2003. Products serving the same purpose might have different attributes in different countries. In the sample of this study, the forms, strength levels, and pack sizes are the quality and market characteristics of drugs that vary across countries (Timur et al., 2011).

Pharmaceutical prices are expected to differ systematically across countries, reflecting differences in health care regimes. Because some price variation across countries is explained by factors other than observed product characteristics that change very little over time, the model includes country-specific intercepts. Moreover, drug prices also vary across countries because of time-varying differences in regulatory and reimbursement environments. To address these, the model specifies market competition measures, as additional explanatory variables (Danzon and Chao, 2000; Timur et al., 2011).

In the fully interacted model, quality and competition (market) characteristics have different effects across different countries over time. The regression includes controls for product characteristics that vary over time within a drug. Thus, the model controls for drug quality and market characteristics that varies across drugs. The model includes interactions between product characteristics and country fixed effects; product characteristics and year fixed effects; and finally interactions between product characteristics, country fixed effects and year fixed effects. This model includes product fixed effects to control for unobserved drug heterogeneity, and year fixed effects to control for price inflation and for all other unmeasured time effects. Rather than estimate separate regressions for each country, the study pools the data for all five countries and estimates a fully interacted model as follows:

Similar to Danzon and Chao (2000) and Timur et al. (2011), this model uses log transformations of product prices and characteristics as defined in Equation (1);

$$
\begin{aligned}
lnP_{k,j,t} = \alpha_0 &+ \sum_{c=1}^{9} \beta_c lnX_{c,k,j,t} + \sum_{j=1}^{4} \phi_j d_j + \sum_{t=1}^{9} \varphi_t d_t + \sum_{t=1}^{9}\sum_{j=1}^{4} \lambda_{j,t} d_j d_t \\
&+ \sum_{c=1}^{9}\sum_{j=1}^{4} \rho_{c,j} d_j lnX_{c,k,j,t} + \sum_{c=1}^{9}\sum_{t=1}^{9} \gamma_{c,t} d_t lnX_{c,k,j,t} \qquad (1) \\
&+ \sum_{c=1}^{9}\sum_{t=1}^{9}\sum_{j=1}^{4} \theta_{c,j,t} d_j d_t lnX_{k,j,t} + \sum_{k=1}^{K} \delta_k d_k + u_{k,j,t}
\end{aligned}
$$

Mean values of the quality and competition (market) characteristics, parameter values and fixed country effects represent heterogeneity across different countries over time, therefore this model measures price differences between the baseline country Germany and all other countries by considering all these discrepancies for consistent estimations. All the product quality and competition (market) characteristics appear on the right hand side of Equation (1). Accordingly, k, j, and t represent an individual product, country and year respectively. P measures the average price per standard unit for each product that is the volume-weighted average over all forms and packs of the product. Xc indicates a vector of quality and competition characteristics of products. βc captures the different impact of the imperfectly competitive market for pharmaceuticals in different countries and thus measures the country-specific differences between parameter effects for the baseline country Germany and other countries j. Net implicit prices for product characteristics are β for Germany in 1994, (β + γt) for Germany in year t =1995 – 2003, (β + ρj) for other countries j in 1994, and (β + γt + ρj + θj,t) for other countries j in year t = 1995 – 2003 (Danzon and Chao, 2000; Timur et al., 2011). The model also includes d variables that are indicators for country j, year t and product k. λj,t is the parameter that estimates the average price difference in time t between the baseline country Germany and country j, which is omitted from the country indicator vector, across products. This price gap is net of variation induced by differences across quality and competition characteristics, products, time and countries (Timur et al., 2011). The model uses coefficients ρ, γ, and θ for the interactions between the product characteristics and the country and year indicators. And, finally u is the regression error in the model. As stated previously, Germany is used as the baseline country, because it is the least regulated market for both manufacturer prices and pharmacy margins and it has the most products in the sample. This fully interacted model yields the same coefficient estimates with separate, country-specific regressions.

This study uses panel data analysis where the product-specific intercepts are treated as fixed effects. In the case of panel data analysis, fixed effects estimators are considered to be quite efficient. The fixed effects model refers to the possibility that each unit of observation, market, quality, and time period, would have unique parameters. Following this, in this model, there are market, quality, and time specific "fixed" effects. It is important to note that drug prices also reflect intrinsic value that is not observable. If these are time-invariant and product-specific, then the fixed effects model is efficient (Wooldridge, 2001). The econometric model used in this analysis accounts for the endogeneity of market entry by employing a fixed effects model, which controls for all observed and unobserved time varying and time-constant variables, and the econometric model also takes advantage of the panel data to eliminate both observed and unobserved heterogeneity and to remedy the problems with error terms. Thus fixed effects model explicitly accounts for endogeneity resulting from time variant and time-invariant omitted variables. Tab. 12.2 reports fully interacted regressions for product-level prices for 1994 and 2003 in five countries, which allows all parameters to differ across countries. Tab. 12.3 reports complete annual results with the fully interacted model for the major variable of interest – generic competition – in five countries between 1994 and 2003. All variables are specified in log form; thus each coefficient is interpreted as the elasticity of price with respect to the quality or market characteristics.

4. Empirical Results

The model yields the expected coefficients with consistent fixed effects results. The elasticity of unit price P with respect to strength increases in all countries and over both years, due to the fact that therapeutic value increases with strength, and strength is a direct measure of relative prices. Molecule Age is significantly negatively related to product price in all five countries. Competitive generic prices in Germany are expected to estimate the marginal cost of production, which is related to the therapeutic value of the molecule (Danzon and Chao, 2000). Additionally, renegotiation of fixed prices as molecules age is the source of large effects in the more strictly regulated countries (Mossialos et al., 2004; Seget, 2003; Timur et al., 2011); consistent with the hypothesis that molecule age is an inverse indicator of relative quality. In the United Kingdom, France, Italy, and Spain the Molecule Age interactions are significantly negative

Tab. 12.2: Product Level Pharmaceutical Prices: Log Price Per Unit Fully Interacted Model – Fixed Effect, 1994 – 2003, Source: Author's own calculations

Variable	Year	Germany	France	U.K.	Italy	Spain
Quality:						
Strength (ln)	1994	0.1344* (0.004)	0.0619** (0.015)	0.1580* (0.000)	0.1126* (0.003)	0.1557** (0.011)
	2003	0.1259* (0.001)	0.0353* (0.006)	0.1598* (0.000)	0.0596* (0.000)	0.1502* (0.004)
Molecule Age (ln)	1994	-0.6797* (0.000)	-0.0970* (0.001)	-0.4834 (0.180)	-0.0367* (0.000)	-0.5392* (0.000)
	2003	-0.9603* (0.003)	-0.5663* (0.000)	-0.3968* (0.001)	-0.2144* (0.000)	-0.7134* (0.000)
Form Codes (ln)	1994	0.0089*** (0.080)	0.1763** (0.014)	0.0004 (0.157)	-0.0787** (0.024)	0.1400*** (0.085)
	2003	0.0756* (0.000)	-0.0538* (0.000)	-0.0207* (0.000)	0.0728* (0.000)	0.1458* (0.000)
Competition (Market):						
Pack Size (ln)	1994	-0.2527* (0.000)	-0.5135* (0.000)	-0.4787* (0.000)	-0.3385* (0.000)	-0.6818* (0.000)
	2003	-0.2198* (0.000)	-0.4273* (0.000)	-0.5768* (0.000)	-0.3294* (0.000)	-0.8127* (0.000)
Generic Competition (ln)	1994	-0.0263** (0.022)	0.0973** (0.017)	0.2252* (0.003)	0.1332* (0.003)	0.1052* (0.001)
	2003	-0.1775* (0.000)	0.0374* (0.000)	0.1118* (0.000)	0.0006* (0.000)	0.0039* (0.000)
Therapeutic Substitute Molecules (ln)	1994	0.5159** (0.016)	-0.3138* (0.000)	-0.1373** (0.031)	-0.4497* (0.000)	-0.0478** (0.039)
	2003	0.4970** (0.032)	-0.0932* (0.000)	-0.3608* (0.000)	0.1193* (0.000)	-0.1134** (0.029)

Note: Adjusted R^2=0.539; p-values in parentheses.
*, ** and *** reflect $p < 0.01$, $p < 0.05$ and $p < 0.10$ respectively.

due to regulatory restrictions on post launch price increases and due to weaker generic competition. Form Codes are positively related with price in all countries. The number of formulations increases price in Germany and Spain throughout the period, which indicates that introducing line extensions is an effective tool for a price increase in countries that do not allow price increases for established products (Danzon and Chao, 2000). In France, Italy and the

Tab. 12.3: Product Level Pharmaceutical Prices: Generic Competition Log Price Per Unit, Fully Interacted Model, Source: Author's own calculations

Year	Germany	France	United Kingdom	Italy	Spain
1995	-0.0261 (0.173)	0.0981 (0.447)	0.1808* (0.005)	0.1104* (0.007)	0.0923* (0.004)
1996	-0.0081*** (0.094)	0.0684*** (0.056)	0.1849* (0.002)	0.1083* (0.004)	0.0876* (0.002)
1997	-0.0579* (0.004)	0.0382* (0.006)	0.1687* (0.000)	0.1076* (0.000)	0.0794* (0.000)
1998	-0.0882* (0.000)	0.0087* (0.000)	0.1504* (0.000)	0.0960* (0.000)	0.0712* (0.000)
1999	-0.1079* (0.000)	0.0316* (0.000)	0.1780* (0.000)	0.0966* (0.000)	0.0605* (0.000)
2000	-0.1188* (0.000)	0.0373* (0.000)	0.1915* (0.000)	0.0844* (0.000)	0.0564* (0.000)
2001	-0.1336* (0.000)	0.0394* (0.000)	0.1584* (0.000)	0.0663* (0.000)	0.0338* (0.000)
2002	-0.1581* (0.000)	0.0329* (0.000)	0.1242* (0.000)	0.0235* (0.000)	0.0152* (0.000)

Note: Adjusted R^2=0.539; p-values in parentheses.
*, ** and *** reflect $p < 0.01$, $p < 0.05$ and $p < 0.10$ respectively.

United Kingdom, the price elasticity with respect to the number of forms also indicates a positive relationship for many years since manufacturers have an incentive to introduce new forms where expected prices are sufficient to cover the fixed costs of introducing a new form. Price significantly decreases with Pack Size in all countries and years, implied by economies of scale in packaging, EMEA packaging and labeling regulations, and use in reference pricing calculations. Consistent with this negative estimation, patient co-payment is based on pack size in Germany and maximum price is based on maximum pack size in the United Kingdom (Timur et al., 2011). In Tab 12.2, price is positively related to the number of Therapeutic Substitute Molecules for Germany indicating that the number of Therapeutic Substitute Molecules does not have a competitive pressure on price. On the other hand, the price elasticity with respect to Therapeutic Substitute Molecules is significantly negative for the United Kingdom, France, Italy, and Spain. In these countries, therapeutic reference pricing regulations are present to encourage across-molecule competition by therapeutic substitute molecules. In these regulated countries, there is evidence of competition between therapeutic substitutes in the form of lower prices for successive entrants. Competition, under therapeutic reference pricing, decreases drug prices (Brekke et al., 2007). These countries do not have as much generic competition, although generics are much closer substitutes.

Tabs. 12.2 and 12.3 report empirical results for the elasticity of unit price with respect to Generic Competition at the product level between 1994 and 2003. Germany is the only country that demonstrates a decrease in prices as a result of generic competition. An increase in generic competition by 10 % leads to a decrease in drug prices by about 1 %-2 %. German pharmaceutical markets are relatively least regulated where originator market prices are set freely. Therefore, originator drug prices are higher in Germany than originator drug prices in strictly regulated markets. Following patent expiration, generic drugs enter the market at a lower price and introduce price competition to originators due to a high price gap between originators and generics. In this case, generic firms are able to steal market share from originators via price competition. Originators often decrease their prices to match with generic drug prices. As time passes, market share of originators also decrease and market share of generic drugs increase. Overall, average price per standard unit decreases in Germany. Thus, generic competition effectively reduces prices in Germany, where originator prices are high and relatively free from regulations. By contrast, in the United Kingdom, the coefficient of the variable representing generic entry is positive and statistically significant; an increase in generic entry by 10 % leads to an increase in prices by between 1.1 % and 2.2 % over 10 years. This study finds evidence that the generics paradox is present in the United Kingdom, as originator prices increase post-generic entry. In the United Kingdom, originator prices are subject to rate of return regulation that is profit controls, which were introduced in 1993. Additionally, price caps were introduced in the United Kingdom at the end of 1990s, and price caps were found not being effective price regulation in lowering drug prices. There is some evidence in the literature that price caps have a positive effect on prices. Frank and Salkever (1992) find that the price of generic products decreases as a result of price caps regulation. However, while more patients use generics, many still use the originators. The group using the originators has an inelastic demand, providing the producer the incentive to raise price and therefore revenue. Thus, the average price of the drug may be higher with a price cap. In Spain, Italy, and France, where direct price regulations are present, generic entry has a positive effect on prices. A 10 % increase in generic entry in these countries leads to an increase in prices by 1.0 % or less over all years. In these countries, originator markets are heavily regulated; therefore;

originator drug prices are low. Following patent expiration, when generics enter the market, they cannot introduce price competition to originators due to low originator prices and thus due to a low price gap between originators and generics. Therefore, they are not able to capture market share from originators by competing via price. In this case, generic competition is typically non-price competition. They cannot compete via price but compete with different form codes and pack size, thus they compete via product differentiation, often with higher price per standard unit. Overall, the prices are not affected negatively by increasing generic competition; consistent with the theory that generic entry does not necessarily lead to a reduction in prices in the regulated markets and may only slow down the increase in these prices. This theory is consistent with the results showing that strict pricing and reimbursement regulations lead to an increase in prices in the United Kingdom and France and also slow down the increase in prices in Italy and Spain throughout the study period. In the regulated markets (United Kingdom, Spain, Italy and France), fixed prices protect generic entrants from price competition from other generic entrants, thus there is no incentive to lower prices as the number of generic entrants increases (Sloan and Hsieh, 2012).

Looking at the effect of the generic entry on the post generic entry price per standard unit, there are two facts observed in the study. In Germany, where the prices of the originator drugs are high to begin with and where the generic entry leads to a decrease in the price per standard unit, as the time goes by from 1994 to 2003, the magnitude of this negative effect monotonically increases from -0.0263 to -0.1775 (see Tab. 12.3). On the other hand, in the other four more regulated countries, where the prices of the originators are lower before the generic entry and in general the prices per standard unit increase following the generic entry, the magnitude of this positive effect decreases over time; for instance, in the case of Italy from 0.1332 to 0.0006 (see Tab. 12.3).

One possible explanation for the monotonic increase in the negative effect of generic entry in Germany is that over time the generics become more acceptable substitutes for the originator drugs. This would both lead to lower prices for originator drugs post generic entry and lower market shares for these originator drugs. If that is the case in less regulated market Germany, as time passes, the competition brought about by generic drugs become more intense and thus the price of the originators decreases more significantly in response to the entry of the generic drug, lowering the overall price per standard unit (a weighted average price of the originator drug prices and generic drug prices) which is observed in the data. In addition, the market share of the generics would have also increased over time, which would have further lowered the average price.

There are several possible explanations for why generic drugs become more acceptable substitutes of the originators over time. First, the consumers become more informed of the existence of these generics. Second, the consumers' perception of generics becomes more favorable over time because they become more aware of the fact that generics are indeed good substitutes for the originator drugs. Third, the doctors are more likely to prescribe generics either by their own will or because of government regulations (or health insurers) that require them to prescribe generics. Fourth, if the prices of the originators increase sufficiently over time, either consumers or doctors or insurers or the regulators are more likely to consider alternatives.

On the other hand, in more regulated countries, where the prices of the originators are lower before the generic entry, in general the prices per standard unit increase following generic entry, but the magnitude of this positive effect decreases over time. One possible explanation is that following patent expiration generics enter the market in different form codes and pack sizes with a higher price per standard unit. As more generics enter the market, they capture market share with product differentiation and increase the price per standard unit. As time passes generics continue to enter with higher price per standard unit but they start to capture smaller market share because they face more stringent spatial competition; more generic entry leaves smaller product space for firms that compete via product differentiation. Therefore, in these regulated countries the prices per standard unit still increase following the generic entry, but the magnitude of this positive effect decreases over time. The above conjecture regarding a possible explanation for the change over time in the effect of the generic entry on the average drug price is only few of the possible explanations, which at this moment this study cannot test because of the lack of specific data on the evolution of the price and market shares of the originator drugs over time.

The number of generic entrants depends on drug prices in the market; when prices are high, firms enter due to higher expected profits (Danzon and Chao, 2000). This could lead to a reverse causation problem and bias the estimates. Other studies have posited that such a bias would understate the price-lowering effects of generic entry. Thus the true effects in Germany would be more negative, while the positive effects in the other countries are overstated. Danzon and Chao (2000) make the claim that this bias would be larger in the less regulated countries. This endogeneity problem in this analysis is limited by two things: First, firms cannot obtain a production permit immediately, it takes time due to regulatory delay for the approval of drug in the industry, and therefore the number of generic competitors is predetermined when price is set. Second, this study controls for country and product fixed effects as well as interaction between the country and the time effects. Thus, the analysis allows for a great amount of heterogeneity that can be correlated with generic entry.

5. Conclusion

This study focuses on how drug prices change over time as a consequence of generic competition. The results suggest that the relationships between the dynamics of drug prices and generic competition are complex and differentiated across EU countries.

When including all five countries in panel data models, this study finds evidence that generic price competition is not present in the United Kingdom, France, Italy, and Spain as prices increase with generic entry post-patent expiry. Generic entry and product price are positively related in these more regulated markets. These positive elasticities in the United Kingdom, France, Italy, and Spain are consistent with evidence that multi-source suppliers in these countries are usually licensed co-marketers rather than competing generic manufacturers or minor new products that enter to obtain a higher regulated price. The only country in which generic entry leads to lower prices is Germany. Germany has a free-pricing originator market, it thus has generic price competition and more generic competitors compared to the other more regulated regimes. The elasticity of product price with respect to Generic Competitors is negative and significant. One would expect more entry and price competition in Germany and the results confirm this. In sum, this analysis does not find any evidence that prices decrease as a result of generic entry in the heavily regulated other pharmaceutical markets. The findings are very clear and also show the presence of the generics paradox. Evidence of the generic paradox should signal to policy makers that under their regulatory structure, generic entry will not lead to price-reducing competition. Across the four countries the elasticity estimates for generic competition are positive, but differ in magnitude, with a much larger coefficient in the U.K. than in France, Italy, and Spain.

The most important factor that increases prices in regulated countries relative to Germany is non-price competition. The relatively small number of generic entrants and fewer generics are consistent with the results found in the regulated pharmaceutical markets: generic entry is not attractive once patent expires due to low regulated prices for originator products. Danzon and Chao (2000) say that "the incentives for price-competitive generic strategies are less owing to price- insensitive purchasers, and the incentives for price-increasing generic strategies are greater". The estimates of generic competition in Germany show that reference pricing policy and free originator pricing together increase generic entry and price competition. In the United Kingdom, the total generic effect is found to be weaker compared to Germany, due to the lower number of generics per molecule and most importantly due to profit control and price caps regulations.

There is evidence of competition between therapeutic substitutes in the form of lower prices for successive entrants. This study shows that the number of Therapeutic Substitute Molecules has a negative effect on price in the more regulated markets, but this is mostly attributable to their regulation systems rather than to competition, since prices of established products are quite effective in regulation of new product prices. Generic price competition does not exist in these regulated countries; even though generics are much closer substitutes. Danzon and Chao (2000) say, "these pricing and reimbursement regulations cause indistinguishable price incentives for investment in innovative and imitative R&D". The results of this work are consistent with Danzon and Chao's findings that the more regulated countries have produced a large number of minor new products but few truly innovative molecules that have achieved global diffusion.

There are few important points that need to be emphasized at this point. First, this paper focuses on an empirical analysis of generic competition and prices, considering the role of several fundamental features of the European pharmaceutical market. Second, this study does not look at comparisons of price levels across countries, but focuses on price changes within countries. Third, this study does not analyze the determinants of generic entry; this would be an important and interesting issue for future research. Fourth, quality and market characteristics employed in the empirical analysis are based on the measurability of variables in the data set. A different competition characteristic factor, such as an "index" variable considering all the different regulations and reimbursements in different countries, may be very useful in order to better capture the generic price competition (Timur, 2006). Finally, although this study has identified certain factors like returns to age, therapeutic substitutes, and competition, controlling for these measured factors leaves some unmeasured country effects. For instance, the contribution of patent expiration and other factors to these unexplained differences is an important subject for future research.

Acknowledgments

I gratefully acknowledge financial support from Aysegul Timur, Ph.D., for providing me the IMS data set used in this study and for her unlimited assistance in understanding the data set. I gratefully acknowledge invaluable support and advice from Bradley P. Kamp, Ph.D., Gabriel Picone, Ph.D., Andrei Barbos, Ph.D., and Aysegul Timur, Ph.D. for their unlimited assistance in my research.

References

Adriaen, M., De Witte, K., & Simoens, S. (2008). Pricing Strategies of Originator and Generic Medicines Following Patent Expiry in Belgium. Journal of Generic Medicines 5: 175–87.

Anis, A. H., Guh, D. P., & Woolcott, J. (2003). Lowering Generic Drug Prices: Less Regulation Equals More Competition. Med Care 2003 41(1): 135–141.

Augurzky, B., Göhlmann, S., Gress, S., & Wasem, J. (2009). Effects of the German Reference Drug Program on Ex-Factory Prices of Prescription Drugs: A Panel Data Approach. Health Economics 18(4): 421–436.

Brekke, K. R. (2007). Regulation and Pricing of Pharmaceuticals: Reference Pricing or Price Cap Regulations? CESifo Working Paper No. 2059.

Caves, Richard E., Whinston, Michael D., & Hurwitz, Mark A. (1991). Patent Expiration, Entry, and Competition in the U.S. Pharmaceutical Industry. Brookings Papers on Economic Activity: Microeconomics 1–48.

Danzon, P. M., & Chao, L. W. (2000). Does Regulation Drive Out Competition in Pharmaceutical Markets? Journal of Law and Economics 23(2): 311–358.

Danzon, P. M., & Furukawa, M. F. (2003). Prices and Availability of Pharmaceuticals: Evidence from Nine Countries. Health Aff (Millwood), 521–536.

Ephmra.(2006). Anatomical Classification Guidelines. Retrieved from http://farmacia.udec.cl/wp-content/uploads/2015/09/atc.pdf (01.04.2014).

Frank, R. G., & Salkever, D. S. (1992). Pricing Patent Loss and the Market for Pharmaceuticals. Southern Economic Journal, 59(2), 165–179.

Garattini, L., & Tediosi, F. (2000). A Comparative Analysis of Generic Markets in Five European Countries. Health Policy 51: 149–162.

Grabowski, Henry G., & Vernon, John M. (1992). Brand Loyalty, Entry, and Price Competition in Pharmaceuticals after the 1984 Drug Act. Journal of Law and Economics, 35(2) 331–350.

Jönsson, B. (1994). Pricing and Reimbursement of Pharmaceuticals in Sweden. Pharmacoeconomics 6 (Suppl 1): 51–60.

Kanavos, P., & Srivastava, D. (2008). The Impact of Patent Expiry on Product Competition and Generic Market Entry: Evidence from Four European Countries. Unpublished work, mimeo, London School of Economics and Political Science.

Magazzini, L., Pammolli, F., & Massimo, R. (2004). Dynamic Competition in Pharmaceuticals: Patent Expiry, Generic Penetration, and Industry Structure. European Journal of Health Economics 5(2): 175–182.

Mossialos, E., Walley, T., & Mrazek, M. (2004). Regulating Pharmaceuticals in Europe: An Overview. London, UK: Open University Press.

Podnar, K., Molj, B., & Golob, U. (2007). How Reference Pricing for Pharmaceuticals Can Increase Generic Share of Market: The Slovenian Experience. Journal of Public Policy and Marketing 26(1), 89–101.

Puig-Junoy, J. (2010). Impact of European Pharmaceutical Price Regulation on Generic Price Competition: A Review. Pharmacoeconomics 28(8): 649–663.

Reekie, W. Duncan. (1996). Medicines Prices and Innovations. London: Institute of Economic Affairs, Health and Welfare Unit.

Rizzo, J. A., & Zeckhauser, R. (2009). Generic Scrip Share and the Price of Brand-Name Drugs: The Role of the Consumer. International Journal of Health Care Finance and Economics, 9, 291–316.

Rovira, J., & Darba, J. (2001). Pharmaceutical Pricing and Reimbursement in Spain. European Journal of Health Economics 2(1): 39–43.

Scherer, F. M. (2000). The Pharmaceutical Industry. In A. J. Culyer, & J. P. Newhouse (Eds.), Handbook of Health Economics (1297–1336). Philadelphia: Elsevier.

Seget, S. (2003). Pharmaceutical Pricing Strategies: Optimizing Returns Throughout R&D and Marketing. Reuters Business Insight – Healthcare.

Sloan, F., & Hsieh, C. R. (2012). Health Economics. Cambridge, MA: Massachusetts Institute of Technology.

Timur, A. (2006). The Single Market and Pharmaceutical Industry in the European Union: Is There Any Evidence of Price Convergence? University of South Florida, Doctoral Dissertation.

Timur, A., Picone, G., & DeSimone, J. S. (2011). Has the European Union Achieved a Single Pharmaceutical Market? International Journal of Health Care Finance and Economics, 11, 223. Retrieved from https://doi.org/10.1007/s10754-011-9100-z (10.02.2013).

Vandoros, S., & Kanavos, P. (2013). The Generics Paradox Revisited: Empirical Evidence from Regulated Market. Applied Economics 45(22), 3230–3239.

Wooldridge, J. M. (2001). Econometric Analysis of Cross Section and Panel Data. Massachusetts Institute of Technology.

Merve Ertok Onurlu and Frank Windmeijer

Chapter 13 The Use of Aggregate Data in the Evaluation of Hospital Interventions: The Case of Payment by Results for Maternity Care in England*

Abstract: It is common to use individual level data (e.g. patient, practice or hospital admission) for the evaluation of health policies. Individual level data allow health care researchers to keep track of patients over time. However, the authorization of the use of patient level data from public bodies is usually a long process and can be costly. Whilst aggregate data, for example at hospital or trust level, are generally considered to provide less information, we discuss here under what conditions aggregate and individual level data can provide the same level of information for estimation of treatment effects. We compare use of the Hospital Episode Statistics individual spell level data with the National Health Services (NHS) trust level data at the English NHS setting to evaluate the impact of Payment by Results (PbR) in maternity care. We exploit a short panel of two years from the Hospital Episode Statistics database and our identification strategy is based on the differences in the roll out of the policy across NHS trusts. We investigate under what circumstances trust level and individual spell level analyses provide identical results once appropriate weights are used at trust level. We examine when the estimated impact of PbR is identical comparing ordinary least square (OLS) and fixed effects models and how the use of fixed effects models contributes to our identification strategy by correcting for unobservable time invariant factors at hospital level. We show how to switch from individual level data to aggregate level data analysis within a difference in differences setting for OLS estimation with and without fixed effects.

Keywords: Policy Evaluation, Panel Data, Aggregate Hospital Level Data, Individual Spell Level Data, Econometric Modelling, DiD Approach

1. Introduction

The use of individual level data (e.g. patient, practice or hospital admission) in the evaluation of health care interventions is popular in the social sciences.

---

* This study is produced from Merve Ertok Onurlu's PhD thesis named "Essays on the Economics of Maternity Care in England" submitted to the University of Bristol, UK in 2015.

Individual level data allow health care researchers to keep track of patients over time and they can provide a wide range of information on patient characteristics and a history of patients' health status at different time intervals (e.g. diagnoses, surgeries, ethnicity, weight, age, gender, place of residence, GP practice). Although the authorization of the use of patient level data from public bodies is usually time consuming due to confidentiality concerns, and costs to obtain such data are high, they are attractive to many health care researchers, more so than the higher (aggregate) level data (e.g. National Health Service (NHS) trust level, hospital level) (Goddard et al., 2014). Hospital and/or NHS trust level data are usually in the public domain and easily obtained. However, researchers are usually less willing to use aggregate data due to a problem that such data do not provide sufficient information for hospital-based policy interventions (Goddard et al., 2014).

The Hospital Episode Statistics (HES) database is a comprehensive database accommodating a broad range of details on admitted inpatient admissions (i.e. maternity admissions, both babies and mothers), outpatient admissions as well as A&E and private hospital admissions (NHS Digital website-HES statistics, 2020). It is one of the most-commonly used data sources by health care researchers in England.

This study discusses the use of HES individual spell[1] level data and NHS trust level data at the English NHS setting to evaluate the impact of Payment by Results (PbR) in maternity care. The roll-out of PbR in maternity care started only among NHS Foundation Trusts (FTs) in 2005/06. It was 2006/07 when the policy started also among non-Foundation Trusts (non-FTs). Therefore, we exploit a short panel of two years from the Hospital Episode Statistics database since our identification strategy is based on the differences in the roll-out of the policy across NHS trusts. We treat 2004/05 as pre-policy and 2005/06 as post-policy years respectively.

Our research design allows us to investigate important issues contributing to the existing literature in two ways. First, this is the first paper discussing the use of spell level and trust level data in the evaluation of PbR by providing evidence for how to switch from spell level analysis to trust level analysis. In a simple set up, we investigate under what circumstances trust level and individual spell level analyses provide identical results once appropriate weights are used at the trust level.

1 A spell is the duration of hospital stay from admission to discharge.

To our knowledge, the closest work to our paper is by Goddard et al. (2014), who investigate the use of individual student and school achievement data in the US and show how to switch from student level data to school level data in the evaluation of school based policies. We build upon their work by examining whether the estimated impact of PbR is identical for ordinary least squares (OLS) and fixed effects models when the number of time periods T = 2, (trust level vs. spell level analysis) and whether the use of the fixed effects model contributes to our identification strategy by correcting for unobservable time invariant factors at hospital level.

Second, our study is connected to a large empirical literature on the evaluation of PbR in England, which we discuss in Section 3.2. This is the first study specifically focusing on maternity care in the evaluation of PbR. Our empirical approach exploits a Difference in Differences (DiD) model to assess the impact of PbR on maternity outcomes such as volume of admissions, length of stay and emergency readmissions within 28 days of discharge.

We first present a historical background on PbR in England in Section 2 along with its implications for maternity and neonatal care. We then discuss previous literature from both an empirical and econometrics point of view in Section 3. We present our modelling approach in Section 4. Section 5 provides information on the HES data and outcome measures used in the study. Main results and some robustness checks presented are presented in Section 6. Section 7 concludes.

2. The History of Payment by Results

2.1. Background

The UK government provides tax funded health care services, which are free at the point of use (NHS Website, NHS Payment System, 2020)[2]. The majority of health care services including maternity services are provided by the National Health Service (NHS) providers (NHS Trusts) (Propper et al., 2013). Under this health care setting, PbR was announced by the Labour Government in October 2002 for only England as a part of "Reforming NHS Financial Flows" policy package. It commenced among a small proportion of hospitals (Propper et al., 2013). It was then gradually extended to all acute NHS Trusts by the end of 2007/08. The program started with 15 elective procedures in 2003/04 among FTs and was then extended to an additional 33 elective procedures in

2 NHS website: accessed 18th March 2020. https://www.england.nhs.uk/pay-syst/.

2004/05 (Appendix, Tab. 13.A1). It was 2005/06 when all NHS Trusts started implementing PbR for elective services. The PbR tariff was intended to cover most health care services, that is non-elective services (including maternity care), A&E, outpatient services among NHS trusts by 2005/06. However, this did not happen due to the uncertainties regarding the costs of these services from previous years (Department of Health (DoH), 2005a)[3]. Therefore, the implementation of non-elective care among NHS trusts was amended for the 2005/06 financial year with the exclusion of FTts (DoH, 2005a; Boyle, 2005).

PbR is an activity based payment system requiring all commissioners (primary care trusts) to pay national fixed prices pegged for each health care resource group (HRG) (Dixon et al., 2012). These prices within an individual HRG are allowed to differ depending on whether it is an elective or non-elective activity (i.e. emergency activity). Health care resource groups are "clinical groups of hospital activities requiring similar levels of treatment and health care resources and each HRG is assigned to a spell of care" (DoH, 2012, p. 8). A hospital spell is the period of care under a health care provider from admission to discharge and is the unit for PbR reimbursements (Sutton et al., 2007). These groups are similar to the diagnosis related groups in the US (Dixon et al., 2012; Sussex et al., 2009). The tariff prices are based on previous years' average costs and regional differences in the market are taken into account through the adjustment of those prices by a Market Forces Factor (MFF) (DoH, 2012). PbR makes a link between the number of patients, case mix and hospital's income (Sussex et al., 2009). The motivation behind the fixed price payment systems is to reward hospital providers who succeed in increasing the volume of their hospital activity (reduction in waiting times), hospital quality and efficiency (reduction in hospital costs). As the price of each procedure undertaken is centrally fixed, hospitals would therefore have to focus on quality of services to attract more patients and to increase their income (Maybin, 2007).

In addition to the volume of hospital activity and quality of services, if the cost of a specific procedure is lower than the national tariff price, the hospital can keep the surplus which then can be used to re-invest in the following year's hospital services (Maybin, 2007). Therefore, the whole payment scheme is motivated by "increases in volume of hospital activity, improvements in quality and efficiency of services" (Sutton et al., 2007). Nevertheless, one of the unintended impacts of PbR could be "gaming" where health care providers deliberately

3 Letter from Richard Douglas (Director of Finance and Investments at the DoH) to Strategic Health Authority Chief Executives.

group their patients into specific HRGs with a higher tariff price (i.e. HRGs with complications vs. HRGs without complications) (Farrar et al., 2011). This is also known as up-coding.

2.2. Payment by Results in Maternity and Neonatal Care

The Department of Health introduced PbR in maternity care in April 2005. Foundation Trusts are the first implementers of PbR in maternity care. As for other non-elective services, it was gradually extended to other acute NHS Trusts (Appendix, Tab. 13.A1.). There are 12 birth related HRGs (HRG version 3.5) named under obstetrics and neonatal care in the PbR inpatient tariff. The first five HRGs are defined for the treatment of un-well newborn babies whereas the remainings (N06 to N011) are defined for the actual delivery event (Appendix, Tab. 13.A2.). In addition, antenatal admissions not related to a delivery event are grouped under N12.

The 2005/06 PbR tariff included only obstetric services among NHS FTs. Neonatal care was not in the scope of the payment system due to the complicated nature of these services and the need to develop separate tariffs for each level of neonatal care (Memorandum by BLISS 2009). Neonatal care was included in the scope of PbR in the 2009/10 financial year (National Audit Office, 2013). Well babies also remained outside the scope of the PbR tariff and their costs were included in the cost of their mother's treatment (DoH, 2005b). Home births were included in the tariff in April 2008 and were indemnified at the same tariff price as normal deliveries taking place at hospitals (DoH, 2007a).

The transition to PbR for acute NHS Trusts was completed in 2008/09 with the exclusions of specific services such as primary care, mental health, critical care and ambulance services (DoH, 2007a; Dixon et al., 2012). Although the transition of PbR was completed for most of the secondary care services, PbR did not cover all aspects of maternity services such as antenatal and postnatal care and most of the community midwifery care.

3. Previous Literature

3.1. The Use of Aggregate Data vs. Individual Level Data

Our study is the first to examine the relation between the use of aggregate data and individual level data in health care under certain assumptions in a quasi-experimental design. We further make comparisons between the uses of ordinary least squares, and fixed effects methods to discuss that these models can provide the same point estimates and standard errors using weighted aggregate trust level data or individual spell level data.

Kmenta (1997) shows that as long as there is no variation in independent variables across individuals nested in the same group, then point estimates obtained via both individual level and aggregate level analyses are identical. However, this study misses the variation in weights across groups and the use of covariates in aggregate level analyses (Goddard et al., 2014).

Goddard et al. (2014) investigates the use of aggregate school level and student level data in the evaluation of school based interventions in the context of a randomized controlled trial in the US. The 2005 Michigan Educational Assessment Programme fourth grade maths and reading test scores are used in the conducted study. Schools were randomly assigned as treated under various treatments to explore the relation between student achievement and school-based interventions. Different from Kmenta (1997), Goddard et al. (2014) specifically examine (a) how much the degree of variation in weights across schools and the inclusion of covariates affect the parameters of interest in a school-level aggregate OLS model, a weighted school level aggregate OLS model, for which weights are defined as the number of students per school, and a hierarchical linear model at student level in a school based intervention; (b) the comparison of these three models in the presence of heterogeneous treatment effects. They find that if the number of students remains constant across each school, then micro level student achievement data in the context of hierarchical linear modelling and weighted/unweighted school level data analyses often provide very similar results even if the sample size is fairly small. They further show if there is a high variation in the number of students per school, then weighted aggregate school level OLS provides smaller standard errors compared to other models but point estimates remain almost the same. In addition, they find that under the presence of heterogeneous treatment impacts, these three models provide very similar estimates. Their study also reports that the inclusion of school and student level characteristics hardly change point estimates and standards errors.

Our study differs from the Goddard et al. (2014) study in three main ways. Firstly, we examine the adequacy of aggregate level data in a quasi-experimental design with empirical data rather than in a randomized control trial setting. Secondly, the inclusion of covariates is not examined in the context of PbR. This is due to the fact that PbR payment is spell specific rather than patient specific and no spell level characteristics are available in our data. However, we provide assumptions with regards to the inclusion of hospital and patient level covariates in our specifications.

Finally, we investigate how to switch from micro level models with fixed effects to aggregate level models with non-constant weights in a simple DiD setting. We also discuss whether the use of fixed effects provides any additional information in a simple DiD design with two years of data while switching from spell level fixed effects analysis to trust level analysis.

3.2. Payment by Results in England

Our study contributes to the literature on the evaluation of the introduction of PbR with respect to the use of spell level and aggregate level data in maternity care. This is the first paper to exame the impact of PbR specifically on maternity care in England. There is a small number of papers and DoH reports looking at the evaluation of PbR in England but the focus of these studies is mainly on elective care (Appleby et al., 2004; Sutton et al., 2007; Sussex et al., 2009; Yi et al., 2010).

Appleby et al. (2004) investigate the impact of PbR on hospital activity and waiting times using data on 15 elective HRGs in 2003/04. They find that the introduction of PbR increased the volume of activity in these HRGs; however, there was no evidence of a significant association between waiting times and the proposed payment system. As their study was conducted at the very initial stage of PbR, their data are therefore not able to indicate whether the new payment system affected the way English NHS hospitals operated.

Sutton et al. (2007) examine the impact of the introduction of PbR on a wide range of health care services including maternity care using the data from 2002/03 to 2005/06 for England and Scotland. The gradual transition to PbR at the NHS provides a quasi-experimental design for researchers; as PbR was not adopted by Scotland and by English NHS non-FTs at the time of the analysis, differences in the phasing-in of PbR are used to make comparisons (Sutton et al., 2007). Difference in differences method with HRG and trust fixed effects (at spell level) are adopted in the study. Their results indicate a reduction in unit costs across different DiD analyses, where length of stay and proportion of day cases were used as proxies of unit costs as suggested by Donaldson and Gerard (2005), and an increase in the volume of spells for both FTs and non-FTs compared to Scotland between 2004/05 and 2005/06. Sutton et al. (2007) find a statistically significant reduction only in in-hospital mortality as an indication of improvement in quality of care, which is attributable to the introduction of PbR for FTs compared to Scotland. A more recent version of that study is by Sussex et al. (2009) which uses HES data for England and Scottish Morbidity records from 2002/03 to 2005/06. The study exploits the same setting as Sutton et al. (2007) does. The introduction of PbR is associated with a reduction in unit costs across a majority of DiD specifications among FTs and non-FTs compared to Scotland. Volume of spells grows by 1.33 and 2.57 percentage points for FTs and non-FTs respectively (Sussex et al., 2009). They find that PbR is associated with a reduction in in-hospital mortality for FTs. Their study does not explicitly focus on maternity care.

4. Modelling Approach

The Difference in Differences method (DiD) is used to test the hypothesis that PbR affected the way maternity services operated during the transition to PbR, investigating whether length of stay was reduced, volume of maternity admissions increased and quality of maternity services. To do this, we exploit an empirical approach similar to those adopted by previous studies examining the impact of PbR (Sutton et al., 2007; Sussex et al., 2009; Yi et al., 2010). A basic DiD setting allows us to compare the outcomes of two groups over a two year period where one group (treatment group) is exposed to a particular policy in year two and the other group (control group) remains outside the scope of the policy in either year (Propper et al., 2013). Our study uses the differences in the phasing in of PbR across FTs (treatment group) and non-FTs (control group) in England. As we do not have access to the Scottish morbidity records (SMR02), non-FTs are the only control group in the study. The transition to PbR in maternity care started with FTs in 2005/06. It was extended to all acute NHS Trusts in the 2006/07 financial year. We therefore have to limit our study to actual delivery events (N06 to N11 and N12, Tab. 13.A2, Appendix) for the two- year period from 2004/05 to 2005/06.

First of all, we present a trust level model with and without fixed effects and discuss the use of fixed effects with aggregate data for a DiD design. Second, we examine how to switch from spell level data to trust level data with appropriate weights using simple ordinary least squares estimation. Then, we provide information on how to obtain the spell level data fixed effects results from trust level data using the same set up (Section 4.3.2). The estimation results of the impact of PbR on maternal outcomes are presented in Section 6.

4.1. Spell Level Model

A spell level model provides estimates of the impact of PbR on maternal outcomes with spell level data. As spell level data without trust fixed effects fail to capture trust level time invariant unobservable factors (i.e. hospital resources, hospital technology, staffing and spare capacity) affecting observed spell level quality, we provide controls for these unobservable confounders by including trust level

fixed effects, θ_j (Pérotin et al., 2013). Throughout our specifications, we assume that our models are linear.
We express spell level model without trust fixed effects:

$$Y_{ijt} = \alpha_0 + \beta_1 T_t + \beta_2 D_j + \beta_3 T_t D_j + e_{ijt} \tag{1}$$

and spell level model with trust fixed effects:

$$Y_{ijt} = \alpha_0 + \beta_1 T_t + \beta_2 D_j + \beta_3 T_t D_j + \theta_j + e_{ijt} \tag{2}$$

Where Y_{ijt} is the outcome for spell i, year t and trust j, α_0 is the intercept, T_t is a dummy variable taking the value 1 for the 2005/2006 and 0 for the 2004/2005 HES financial year. D_j is an indicator for Foundation Trust status. $T_t D_j$ is the interaction between time and FT status. θ_j is the fixed effect for trust j, and e_{ijt} is the residual.

4.2. Trust Level Model

A trust level model without fixed effects is given by:

$$\bar{Y}_{jt} = \alpha_0 + \beta_1 T_t + \beta_2 D_j + \beta_3 T_t D_j + \bar{e}_{jt} \tag{3}$$

A trust level model with fixed effects is given by:

$$\bar{Y}_{jt} = \alpha_0 + \beta_1 T_t + \beta_2 D_j + \beta_3 T_t D_j + \theta_j + \bar{e}_{jt} \tag{4}$$

Where $\bar{Y}_{jt}$ is the trust level average of an outcome measure for trust j in year t, and is the residual.

4.3. How to Obtain Spell Level Results from Trust Level Data

To obtain individual level results from aggregate level data, researchers should make sure the aggregate data are constructed correctly from the spell level data as implied in models (1)–(4) (Goddard et al., 2014). This holds in our example. Our models are presented below.

4.3.1 Spell Level Model without Trust Fixed Effects

If we re-write equation (1):

$$Y_{ijt} = \alpha_0 + \beta_1 T_t + \beta_2 D_j + \beta_3 T_t D_j + e_{ijt}$$

We can obtain the estimation results by two separate regressions:

$$D_j = 0 : Y_{ijt} = \alpha_0 + \beta_1 T_t + e_{ijt}$$

$$D_j = 1 : Y_{ijt} = \delta_0 + \delta_1 T_t + e_{ijt}$$

Where $\delta_0 = \alpha_0 + \beta_2$ and $\delta_1 = \beta_1 + \beta_3$, or $\beta_3 = \delta_1 - \beta_1$ and the estimates are $\hat{\beta}_3 = \hat{\delta}_1 - \hat{\beta}_1$.

Consider the sample for trusts with $D = 0$. Let J_0 be the number of trusts with $D = 0$, I_{jt} the number of spells for trust j in period t, and let $n_{0t} = \sum_{j=1}^{J_0} I_{jt}$. As we only have two periods, the OLS estimator β_1 is given by

$$\hat{\beta}_{1,spell} = \frac{1}{n_{02}} \sum_{j=1}^{J_0} \sum_{i=1}^{I_{j2}} Y_{ij2} - \frac{1}{n_{01}} \sum_{j=1}^{J_0} \sum_{i=1}^{I_{j1}} Y_{ij1}$$

Using trust level data, we would estimate the model using averages at the trust level, which are given by

$$\bar{Y}_{jt} = \frac{1}{I_{jt}} \sum_{i=1}^{I_{jt}} Y_{ijt}$$

The unweighted model for the trust level averages is

$$\bar{Y}_{jt} = \alpha_0 + \beta_1 T_t + \beta_2 D_j + \beta_3 T_t D_j + \bar{e}_{jt}$$

and the estimator for β_1 in this model is given by

$$\hat{\beta}_{1,trust,unweighted} = \frac{1}{J_0} \sum_{j=1}^{J_0} \overline{Y}_{j2} - \frac{1}{J_0} \sum_{j=1}^{J_0} \overline{Y}_{j1}$$

If we scale the data by $\sqrt{I_{jt}}$, the model for $D_j = 0$ trusts is given by

$$\sqrt{I_{jt}}\overline{Y}_{jt} = \sqrt{I_{jt}}\alpha_0 + \beta_1 \sqrt{I_{jt}} T_t + \sqrt{I_{jt}} \bar{e}_{jt}$$

and the weighted least squares estimator for β_1 is given by

$$\hat{\beta}_{1,trust,weighted} = \frac{1}{\sum_{j=1}^{J_0} I_{j2}} \sum_{j=1}^{J_0} I_{j2}\overline{Y}_{j2} - \frac{1}{\sum_{j=1}^{J_0} I_{j1}} \sum_{j=1}^{J_0} I_{j1}\overline{Y}_{j1}$$

$$= \frac{1}{n_{02}} \sum_{j=1}^{J_0} \sum_{i=1}^{I_{j2}} Y_{ij2} - \frac{1}{n_{01}} \sum_{j=1}^{J_0} \sum_{i=1}^{I_{j1}} Y_{ij1}$$

$$= \hat{\beta}_{1,spell}$$

Of course, we obtain the same result for the estimator δ_1. Hence we can get the non-fixed effects spell level estimator by simply doing a weighted least squares regression on the trust level average data. For this, we need of course the information on the number of spells by trust.

Throughout, we implicitly assume that we do not observe any spell level covariates, X_{ijt}. However, if one goes from spell level to aggregate level data, then spell level covariates should not be correlated with the treatment status,D_j. In the case of included trust level covariates, the model works again under the assumption that there is no correlation between D_j and X_{jt}.

4.3.2 Spell Level Model with Fixed Effects

A spell level model may fail to capture unobservable time invariant trust level factors affecting the level of quality at spell level. Therefore, we next investigate how we can obtain the spell level fixed effects estimator from trust level averaged data.

The spell level model with fixed effects is given by

$$Y_{ijt} = \alpha_0 + \beta_1 T_t + \beta_2 D_j + \beta_3 T_t D_j + \theta_j + e_{ijt}$$

Again, we can get the estimation results from two separate regressions:

$$D_j = 0 : Y_{ijt} = \alpha_0 + \beta_1 T_t + \theta_j + e_{ijt}$$

$$D_j = 1 : Y_{ijt} = \delta_0 + \delta_1 T_t + \theta_j + e_{ijt}$$

The fixed effects transformation for the $D_j = 0$ sample is

$$Y_{ijt} - \overline{Y}_j = \beta_1(T_t - \overline{T}_j) + e_{ijt} - \bar{e}_j$$

Where $\overline{T}_j = I_{j2}/(I_{j1} + I_{j2}) = I_{j2}/I_j$, with $I_j = I_{j1} + I_{j2}$. The fixed effects spell level estimator for β_1 is then given by

$$\hat{\beta}_{1,FE,spell} = \frac{\sum_{j=1}^{J_0}\sum_{i=1}^{I_{j2}} \frac{I_{j1}}{I_j} Y_{ij2} - \sum_{j=1}^{J_0}\sum_{i=1}^{I_{j2}} \frac{I_{j2}}{I_j} Y_{ij1}}{\sum_{j=1}^{J_0} I_{j1} I_{j2}/I_j}$$

$$= \frac{\sum_{j=1}^{J_0}\left(\frac{I_{j1}}{I_j}\sum_{i=1}^{I_{j2}} Y_{ij2}\right) - \sum_{j=1}^{J_0}\left(\frac{I_{j2}}{I_j}\sum_{i=1}^{I_{j2}} Y_{ij1}\right)}{\sum_{j=1}^{J_0} I_{j1} I_{j2}/I_j}$$

$$= \frac{\sum_{j=1}^{J_0}\left(\frac{I_{j1}}{I_j}\sum_{i=1}^{I_{j2}} Y_{ij2}\right) - \sum_{j=1}^{J_0}\left(\frac{I_{j2}}{I_j}\sum_{i=1}^{I_{j2}} Y_{ij1}\right)}{\sum_{j=1}^{J_0} I_{j1} I_{j2}/I_j}$$

$$= \frac{\sum_{j=1}^{J_0}\left(\frac{I_{j1}I_{j2}}{I_j}\bar{Y}_{j2}\right) - \sum_{j=1}^{J_0}\left(\frac{I_{j1}I_{j2}}{I_j}\bar{Y}_{j1}\right)}{\sum_{j=1}^{J_0} I_{j1} I_{j2}/I_j}$$

Therefore, analogous to the above, if we do a weighted regression on the trust level data for the $D_j = 0$ sample, where the weights are $\sqrt{I_{j1}I_{j2}/I_j}$,

$$\sqrt{I_{j1}I_{j2}/I_j}\,\overline{Y}_{jt} = \sqrt{I_{j1}I_{j2}/I_j}\alpha_0 + \beta_1\sqrt{I_{j1}I_{j2}/I_j}T_t + \sqrt{I_{j1}I_{j2}/I_j}\bar{e}_{jt}$$

will give exactly the same estimation results as the fixed-effects spell level estimator.

5. Data

Our study analyses Hospital Episode Statistic (HES) maternity data for NHS acute trusts between April 2004 and April 2006. The HES database provides information on all maternity related admissions consisting of either single or multiple finished consultant episodes from the first point of admission to the final discharge of destination of mothers and babies at all English NHS acute trusts. Further ethical approval is not required to access anonymised HES records. The unit of our analysis is a hospital spell as PbR is a spell based payment system. In our study, we only focus on maternal admissions, which were paid under PbR. This allows us to aggregate PbR data at trust level for 2004/05 and 2005/06 respectively.

5.1. Outcome Measures

5.1.1. Volume of Hospital Activity

Hospital activity is measured by number of spells within an acute trust for 2004/05 and 2005/06 financial years respectively. We use the natural logarithm of number of spells at trust level to measure the change in hospital activity as a result of the introduction of PbR. It indicates a percentage change on growth rate of hospital activity at trust level.

5.1.2. Unit Costs

The HES database does not provide any information on hospital costs. Previous studies have used length of stay as a proxy for unit costs (Sutton et al., 2007; Yi et al., 2010; Donaldson and Gerard, 2005). We exploit average duration of spell in days at trust level to investigate the impact of PbR on unit costs.

5.1.3. Quality of Maternity Care

We investigate the change in the level of hospital quality by emergency re-admission rates of mothers within 28 days of discharge after delivery[4]. Emergency re-admissions and mortality rates are widely used outcome based indicators of quality of care and hospital and/or physician performance in the health economics literature (Laudicella et al., 2013; Propper et al., 2013; Friedman and Basu, 2004; Yam et al., 2010; Aylin and Bottle, 2006).

We could only use emergency readmission rates to measure the change in the quality of care at NHS hospital level. However, as the number of maternal deaths is very low (16 deaths for the study period), mortality rates remain outside the scope of our study.

5.1.4. Gaming / Up-coding

One of the unintended consequences we might expect from Foundation Trusts is an increase in the proportion of deliveries with complications as these are

4 Available via National Health and Social Care Information Centre (NHS Digital) National Indicator Library accessible via https://digital.nhs.uk/data-and-information/national-indicator-library.

reimbursed at a higher price. Alongside the deliveries with complications, the introduction of PbR allowed hospitals to record "antenatal admissions not related to an actual delivery event" under N12 although these could be carried out in an outpatient clinic (Sutton et al., 2007). We take our analysis one step further and investigate whether hospitals are likely to game the payment scheme as a result of the PbR payment. To do this, we use the growth rate of N12.

6. Results

6.1. Common Trends Assumption

Our identification is based on a difference in differences setting. One of the important assumptions of DiD approach is the common trend assumption. Therefore, we first would like to show whether the key outcomes have similar trends among FTs or non-FTs before PbR began in 2005/06. We find that the trend in volume of admissions across FTs and non-FTs was different before the policy started. However, the assumption holds for emergency readmission rates within 28 days of discharge and length of stay in days. Therefore, we are comfortable in using non-FTs as a control group in our study.

6.2. From Spell Level Data to Trust Level Data

This section provides empirical evidence for the fact that hospital level data can be sufficient to evaluate health care interventions. Weights derived in Section 4 are used to assess the impact of PbR on average length of stay. Standard errors are corrected for heteroskedasticity and serial correlation within each trust[5]. We start with the spell-level OLS estimation without fixed effects in Column (1). Column (2) presents results for ordinary least squares estimation with unweighted trust level data. As expected, point estimates and standard errors are different for those two models. To obtain results in Table 13.1, Column (1), we scale our regression in Column (2) with $\sqrt{I_{jt}}$ (Column (3)). It is clear from Column (3) that our results become identical to those obtained from the spell level analysis without fixed effects.

5 http://www.stata.com/manuals13/xtvce_options.pdf.

Tab. 13.1: Comparison of spell level analysis vs. weighted trust level analysis (w/o and w fixed effects), Source: Authors' own calculations

Trust level vs. Individual level analysis (Delivery Records only)					
	Spell-level OLS	**Trust level OLS (unweighted)**	**Trust-level OLS (weighted)**	**Spell-level fixed effects**	**Trust level fixed effects (weighted)**
Length of stay (days)	(1)	(2)	(3)	(4)	(5)
Policy = on	-0.075***	-0.094***	-0.075***	-0.087***	-0.087***
	(0.020)	(0.016)	(0.020)	(0.016)	(0.016)
Trusts = FTs	0.057	-0.001	0.057		
	(0.098)	(0.087)	(0.099)		
Policy on among FTs	**-0.008**	**-0.000**	**-0.008**	**-0.001**	**-0.001**
	(0.055)	**(0.049)**	**(0.056)**	**(0.048)**	**(0.048)**
N	1178857	302	302	1178857	302
R^2	< 0.001	0.015	0.011	0.0001	0.015

Note: Delivery records are included. Robust clustered standard errors are in parentheses. * p<0.1, **p<0.05, *** p<0.01. Treatment group is the same across years (w/o switchover). Year is defined as the fiscal year (1st April-31st March in the following year). Policy on = year (2005/2006 HES financial year). For weighted trust level analyses, weights are $sqrt(I_{jt})$ for Column (3).Weight is $sqrt((I_{j1}I_{j2})/I_j)$ for Column (5). Results are authors' own calculations using 2004/2005 and 2005/2006 HES delivery records.

In a simple DiD design with a two-year period, the inclusion of fixed effects at trust level provide identical results to those obtained via OLS estimation, as fixed estimation is then the same as first-differencing. However, at spell level analysis, we want to control for unobservable time invariant trust fixed effects. Therefore, as an extension we examine spell level analysis with fixed effects in Column (4). To obtain these results, we use our derived weights in Section Section 4.3.2. Finally, results from weighted trust level data with fixed effects, Column (5), are identical to those presented in Column (4).

In summary, estimates in Tab. 13.1 provide empirical evidence for the fact that hospital level data can be sufficient to evaluate health care interventions. Therefore, as long as the weights derived in the study are available then they can be used by health care researchers who do not have access to individual hospital admission records. In addition to the use of weights, it is clear that the use of fixed effects estimation in a simple DiD design is superfluous.

6.3. The Impact of the Introduction of PbR in Maternity Care

Tab. 13.2 presents results for the impact of PbR on volume of admissions, emergency readmission rates (per 1000 maternal admissions) and length of stay, in days, at trust level. Column (1) reports results for the unweighted trust level data without fixed effects. Results suggest that there is no causal link between the introduction of PbR and maternal outcomes. The inclusion of fixed effects when $T = 2$ does not provide any additional information to the precision of the estimates as suggested earlier. Therefore, this is not presented in the table. Column (2) presents results with the weighted trust level data (weights are $\sqrt{I_{jt}}$). For volume of admissions, two columns present the same results due to the fact this outcome is expressed as the natural logarithm of the number of admissions at trust level, therefore, scaling is not required.

In summary, PbR does not seem to have a statistically significant effect on quality of maternity services even after controlling for the heterogeneity in the error.

6.4. Up-coding

We investigate the impact of PbR on the proportion of HRGs with complications vs. without complications by delivery type, normal delivery, c-sections or assisted deliveries. Our evidence of up-coding is very limited. Tab. 13.3 suggests that the introduction of PbR in maternity care did not lead to any unintended incentives for the Foundation Trusts to up-code their patients to a higher price health resource group. However, our results do not show evidence of an increase in the level of normal and assisted deliveries with complications, or a significant change in the proportion of c-sections with complications. In contrast, we find evidence that the NHS trusts are more likely to increase the proportion of antenatal admissions, unrelated to the actual delivery event, which could otherwise be treated under an outpatient clinic with a lower cost (Sutton et al., 2007), with a and estimated 30 % increase in N12, which is significant at the 10 % level.

7. Conclusion

We contribute to the health economics literature on the use of aggregate level data by providing evidence on how to switch from individual level data (spell level) to aggregate level data analysis within a DiD setting for OLS estimation with or without fixed effects. We present the derivation of appropriate weights in a weighted least squares estimation. For this, the number of spells per hospital needs to be known. We investigate the impact of PbR on maternal outcomes. The identification comes from the differences in the roll-out of the policy between FTs non-FTs. Our study contributes to the literature by providing explicit evidence on the impact of PbR on maternity care.

We find that the weights we derive in Section 4 can be used to switch from spell level data to trust level data. Therefore, we show that use of aggregate data can be sufficient to investigate health care interventions.

Tab. 13.2: The impact of PbR on maternal outcomes (HES delivery records only), Source: Authors' own calculations

Trust level analysis	**Unweigted DiD**	**Weighted DiD**
	(1)	**(2)**
Volume of admissions (log)		
Policy = on	0.025***	
	(0.009)	
Trusts = FTs	-0.061	
	(0.107)	
Policy on among FTs	0.049	
	(0.039)	
N	302	
R^2	0.003	
Emergency readmissions rates (per 1000 maternal admissions)		
Policy = on	0.750***	0.702***
	(0.237)	(0.215)
Trusts = FTs	1.067	0.394
	(0.979)	(0.873)
Policy on among FTs	0.075	0.881
	(0.925)	(1.132)
N	302	302
R^2	0.018	0.020
Length of stay (days)		
Policy = on	0.018	-0.075***
	(0.016)	(0.020)
Trusts = FTs	-0.001	0.057
	(0.087)	(0.099)
Policy on among FTs	-0.000	-0.008
	(0.049)	(0.056)
N	302	302
R^2	0.015	0.011

Note: Robust clustered (at trust level) standard errors in parentheses. Delivery records are included. * p<0.1, ** p<0.05, *** p<0.01. Year is defined as the fiscal year (1st April-31st March in the following year for 2004/2005 and 2005/2006). Policy on = year (2005/2006 HES financial year). Mortality rates are expressed in terms of per 1000 total births. Results are authors' own calculations using 2004/2005 and 2005/2006 HES delivery records.

Tab. 13.3: The impact of PbR on the proportion of HRGs with complications, up-coding (HES delivery records only), Source: Authors' own calculations

Trust level analysis	**Unweighted DiD**	**Weighted DiD**
	(1)	**(2)**
Proportion of Normal Deliveries with complications vs. w/o complications		
Policy = on	0.005*	0.007
	(0.003)	(0.005)
Trusts = FTs	0.017	0.042
	(0.021)	(0.042)
Policy on among FTs	0.000	-0.001
	(0.006)	(0.008)
N	302	302
R^2	0.009	0.030
Proportion of C-sections with complications vs. w/o complications		
Policy = on	0.002	0.004
	(0.003)	(0.003)
Trusts = FTs	0.009	0.018
	(0.014)	(0.017)
Policy on among FTs	-0.001	0.004
	(0.011)	(0.016)
N	298	298
R^2	0.002	0.011
Proportion of Assisted deliveries with complications vs. w/o complications		
Policy = on	0.002	0.001
	(0.002)	(0.003)
Trusts = FTs	0.003	0.004
	(0.010)	(0.012)
Policy on among FTs	0.020	0.041
	(0.017)	(0.034)
N	298	298
R^2	0.008	0.029
Antenatal admissions not related to a delivery event (Natural logarithm of number of N12s)		
Policy = on	0.042	0.042
	(0.075)	(0.075)
Trusts = FTs	-0.027	-0.027
	(0.258)	(0.258)
Policy on among FTs	0.304*	0.304*
	(0.171)	(0.171)
N	302	302
R^2	0.004	0.004

Delivery records are included. Roust clustered standard errors are in parentheses. * $p<0.1$, ** $p<0.05$, *** $p<0.01$. Weights are the square root of volume of each delivery/admission type at trust level. *Year* is defined as the fiscal year (1st April-31st March in the following year for 2004/2005 and 2005/2006). Policy on = year (2005/2006 HES financial year). Results are authors' own calculations using HES 2004/2005 and 2005/2006 HES delivery records.

With respect to the evaluation of PbR on maternal outcomes, we do not find any statistically significant association between the introduction of PbR and maternal outcomes. However, we find evidence that trusts are more likely to record antenatal admissions not related to an actual delivery event, which could otherwise have been treated under outpatient admissions, under inpatient admissions.

Overall, the evidence points to no causal impact of PbR on quality and efficiency of maternity services. However, our research adds to the literature on weighted least square estimation on grouped data by providing weights to switch from an individual level fixed effects estimation to aggregate level first-difference and fixed effects estimations.

References

Appleby, J. and Jobanputra, R. (2004). Payment by Results the NHS financial revolution. *New Economy*. 11, 195–200.

Aylin, P. and Bottle, A. (2006). Mortality associated with delay in operation after hip fracture: Observational study. *British Medical Journal*. 332, 947–951.

Boyle, S. (2005). Payment by Results in England. Euro observer newsletter of the European observatory on health. *Systems and Policies*. 7(4), 1–4.

Department of Health. (Douglas, R.) (2005a). The scope of Payment by Results in 2005/06. [Accessed 21st October]. Available from: http://webarchive.nationalarchives.gov.uk/20130107105354/http://www.dh.gov.uk/prod_consum_dh/groups/dh_digitalassets/@dh/@en/documents/digitalasset/dh_4100934.pdf.

Department of Health. (2005b). Implementing Payment by Results. [Accessed 21st September 2014]. Available from: http://webarchive.nationalarchives.gov.uk/20130107105354/http://www.dh.gov.uk/prod_consum_dh/groups/dh_digitalassets/@dh/@en/documents/digitalasset/dh_4097994.pdf.

Department of Health. (2007a). Payment by Results guidance 2008/09. [Accessed 12th August 2014]. Available from: http://webarchive.nationalarchives.gov.uk/20130107105354/http://www.dh.gov.uk/prod_consum_dh/groups/dh_digitalassets/@dh/@en/documents/digitalasset/dh_081334.pdf.

Department of Health. (2012). A simple guide to Payment by Results. [Accessed 19th November 2014]. Available from: https://www.gov.uk/government/uploads/system/uploads/attachment_data/file/213150/PbR-Simple-Guide-FINAL.pdf.

Dixon, A., Appleby, J., Harrison, T. and Hawkins, L. (2012). Payment by Results how can payment systems help to deliver better care? King's Fund. [Accessed

18th March 2020]. Available from: http://www.kingsfund.org.uk/sites/files/kf/field/field_publication_file/payment-by-results-the-kings-fund-nov-2012.pdf.

Donaldson, C. and Gerard, K. (2005). The economics of health care financing: The visible hand.

Farrar, S., Yi, D. and Boyle, S. (2011). Payment by Results. *In Understanding new labour's market reforms of the English NHS.* Edited by Mays N., Jones L. and Dixon A. London: King's Fund.

Friedman, B. and Basu, J. (2004). The rate and cost of hospital readmissions for preventable conditions. *Medical Care Research and Review.* 61, 225–240.

Goddard, R. D., Jacop, R. T. and Kim, E. K. (2014). Assessing the use of aggregate data in the evaluation of school-based interventions: Implications for evaluation research and state policy regarding public-use data. *Educational Evaluation and Policy Analysis SAGE.* 36(1), 44–66.

Hawe, E. (2009). Compendium of Health Statistics. Office of Health Economics. Abingdon: Radcliffe Publishing.

Kmenta, J. (1997). Elements of Econometrics. 2nd Ed. New York, NY: Macmillan Publishing Co.

Laudicella, M., Donni, L. P. and Smith, P. C. (2013). Hospital readmission rates: Signal of failure or success? Journal of Health Economics. 32(5), 909–921.

Maybin, J. (2007). Payment by Results. *King's Fund.* [Accessed 1st February 2020]. Available from: http://www.kingsfund.org.uk/sites/files/kf/field/field_publication_file/briefing-payment-by-results-jo-maybin-19-october-2007.pdf.

Memorandum by BLISS. (2009). Commissioning: Written evidence by Great Britain. *Parliament House of Commons. Health Committee Session 2008–09 (2009).* [Accessed 1st February 2020]. https://publications.parliament.uk/pa/cm200809/cmselect/cmhealth/1020/1020w153.htm.

National Audit Office. (2013). Maternity services in England. Department of Health. [Accessed 25th September 2019]. Available from: http://www.nao.org.uk/wp-content/uploads/2013/11/10259-001-Maternity-Services-Book-1.pdf.

National Health Service Digital website. (2020a). Hospital episode statistics. [Accessed 18th March 2020]. Available from: https://digital.nhs.uk/data-and-information/data-tools-and-services/data-services/hospital-episode-statistics.

National Health Service Digital website. (2020b). National indicator library. [Accessed 18th March 2020]. Available from: https://digital.nhs.uk/data-and-information/national-indicator-library.

National Health Care Services Digital website. (2020). SB 0070: Healthcare Resource Groups (HRGs). [Accessed 1st February 2020]. Available from: https://digital.nhs.uk/data-and-information/information-standards/information-standards-and-data-collections-including-extractions/publications-and-notifications/standards-and-collections/isb-0070-healthcare-resource-groups-hrgs.

National Health Service Data Dictionary. (2020). [Accessed 18th March 2020]. Available from: http://www.datadictionary.nhs.uk/data_dictionary/nhs_business_definitions/h/hospital_provider_spell_de.asp?shownav=1.

National Health Service Website, NHS Payment System. (2020). [Accessed 18th March 2020]. Available from: https://www.england.nhs.uk/pay-syst/.

Pérotin, V., Zamora, B., Reeves, R., Bartlett, W., et al. (2013). Does hospital ownership affect patient experience? An investigation into public–private sector differences in England. *Journal of Health Economics*. 32(3), 633–646. [Online] [Accessed 23rd November 2014]. Available from: http://www.sciencedirect.com/science/article/pii/S0167629613000337#

Propper, C., Gaynor, M. and Moreno-Serra, R. (2013). Death by market power: Reform, competition and patient outcomes in the National Health Service. American Economic Journal: Economic Policy. 5(4), 134–66.

Stata Official Website. (2020). Stata Manuals. [Accessed 18th March 2020] Available from: https://www.stata.com/manuals13/xtvce_options.pdf.

Sussex, J., Yi, D., Chalkley, M., Sutton, M., Farrar, S. et al. (2009). Has Payment by Results affected the way that English hospitals provide care? Difference-in-differences analysis. *BMJ* [Online]. [Accessed 11th November 2014]. Available from: http://www.bmj.com/content/bmj/339/bmj.b3047.full.pdf.

Sutton, M., Farrar, S., Sussex, J., Yi, D. and Chalkley, M. (2007). National evalution of Payment by Results, report to the Department of Health. Available from: http://hrep.lshtm.ac.uk/publications/PaymentByResultsFinal.pdf

Yam, C. H., Wong, E. L., Chan, F. W., Wong, F.Y. et al. (2010). Measuring and preventing potentially avoidable hospital readmissions: A review of the literature. *Hong Kong Medical Journal*. 16, 383–389.

Yi, D., Farrar, S., Chalkley, M. and Ma, A. (2010). Payment by Results: *Consequences for key outcomes measures and variations across HRGs, providers and patients. Report to Department of Health.* Health Economics Research Unit.

Appendix

Tab. 13.A1: The roll out of Payment by Results and HRGs in maternity care, Source: Authors' own calculations

Tab. 13.A.1. The roll out of Payment by Results (PbR) including maternity care in England

	2003/2004		2004/2005		2005/2006		2006/2007		2007/2008		2008/2009
	FTs	Non-FTs	FTs	Non-FTs	FTs	Non-FTs	FTs	Non-FTs	FTs	Non-FTs	Transition completed
Elective care	15 HRGs		+33 HRGs (48HRGS)								
All remaining elective services											
Non-Elective services[a]											
Maternity services	*Births at NHS premises*										
	Home births										
A&E services & minor injuries units											
Outpatient services											
Maternity services[b]	*Midwifery led clinics*										
	Consultant led clinics										
Maternity services	Pre and post natal home visits										

Note for Tab. 13.A1: Figures are based on DoH PbR guides (2003/2004–2008/2009) available via the Health and Social Care Information Centre's website(Now called NHS Digital) and Sussex et al., 2009. HRGs: Health Resource groups, FTs: Foundation trusts, Non-FTs: Non-Foundation trusts, A&E: Accident and Emergency. Blue cells refer to the health services where PbR was introduced for a given financial year. a The scope of the maternity related PbR tariffs exclude midwifery led clinics, well-babies, community midwifery and home birth; well-babies are included in the cost of mother's care (DoH, 2005b). b i.e. pre-booked antenatal visits and obstetric outpatient services.

Tab. 13.A2: Health resource groups in maternity & neonatal care (v3.5 HRG), Source: Authors' own calculations

Panel A		
Admitted patient care		
HRG code	**HRG name**	**Source of the data within HES**
Baby condition (unwell babies)		Birth Records
N01	Neonates – Died <2 days old	
N02	Neonates with Multiple Minor Diagnoses	
N03	Neonates with one Minor Diagnosis	
N04	Neonates with Multiple Major Diagnoses	
N05	Neonates with one Major Diagnosis	
Main delivery event		
N06	Normal delivery w cc	Delivery Records
N07	Normal delivery w/o cc	
N08	Assisted delivery w cc	
N09	Assisted delivery w/o cc	
N10	Caesarean section w cc	
N11	Caesarean section w/o cc	
Non-delivery event		
N12	Antenatal admissions not related to delivery event	Delivery Records
Panel B		
Outpatient care		
Treatment function code	Treatment function name	Source of the data
501	Obstetrics	NA

Source: NHS data dictionary, National Health Care Services Digital website, HRGs (2020), Hawe, E. (2009). "w cc" with complications, "w/o cc". without.complications, "NA" not available.

List of Tables

List of Figures

www.ingramcontent.com/pod-product-compliance
Ingram Content Group UK Ltd.
Pitfield, Milton Keynes, MK11 3LW, UK
UKHW020153290926
15471UKWH00005B/849

9 783631 831915